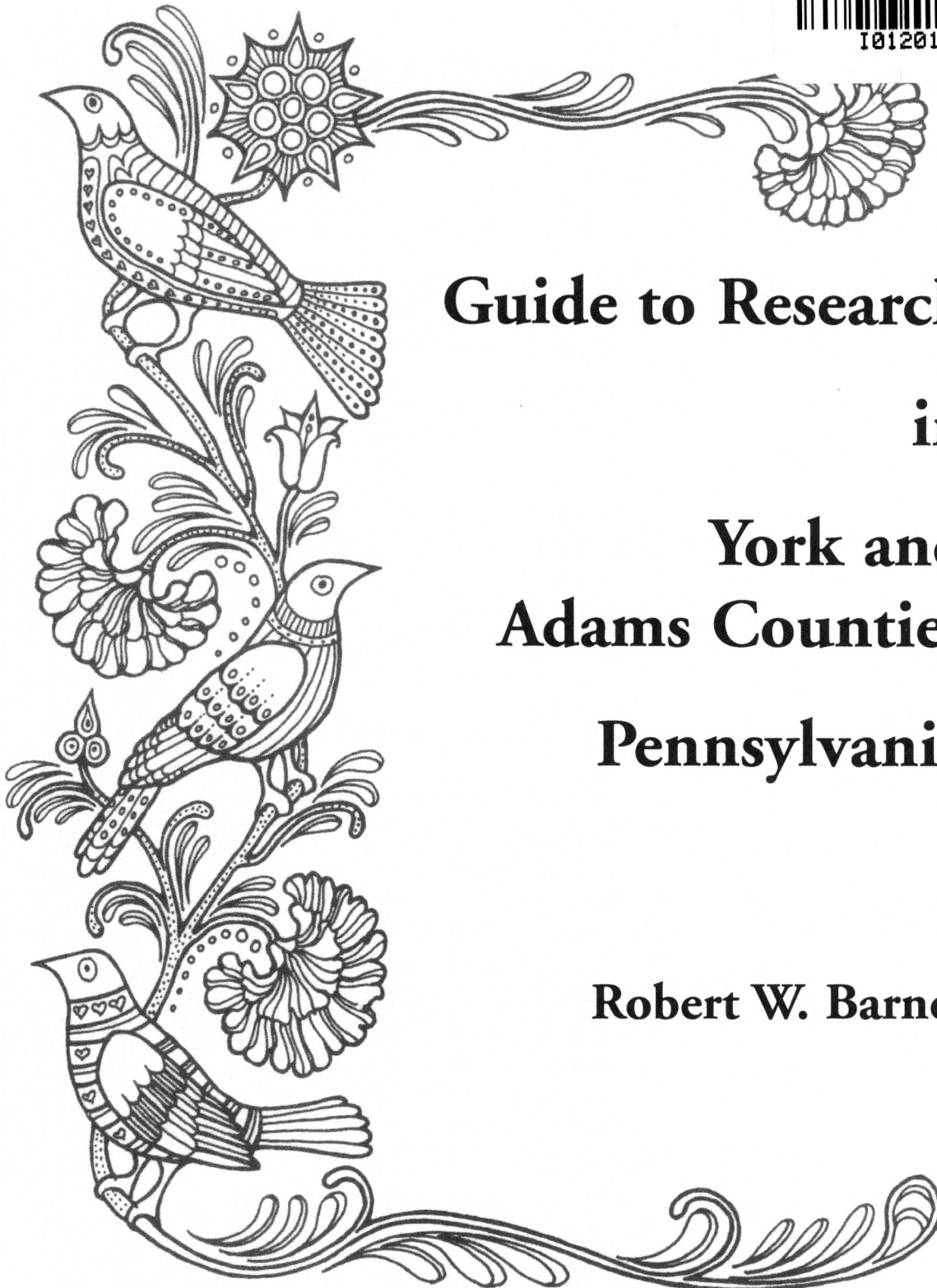

Guide to Research

in

York and Adams Counties

Pennsylvania

Robert W. Barnes

HERITAGE BOOKS
2019

HERITAGE BOOKS
AN IMPRINT OF HERITAGE BOOKS, INC.

Books, CDs, and more—Worldwide

For our listing of thousands of titles see our website
at
www.HeritageBooks.com

Published 2019 by
HERITAGE BOOKS, INC.
Publishing Division
5810 Ruatan Street
Berwyn Heights, Md. 20740

Heritage Books by Robert W. Barnes:

1783 Tax List of Baltimore County
Robert W. Barnes and Bettie S. Carothers

Baltimore and Fell's Point Directory of 1796

Baltimore County, Marriage References, 1659–1746

Baltimore County, Maryland Deed Abstracts, 1659–1750

Colonial Families of Anne Arundel County, Maryland

Colonial Families of the Eastern Shore of Maryland, Volumes 1–3
Robert W. Barnes and F. Edward Wright

Gleanings from Maryland Newspapers, 1776–85

Gleanings from Maryland Newspapers, 1786–90

Gleanings from Maryland Newspapers, 1791–95

Guide to Research in York and Adams Counties, Pennsylvania

Index of Baltimore County Wills, 1659–1850
Robert W. Barnes and Bettie S. Carothers

Index to Marriages and Deaths in the Baltimore County Advocate, *1850–1864*

International Standard Book Number
Paperbound: 978-1-58549-326-5

CONTENTS

Introduction vii

Chapter 1: Archives, Court Houses and Institutions 1

   York County 1
      The Historical Society of York County 1
      The South Central Pennsylvania Genealogical Society 3
      The York County Court House 5
      The York County Archives 5
      Martin Memorial Library 6
      Hanover Area Historical Library 6
      Hanover Public Library 6
      Kaltreider Library 7
      The Old Line Historic Library 7
      Red Lion Area Historical Society 7
      John Timon Reily Historical Society 7
      The Stewartstown Historical Society 7
      The LDS Family History Center 7
   Adams County 9
      The Adams County Historical Society 9
      The Adams County Court House 11
      The A. R. Wentz Library 11
      Lancaster County 11

Chapter 2: Atlases, Maps and Gazetteers 13

Chapter 3: Bibliography 15

   General 15
   Regional Histories 15
   Guides 15
   Business Records 15
   Community Histories 16
   County Histories 16
   Ethnic Groups 17
   Houses and Structures 17
   Migration of York Countians 17
   Occupations 18

Chapter 4: Cemeteries 19

    Cemetery Records Held by Historical Society of York County 19

    York County Cemetery Records 19

    Adams County Cemetery Records (Held at HSYC) 33

    Other Copies of Tombstone Records 38

Chapter 5: Censuses, Directories and Tax Lists 40

    Tax Lists by Township 40

    Tax Lists by County 41

    Directories and Lists 41

Chapter 6: Churches 42

    Compiled Church Records and Guides 42

    Original Church Records of York and Adams Counties 43

    Pastoral Registers 51

    Original Church Records of Adams County 52

    Church Records Outside York and Adams Counties 55

Chapter 7: Families Histories 57

    Collections of Family Histories 57

    Individual Family Histories 57

    Family Reports 67

Chapter 8: Land 71

Chapter 9: Military 73

Chapter 10: Naturalization 74

Chapter 11: Newspapers 75

Chapter 12: Origins of Settlers 89

Chapter 13: Other Court Records 101

Chapter 14: Passenger Lists and Immigration Records 102

Chapter 15: Periodicals and Other Publications 103

    Special Publications of the South Central Pennsylvania Genealogical Society 103

    Ancestral Charts of Members of the SCPGS 106

    Codorus Chronicles 106

    Our Name's the Game 106

Chapter 16: Probate Records 107

Chapter 17: Townships 108

Chapter 18: Vital Records 113

Chapter 19: Visiting York County 114

Index 115

INTRODUCTION

Purpose

For many years the compiler of this guide has enjoyed doing research at the Library of the Historical Society of York County. The facilities, the materials and the staff -- paid and volunteer -- combine to make it an excellent place to do research.

Located on the first floor of the Historical Society, the Library has many stacks open to the public where family histories, county and regional source materials (including an outstanding collection of church and cemetery records of York and Adams Counties), periodicals and finding aids may be found.

The Historical Society also has a large microfilm collection of newspaper and census records. The family file folders, vital statistic cards and other card indices are quickly retrieved for patrons by the staff.

An active group of volunteers accession and file new materials. The following story will illustrate the attitude of the staff. Some years ago, I sent to the Library an updated report on one of my families. Several months later I received letters from researchers thanking me for placing my report in the library and adding some new information. Subsequently, one of those volunteers sent me a letter saying: "I remember your report on the Family and that your grandmother's parents were mentioned. We just received a copy of some church records, and I found an entry for the marriage of those parents. Here's a photocopy of the page." That volunteer not only remembered one of the families mentioned in my report but took the trouble to send me some new information.

Many times I have gone to the York County Court House and the Martin Public Library. I have been met with cooperation and helpfulness.

I expect that the staff of the new County Archives, when it opens in a few weeks will exhibit the same attitude of willingness to help.

Historical Notes

York County, the fifth county to be created in colonial Pennsylvania was erected in 1749 out of Lancaster County. At its inception it included all of present day York and Adams Counties. Adams County was a cut off from York in 1800.

Researchers whose families have been in Pennsylvania prior to 1749 may want to check the records of Lancaster County. Lancaster was created in 1729 from Chester County. Chester County, with Philadelphia and Bucks Counties, made up the three original counties of Pennsylvania.

Glatfelter, in Volume 1 of *Pastors and People,*[1] points out that the Penns did not officially open the area west of the Susquehanna for settlement until October 1736. However, they had been encouraging settlers to move into the area for several years prior to this date as the Proprietors of Pennsylvania wanted to strengthen their claims to land which was deemed by the Lords Baltimore to part of their grant from the King. The boundary dispute was somewhat settled by 1739 with the establishment of a temporary dividing line. This was followed by the surveying of the Mason-Dixon Line.

Most of the early settlers in present day York county were Germans. largely members of Lutheran and Reformed congregations. By 1748 there were six congregations. Two were at Codorus at Yorktown, two were in Kreutz Creek, and two were in present day Adams County, at Conewago.

Scotch-Irish settlers came primarily to the southeastern part of the county. Presbyterian churches were founded at Guinston and Slate Ridge c1747, and at Chanceford by 1760 The First Presbyterian Church at York was also established in the 18th Century as were churches at Dillsburg, c1737 and Centre, c1780.[2]

Other denominations were in York County prior to the outbreak of the American Revolution. Moravian missionaries were holding services in York as early as 1744, and the first Moravian Church was built in York in 1755. Members of the Society of Friends settled in York County in 1734, in the eastern parts of Manchester and Newberry Townships and in the Redland Valley around Lewisberry. John Barton, an Anglican missionary, visited York in 1755 and established several congregations in York, Adams and Cumberland Counties. The Catholic Church was represented by Jesuit missionaries as early as 1720, Conewago Chapel served York County and parts of northern Frederick County, MD. Mennonite Societies were established at Dover (1753), Bairs (1774), Hanover (by 1773) and Manchester (by 1810). German Baptist Congregations were established in 1738, 1741 and 1758.

After American independence was established, the Methodists (1782), Baptists (after 1800), and United Brethren (after 1800) also established Congregations.

Organization

This Guide is primarily organized by types of records and where they may be found, in original, microfilm or published form. However, no Bibliography is ever complete and the compiler welcomes any suggestions for new material in the event that a revised edition is published. The opening pages identify the major resource facilities in York and Adams Counties. For the convenience of travellers, a list of places to eat, stay, and visit are also included. The list is far from complete, and again, any suggestions for new information are welcome.

The Index

Specific topics and subtopics within the chapters and names of authors and compilers of books and articles are included in the index.

Acknowledgements

No book of this sort is ever the product of one person only.

Richard Konkel read the text and made innumerable suggestions and corrections. He also generously made available his list of York County Newspapers, which have greatly enhanced the usefulness of the chapter on newspapers.

Dr. Charles H. Glatfelter of the Adams County Historical Society contributed much helpful information about the holdings of that Society.

June Lloyd, Librarian of the Historical Society of York County, made many resources available for inclusion in the book.

Jonathan Stayer of the Pennsylvania Archives and the staff of the new County Archives contributed helpful information.

Many helpful suggestions came from Wendy Bish and Henry Retzer of the Hanover Public Library, Rev. Dr. Neal Hively, and Roberta Hudson, former Librarian of the Historical Society of York County.

A large debt of gratitude is due to the many unnamed volunteers who have spent untold hours cataloging and indexing the church and cemetery records at the Historical Society, making them available for researchers.

Robert Barnes
Perry Hall, MD
February 1996.

1. *Pastors and People: German Lutheran and Reformed Churches in the Pennsylvania Field, 1717-1793*, by Charles H. Glatfelter (Breinigsville: The Pennsylvania German Society, 1980), p. 457.

ABBREVIATIONS

CC   - *Codorus Chronicles*.

CVR - Calendar of Vital Records, at HSYC.

GSP - Genealogical Society of Pennsylvania.

HSP - Historical Society of Pennsylvania.

HSYC - Historical Society of York County.

NGSQ - *National Genealogical Society Quarterly*.

ONTG - *Our Name's the Game*.

PA   - *Pennsylvania Archives*

PGM - *Pennsylvania Genealogical Magazine*

PMHB - *Pennsylvania Magazine of History and Biography*

PSL - Pennsylvania State Library

SASE - Self Addressed Stamped Envelope.

SCPGS - South Central Pennsylvania Genealogical Society

YC   - York County.

Chapter 1
ARCHIVES, COURT HOUSES AND INSTITUTIONS

When planning to visit any of the resource facilities listed below call ahead to confirm the hours, since any of the times of opening given below are subject to change. When writing to the facility be sure to enclose a SASE to help to ensure a prompt reply.

YORK COUNTY

THE HISTORICAL SOCIETY OF YORK COUNTY

Address: 250 East Market Street, York, PA.
Hours: Mon.-Sat., 9:00-5:00.
Phone: (717) 848-1587.

Rules: pencils only; patrons leave briefcases at or near lockers; non-members pay $4.00 a day or purchase a year's membership for the library for $15.00. Membership dues in the Society are $25.00 (individual) or $35.00 (family).

Parking on Market Street is regulated by meters, but many side streets have available parking.

Research Aids

Family File Folders
Researchers should check the card catalog for the control number. These folders may contain family group sheets, correspondence, Bible records, reports, clippings and typed family histories not bound as books.

Vital Statistics Card File
Birth, baptism, marriage and death and burial notices abstracted from church registers are found on these cards. Entries from the 1850 and 1880 censuses and some naturalizations are also found, as are abstracts of wills from 1850-c1900.

Censuses of 1850 and 1880 Card File.
These files are now included in the Vital Statistics Card File.

Naturalization Card File
Entries list the head of the family, former country of origin, and date of naturalization. This file is now included in the Vital Statistics Card File.

Abstracts of York County Wills and Orphans Court Dockets
These cards, covering the years 1749-1850, contain abstracts of wills, proceedings of the orphans court, appointment of guardians, and inventories. Petitions to the Orphans Court for sale of real estate of intestate decedents name the heirs. There are abstracts of accounts and reports of court ordered sales of real estate. Abstracts of wills from 1850 to c1900 are included in the Vital Statistics Card File.

Land Record Card File
This file lists name of owner of property and where land is located. Cards refer to warrants and drafts concerning original land grants from the Penns, and refer to photocopies (kept in binders) of the original papers.

Cemetery Inscriptions Card File
The inscriptions of gravestones for most graveyards in York and Adams County are included here. The records are from a survey of cemeteries conducted by the HSYC in the 1930s. Later burials are not recorded.

Cemeteries
There are a number of typed volumes of cemetery inscriptions. Even though all of these

have been abstracted in the cemetery inscription cards, check these transcriptions to confirm where people are buried.

Tax List Cards
These contain abstracts of pre-1800 tax lists. Many Pennsylvania tax lists show the number of acres owned, and give details of livestock and slaves. The tax lists do not always show the number of taxables. For a fuller explanation of the tax lists, see the section on Censuses, Directories and Tax Lists.

Cross References
This file contains mostly marriage cross references from wills and Orphans Court Dockets.

Genealogical Reports
Titled "Evidences of the ... Family in York County prior to 1850," these reports contain typed abstracts of church records, tombstones, probate records, deeds, military service, and newspaper notices. There is a typed list of all Genealogical Reports, indicating the volume of bound reports in which they can be found.

Church Registers
There is a typed list of those bound church registers that are on the shelves. There are church records from York and Adams Counties, PA, and some counties in Maryland. There are also some private registers of ministers. From time to time new church registers are being added. Volunteers card the entries for inclusion in the Vital Statistics Card File.

Newspaper Records
The Society's holdings include newspapers (microfilm or hard copy) for York County and for the borough of Hanover. There are several series of typed indices to marriage and death notices.

Typed indices to wills and administration books
The original books are at the court house, but many early records are on microfilm at the Historical Society.

York County Birth and Death Certificates
These records from the end of the 19th and beginning of the 20th century are on microfilm.

Microfilm records
The Society's holdings include Births 1893-1905; census returns for York and Adams counties, 1800-1920; deaths, 1877-1907; land records; marriage certificates, 1885-1901; orphans court proceedings, 1749-1861; wills, 1749-1858.; York County Tax Records by Township, 1800-1850; York County Federal Direct Tax (The Glass Tax), 1798. There are also some census records (by no means complete) for Cumberland, Lancaster, Franklin, and Dauphin counties, PA, and for Baltimore, Harford, and Carroll counties, MD.

Compiled Military Records of York Countians in the Revolution
There are two series, compiled by Henry James Young: a red and black series. These were taken from original records at HSYC and elsewhere.

Other Pennsylvania Sources
The HSYC has abstracts of wills for many of the early Pennsylvania counties, namely, Adams, Bucks, Berks, Chester, Cumberland, Delaware, Franklin, Montgomery, Lancaster, and Philadelphia. Many of these are photocopies of the abstracts found at the Genealogical Society of Pennsylvania. The Society also has wills for Baltimore County, Maryland, and the *Maryland Calendar of Wills* series. It also has a number of church registers from counties surrounding York County, as well as county histories for many Pennsylvania counties.

Index of Continental European Origins of Pennsylvania Settlers
This multi-volume index contains thousands of names found in books and articles on immigration of Pennsylvania settlers.

THE SOUTH CENTRAL PENNSYLVANIA GENEALOGICAL SOCIETY
Address: P.O. Box 1824, York, Pennsylvania 17405

Purpose
The Society was founded in 1975 to meet the demand for a genealogical society in the south central Pennsylvania area, the SCPGS offers the following services to its members:

Meetings
Meetings are normally held the first Sunday of each month, September through June, except December, usually at the Meeting Hall of HSYC, but sometimes at special locations, announced in the newsletter. When a holiday falls on the first Sunday the meeting date is moved forward or back a week. The short business portion of the meetings begins at 2:15 p.m. It is followed at, or near, 2:30 by the program or activity. This portion is intended to be genealogically educational/ informational/instructional to our members. Non-members are always welcomed.

Ideas, suggestions, etc. from our members for future programs, events, and activities are always welcomed.

Newsletters
Members receive eleven issues (July/August is a combined issue) of the Society's newsletter, *Our Name's The Game*, during each fiscal year (July 1 to June 30). Included in this publication are listings of future programs and events, queries from members, notices of publications by other organizations and individuals that might be of interest, and occasionally, short articles dealing with genealogical research.

Members are invited to submit articles and informational items for inclusion in the newsletter that are of genealogical pertinence to the SCPGS area. Commercial advertisements are not included. However, members in the process of publishing or who have recently published, a family history, etc. are entitled to "coverage" of such in the newsletter.

Special Publications
Each fiscal year members receive Special Publications. These are booklets of varying lengths that contain genealogical resource materials, most of which is from unpublished primary sources. Members are encouraged to submit articles, ideas and suggestions for Special Publications.

Newsletter Queries
Members of SCPGS may have an unlimited number of queries published in the newsletter free of charge. They are printed on a first received, first included basis. While there is no limit on the number of queries submitted the length of space provided in a particular newsletter for queries from one individual is limited. When more than one or two queries are received from a member at the same time one or two will be included in the upcoming newsletter and the remainder in successive issues.

There is no special form that must be followed when constructing queries for submission, however, queries should be brief and "to the point." If handwritten, they must be legible. Include dates, locations (township, county, etc.) and time span whenever possible.

Resource Persons

As they become known to the Society, names are listed in the newsletter of those members who are willing to serve (without charge) as Resource Persons for other members needing research help/advice in areas outside the immediate SCPGS area. They will not answer letters unless they are accompanied with a business or legal size self addressed stamped envelope. These members are willing to share their research knowledge and are considerate enough to help other members. They are not expected to provide you with "mounds" of information you should be paying a professional to provide.

Any member, living outside the SCPGS area who is willing to be listed as a Resource Person need only contact the Society. When writing, identify your area by state/county/township, etc. and briefly state in what way(s) you would be willing to help those needing assistance.

Surname Index File

The Society maintains an up-to-date file on computer of all surnames being researched by members. There is no limit on the number of surnames a member may submit and they may be submitted at any time.

If you are researching a particular surname and desire to know the names and addresses of other members researching the same surname, address your request in care of the Membership Secretary. When requesting this information you should include a business or legal size SASE. There is no limit on the number of times a member may utilize this service.

Research Committee

This committee of volunteers uses the facilities of the Historical Society of York County to answer correspondence pertaining to brief requests for genealogical information referring mainly to the York and Adams county areas of Pennsylvania.

Requests from members and non-members are acknowledged, but only if a business or legal size self addressed stamped envelope is included. Members' requests receive first priority and are given more search time than those of non-members. There is no charge to members for this volunteer service if the request is brief.

A $10.00 donation will be required from members if the request is complex and lengthy. Please state all requests as clearly and precisely as possible, include a Family Group Sheet if possible. A check will be made of a specific name for baptism, cemetery, will and Orphan Court records (1749-1850) for the donation paid in advance. Make check payable to the society. Remember, an unsuccessful search takes as long as a successful one. If a large amount of photocopying is required the correspondent will be informed in advance.

Non-members' requests will be answered if they are simple ones, but a $20.00 fee is charged. A list of Professional Researchers will be sent to those requesting complex research.

CERTAIN RECORDS are available from the York County Court House and County Archives using the following guide lines:

Only requests from members will be honored; non-members requesting research at the Court House will be sent a list of Professional Researchers.

Please list complete name and approximate birth/death date of person being researched. Wills, administration accounts and Orphans Court records will be searched for ten years after death.

A $20.00 donation to SCPGS will entitle a member up to 10 copies and over 10 copies a charge of $.50 per copy (includes postage, etc.).

If a member supplies the book and page number of the document a $10.00 donation will be acceptable with the same limitations as listed above. However, deeds will be searched only if book and page sources are supplied.

THE YORK COUNTY COURT HOUSE

York County Court House, York, PA 17401; open Mon.-Fri., 8:30-4:30. NOTE: In the Fall of 1995 many of the earliest records described below will be moving to the new York County Archives Building. The new archives will have nearly all records prior to 1900.

Birth Records. 1893-1906 are in the Register of Wills Office.

Clerk of Courts Office has Quarter Sessions Dockets, 1749-1800; The Quarter Sessions dealt with criminal activities, and created townships and roads. See article in ONTG 2 (6) 3.

Death Records, 1893-1906, are in the Register of Wills Office.

Divorces
Some records are stored in the attic, but check at the Prothonotary's Office first.

Land Office has current records only, including tax maps of York County and tax lists of boroughs, cities and townships.

Prothonotary's Office. Records include two volumes of oaths of allegiance dating back to 1800. The information has been carded. The office has a record of civil cases (Court of Common Pleas), and naturalization and passport information (ONTG 2 (5) 3).

Recorder of Deeds Office has deeds from 1749 to the present, mortgages, veterans discharges, recorded from 1868 to the present, and respective indices to the above.

Register of Wills Office has records dating from 1749 to the present, including wills (both originals and copies in bound volumes), Orphans Court dockets, administration bonds and accounts, inventories, vendue (sales) lists, guardian accounts, indices to the preceding, and adoptions (the latter are not open to the public).

Marriage Applications and Licenses from 1885 to the present are under the jurisdiction of the Clerk of the Orphans Court, located in the Register of Wills Office.

Sheriff's Office has data on quarter sessions from 1749 and data on criminal cases. The office also has two volumes of deeds beginning in 1875. These are for property sold to pay debts (ONTG 2 (5) 3).

Tax Records are discussed more fully in the Section on Censuses, Directories, and Tax Lists.

Veterans' Office has a record of tombstones for veterans buried in the county from the Revolutionary War to the present.

The York Legal Record begins with court cases of 1880. Copies are also at HSYC.

THE YORK COUNTY ARCHIVES

Address: 150 Pleasant Acres Road
York, PA 17402
Phone: 717-840-7222
This new facility is scheduled to open in April 1996, and will house the older records of York County. Located in the old Juvenile Detention Center, it will have on-site parking for patrons.

MARTIN MEMORIAL LIBRARY

Address: 159 East Market St., York, PA.
Phone: (717) 846-5300.
Hours: Mon.-Thu., 9:00 am to 9:00 pm. Fri., 9:00 am to 5:30 pm. Sat., 9:00 am to 5:00 pm.
Summer Hours: Sat., 9:00 am to 12:00 pm.

The Library does not attempt to duplicate the holdings of the HSYC; for example, it has no church records or court records.

The Library contains general histories of York County by Prowell and Gibson. It also has some basic "how-to" genealogical source books. It has the censuses for York County from 1790 through 1920.

The Library also contains some family histories, and a scrapbook pertaining to the Haines Family (members of which built the Shoe House).

The Library also has copies of *The York Gazette and Daily Record,* 1815 to present, and *The York Dispatch,* from 1924 to the present.

HANOVER AREA HISTORICAL SOCIETY

Located at 105 High Street, Hanover, PA 17331. Phone (717)-632-3207. The Society collects and makes available information on the history and material culture of the area.

HANOVER PUBLIC LIBRARY

Address: Library Place, Hanover, PA, 17331 (off Carlisle St. at the Railroad Crossing).
Phone: (717)-632-5183.
Parking: There is a parking area for the library; when it is filled, use on street parking.
Hours of Library (1 September-30 May): Mon. and Wed.-Thu., 10:00-9:00, Tue., 2:00-8:00, and Fri. Sat., 10;00-5:00. (1 June-1 August): Mon., Wed., and Thu., 10:00-8:00; Tue., 2:00-8:00; Fri., 10:00-5;00, and Sat. 10:00-2:00.

The Pennsylvania Room is staffed by volunteers, and is open to the public at no charge. It is not always open when the library is open, so it is important to call ahead.

The current coordinator of the Pennsylvania Room is Wendy Bish. Holdings of the Pennsylvania Room include church registers, year books of the high school, *The Pennsylvania Archives,* censuses of York and Adams counties, some Carroll County, MD, records, over 150 family histories, and vertical file material. Other materials in the Pennsylvania room include: obituary indices to Hanover newspapers, 1828-1994; a local history index; Hanover tax records, 1778-1817; CD-Rom Census Indices; microfilms of tax and court records; and a very large photograph collection. Passenger lists, family histories, and vertical file material are also to be found. Newspapers are being put on microfilm as an on-going effort.

A number of church records are available at the Pennsylvania Room. These include registers of many of the Roman Catholic churches in the immediate area, and St. Bartholomew's Union and St. Mark's Lutheran churches.

There is a reader printer available to make copies.

There is no charge for using the Pennsylvania Room which is open to the public whenever a volunteer is on duty. A schedule of hours is available each month in the library.

Researchers will find a guide to the collections on entering the room. Patrons are asked to fill out a usage slip for each item used. No materials are to be reshelved by the patrons.

Library staff does not do genealogical research, but volunteers will provide research of the collections as well as materials at the county courthouses for a reasonable fee. All funds are used to increase the holdings of the Pennsylvania Room.

KALTREIDER LIBRARY
Address: 5 Charles, Red Lion, PA, 17356.
Hours: Mon.-Tue., Thu.-Fri., 12:00-8:00; Wed. and Sat., 10:00-2:00.
Phone: (717) 244-2032.

This is the 3rd largest library in the York County Library System. It has published York County histories, but no newspapers, censuses, or vertical file.

THE OLD LINE HISTORIC SOCIETY
Address: 401 Main St., Delta, PA 17314.

RED LION AREA HISTORICAL SOCIETY
Mailing address: P. O. Box 94, Red Lion, PA 17356. **Phone:** (717) 244-2032.
Hours: Sun., 2:00-4:00, Wed., 1:00-3:00, and Fri., 7:00-9:00.

The Society was established in 1980, and collects local history. For additional information call: Shirley Keeports, (717) 244-2122, or Bruce Knisely, (717) 244-2501.

JOHN TIMON REILY HISTORICAL SOCIETY
Address: John Timon Reily Historical Society of the Conewago Valley 363 Main St., Mc-Sherrystown, Adams County, PA. The Library is open the first and third Sundays from 1:00 to 4;00. Non-members are asked to pay $1.00 to use the Library See ONTG 20 (5) 1.

Several publications are noted in ONTG 11 (6)3.
- *Conewago Chapel Marriages & Sponsors, 1796-1863.*
- *Conewago Chapel Deaths and Burials, 1752-1979.*
- *Conewago Chapel Baptisms, Parents and Mother's Maiden Names, 1791-1900.*
- *Adams of the Alleghenies.*
- *Catholic Colonial Conewago.* By John Poist Keffer, Repr. by the Society.

THE STEWARTSTOWN HISTORICAL SOCIETY
Located in the Mason-Dixon Library, Main St., Stewartstown, PA, the Society's mailing address is R.R. 4, Box 4082, Stewartstown, PA 17363. Phone: (717) 993-9210. Founded in the year 1984, the Society has a library devoted to the history of the area. It is open to the public.

THE LDS FAMILY HISTORY CENTER
Address: 2100 Hollywood Drive, York, PA.
Mailing address: Family History Center, c/o Jackson Sonneborn, Director, 4015 Amanda Lane, York, PA 17406.
Phone: (717) 854-9331.

Hours (subject to change): Tue.: 9:30 am to 12:30 pm and 5:30 pm to 8:30 pm. Wed.: 9:00 am to 8:00 pm. Thu.: 12:00 pm to 3:00 pm and 5:30 pm to 8:30 pm. Sat.: 9:30 am to 3:00 pm. The room can be opened at other times by special arrangement. Call the number listed above during regular hours to make arrangements.

Closings: The Saturday before Memorial Day, July 4th, the Saturday before Labor Day; the Wednesday and Thursday of Thanksgiving Week; and the week of Christmas through January 1st. The center is also closed on the Saturday of the semi-annual General Conference broadcast from Salt Lake City which usually takes place the first weekend of October. The center is also closed during inclement weather. Call ahead to ensure the facility is open.

Self-service. The center is a self-service facility, and first time visitors are usually given a tour of the center. Self-help booklets are available for the novice researcher. Volunteer staff members will also provide assistance.

Fees: There is no charge to use the facility, but patrons who wish to order microfiche from Salt Lake City will pay a charge of $.15 a sheet. (The fiche remain in the center as part of their permanent collection.) The fee for ordering microfilm from Salt Lake City is $3.00 for each roll for 1 month, $4.50 per roll for 6 months, and $6.50 for an indefinite period. There is a small charge to extend a film order.

Research Aids

On Microfiche

The International Genealogical Index (IGI). 1992 edition, with 187 million names.

The Family History Library Catalog, updated annually.

Accelerated Indexing Systems (AIS). U.S. census indexes in nine separate "searches," which vary by region and locality.

Reference collection of 200 most used books, arranged by locality.

Miscellaneous records, ordered by patrons, arranged by locality.

Family histories and genealogies ordered by patrons, aranged alphabetically by surname.

On CD-ROM
International Genealogical Index, 1993 edition, with 200 million names. A 1995 addendum contains 40 million additional names.

Ancestral File.

Social Security Death Index. This contains deaths 1962 through 1993.

Military Index. Military dead in Korea, 1950 to 1975; Viet-Nam, 1957 to 1975.

The Family History Library Catalog.

Other Research Aids

Indexes to censuses.

Soundex for 1880, 1900, 1910 (only 21 states), and 1920.

Family Registry Index.

Research outlines for all states and many other countries.

Miscellaneous research outlines.

Resource guides.

Language Helps - Genealogical Word Lists.

Letter writing guides (for German and French).

Passenger and Immigration Index, multi-volumes, compiled by P. William Filby. The collection is not complete.

Old Parochial Register (OPR) Index for Scotland, late 1500s through 1855, contains 10.5 million names.

Parish and vital records, arranged by locality in alphabetical order, showing type of record and time period for which records were extracted for the IGI. (This is the "Controlled Extraction Program.")

Basic book collection.

PAF Users Group. For information on the Susquehanna Trail PAF Users Group (STRAPAFUG), see the Appendix.

ADAMS COUNTY

THE ADAMS COUNTY HISTORICAL SOCIETY

The compiler is indebted to Dr. Charles Glatfelter, Director of the Adams County Historical Society, for supplying much of this information.

The present society was established in 1939 and incorporated in 1940. The Library contains hundreds of books and thousands of manuscripts. There is a vertical file which contains unpublished material.

Mailing Address: Adams County Historical Society, P.O. Box 4325, Gettysburg, PA 17325. When writing please do not use any other designation and include a SASE if a response is requested.
Street Address: 111 W. Confederate Ave., Schmucker Hall, Lutheran Theological Seminary, Gettysburg, PA.
Phone: (717) 334-4723.
Hours: Wed., 1-5 pm, and Sat., 9 am-5 pm.

Parking Facilities: Parking is available across the street in any of the unmarked spaces.

Fees. No fee is charged to use the holdings of the Society, but there is a donation box for contributions.

Dues: Individual members: $15.00; family membership: $25.00; contributing member: $50.00; sponsoring member: $100.00; life member: $350.00; Edward McPherson Society membership: $1000.00.

Research. The Society will undertake research for $20.00 an hour (or portion thereof), with a minimum charge of $20.00. In making an inquiry one should ask the specific questions for which an answer is sought. Copies of specific documents, when requested by mail, cost $1.00 for each search plus $0.30 for each copy made. This includes the cost of postage and handling. A search is an investigation of a particular file, such as one containing papers from a particular estate.

Publications:
The Newsletter is published ten times a year and contains articles of historical interest.

The Society has begun publication of an annual called *Adams County History.*

Holdings of the Society include:
Translations and transcriptions of the records of many Lutheran and Lutheran and Reformed churches, especially those churches that supported the Lutheran Theological Seminary.

Transcriptions of the records of some Reformed, Presbyterian and Methodist churches.

Original estate papers for Adams County from 1800 into the 1980s.

Original marriage returns for Adams County from 1885 to the 1960s. These are arranged alphabetically by male.

Original applications for tavern licenses, 1805-1845. Taverns were located about every five miles along the main roads and the licenses had to be renewed annually. Neighbors had a chance to protest the renewal of a license, and so these applications may contain interesting information on the characters of the tavern-keepers.

Copies of several thousand land surveys for Adams County. These surveys were made when people were making their first claim to the land.

Copies of some 30,000 tombstone inscriptions, made in the 1930s.

A developing card file of marriage and death notices copied from Gettysburg newspapers.

A developing card file of names taken from most surviving pre-1800 tax lists for Adams County, and from all surviving septennial censuses. The Pennsylvania Constitution of 1776 directed that a census of householders be taken every seven years. This census was taken from 1786 through 1863. Most returns have not been preserved, but the returns for York County for 1786, 1793, and 1800 are in the Pennsylvania State Archives. The returns for Adams County exist for the years 1807, 1814 and 1821.

List of Township Officers, 1749-1800, for Adams County, Pennsylvania.
Compiled by Kathryn W. Meals, Adams County Historical Society, 1977. Each township had a constable, two overseers of the poor, two supervisors of highways, and one tax collector. For many Pennsylvanians, holding an office in the township was their first experience of holding a public office.

List of Township Officers, 1749-1800, for York County, Pennsylvania.
Compiled by Tina Fair, Adams County Historical Society, 1984.

Census records for Pennsylvania from 1790 through 1880. Indices for 1790-1860.

Some death certificates for years 1852-1855.

Deeds: The Society has the first 100 original deed books for Adams County, 1800-1925.

Family Genealogies.

Family and individual files, containing over 1500 folders of family data, correspondence and some photographs.

Marriage and obituary indices for Gettysburg newspapers, 1828-1950, and more recently, Hanover newspapers, 1825-1900.

Publications for sale by the Society include:

1858 Map of Adams County: Tracing: Sheet 1. Shows townships and householders. $6.25 by mail.

1858 Map of Adams County: Tracing: Sheet 2. Shows county, towns and villages $6.25 by mail.

1850 Map of Gettysburg. Tracing. Shows householders. $4.25 by mail.

An Adams County Blacksmith: Shop Ledgers of the Eiker Smithy, 1860, 1861, 1865, 1900. 4 volumes. $17.25 by mail.

Atlas of Adams County. 1872. $23.50 by mail.

The Churches of Adams County, Pennsylvania: A Brief Review and Summary. By Charles H. Glatfelter. 1981. $4.00 by mail.

A Glimpse Into Adams County, 1860-1914: A Photographic Record. ed. by C. A. Moore. 1977. $5.00 by mail.

A History of Adams County, Pennsylvania, 1700-1900. By Robert L. Bloom. 1992. $56.00 by mail.

THE ADAMS COUNTY COURT HOUSE
Adams County Court House, Gettysburg, PA 17325; open Mon.-Fri. 8:00-4:30.

THE A. R. WENTZ LIBRARY
Address: Lutheran Theological Seminary, Gettysburg, PA 17325.

Hours: Mon-Thu., 8:30-5:00, 6:00-10:00. Fri., 8:30-5:00. Sat., 9:00-12:00, 1;00-4:30. Sun., 6:00 pm.-10:00 pm. School recesses, Mon-Fri., 8:30-5:00. Summer, Mon-Fri., 8:40-4:30.

The Library is closed on all holidays officially designated by the School, including Labor Day, Thanksgiving, Martin Luther King, Jr., Day, Good Friday, Memorial Day, and Independence Day. The Library is also closed during the Christmas holidays for 8 to 10 days. Any changes in the schedule are posted well in advance.

Smoking, food and beverages are not permitted in the Library.

Non-Seminary patrons are asked to fill out a registration card listing name, address, and telephone number.

Resources

> **The Seminary Archives**, contains materials dating from the General Synod and the Seminary itself. The papers of many past faculty members are also housed here. A notebook containing a listing of the seminary's archives is shelved at the Circulation Desk.

> **The Archives of Region 8 of the Evangelical Lutheran Church** in America. This collection includes proceedings of Synod Assemblies, records of regional and synodical committees and agencies, and the records of defunct congregations.

> **The Congregational History File** is a large collection of pamphlets housed in cabinets near the circulation desk.

> **Parish Registers.** PLEASE NOTE that the parish registers of both current and defunct congregations are NOT available for genealogical research. The library staff will suggest alternative ways to find such information.

Source: *The A. R. Wentz Library at Gettysburg Lutheran Seminary.* S.l., s.n.: Sept. 1995.

LANCASTER COUNTY

Because Lancaster County was a parent County of York County (created in 1749) and Adams County (carved out of York County in 1800) the following facilities should be considered in researching early settlers of York and Adams Counties.

LANCASTER-MENNONITE HISTORICAL SOCIETY (LMHS)
is located at 2215 Millstream Road, Lancaster, PA (off Route 30, near Dutch Wonderland). For a discussion of its holdings, see "Lancaster Mennonite Conference Historical Society Library," ONTG 2 (3) 3.

THE LANCASTER COUNTY HISTORICAL SOCIETY (LCHS)
is located at President and Marietta Avenues, Lancaster, PA (next to Wheatland). The Society holds all original probate documents besides wills: i.e., inventories, accounts, vendue (sales) lists. The society also has family histories, family files (vertical file material), and church and cemetery records.

THE LANCASTER COUNTY ARCHIVES
are located in the basement of the county court house at 50. N. Duke St., Lancaster, PA.

THE PHILIP SCHAFF LIBRARY, LANCASTER THEOLOGICAL SEMINARY (United Church of Christ) is located at 555 W. James Street, Lancaster, PA. The Archives is located on the second floor of the library and holds a large collection of Reformed Church records and many Lutheran records (especially for Union churches).

Township Map of Adams County, Pennsylvania

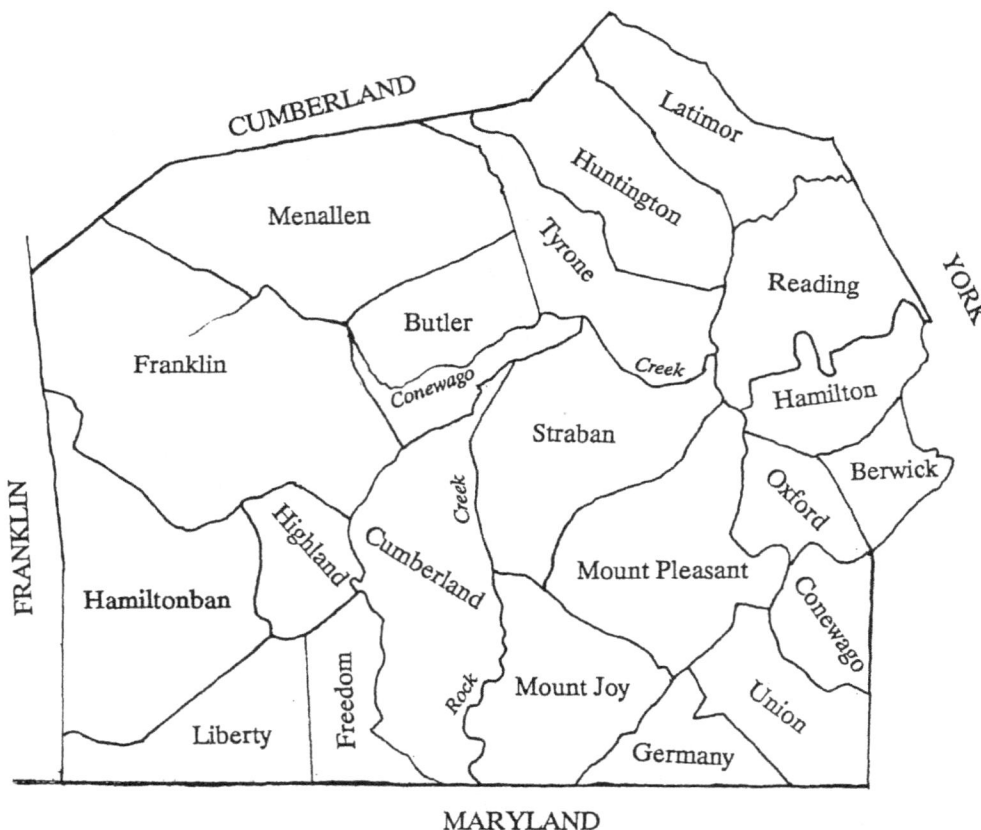

Chapter 2
ATLASES, MAPS AND GAZETTEERS

Alphabetized, Cross References and Coded Indexes to the 1876 Atlas of York County, Pennsylvania, in Two Volumes. Volume 1: Individual Name Index. Compiled and Edited by Patricia R. Gross, Leonard A. Heilman and Samuel J. Saylor (SCPGS Spec. Pub. # 44, 1991).

Alphabetized, Cross References and Coded Indexes to the 1876 Atlas of York County, Pennsylvania, in Two Volumes. Volume 2: Subject Index. Compiled and Edited by Patricia R. Gross, Leonard A. Heilman and Samuel J. Saylor (SCPGS Spec. Pub. # 45, 1991).

Farm Journal Illustrated Farmers' Directory of York County (1915) was published with a road map of the county, mentioned ONTG 7 (5) 1.

Outline Map of York County CC 1(1)cover.

Springettsbury Manor Map. 1810-1812. Repr. by HSYC. Also *Everyname Index*, by Charles Otstot.

York County Map. By (N) Shearer. 1860.

York County Draft Maps. For some time Rev. Dr. Neal Otto Hively of Chambersburg, PA, has been publishing draft warrant maps of tracts in various regions of York County. He has also been compiled indices to the various maps in book form. The following list of Book Indices and Connected Draft Maps will help researchers locate just where their ancestors lived and owned property.

Index Volume 1 - Codorus Township
- Map 1: Steltz Region.
- Map 2: Middle Codorus Region.
- Map 3: Upper Codorus Region.
- Map 4: West Codorus Region.

Index Volume 2 - Manheim and Heidleberg Townships
- Map 5: Manheim - South Region.
- Map 6: Manheim - North Region.
- Map 7: Heidelberg - South Region.
- Map 8: Heidelberg - North Region.

Index Volume 3 - West Manheim and Penn Townships
- Map 9: West Manheim - South Region.
- Map 10: West Manheim - North Region.
- Map 11: Penn Township.

Index Volume 4 - North Codorus Township
- Map 12: North Codorus - South Region .
- Map 13: North Codorus - North Region.
- Map 14: North Codorus - East Region.

Index Volume 5 - Shrewsbury and Springfield Townships
- Map 15: Shrewsbury - Southwest Region.
- Map 16: Shrewsbury - North Region.
- Map 17: Shrewsbury - Middle Region.
- Map 18: Shrewsbury - Springfield Boundary Region.

- Map 19: Springfield - North Region.

Index Volume 6 - The Manor of Springettsbury

The 65,000 acre Proprietary Manor covered 11 townships in central York County. The book traces the history and controversy, and includes a full index of 393 individual land tracts and their early settlers, beginning in 1732.
- Map 20: Manor of Springettsbury.

Index Volume 7 - The Hopewell Townships: Hopewell, East Hopewell, and North Hopewell. (This volume is in progress and was due for completion in the Fall of 1995.
- Map 21: Hopewell - South.
- Map 22: Hopewell - East.
- Map 23: East Hopewell.
- Map 24: North Hopewell.

Township Map of York County, Pennsylvania

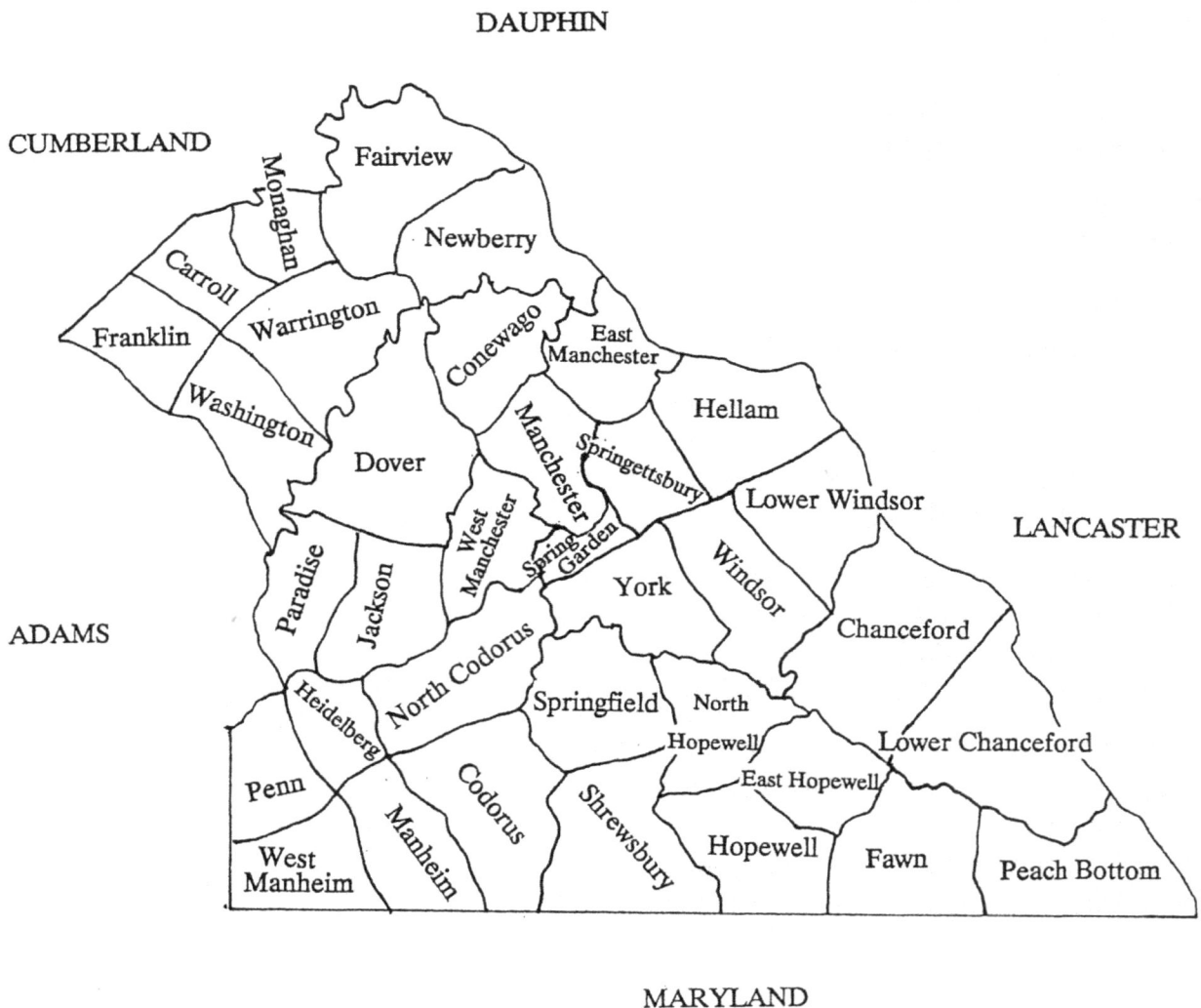

DAUPHIN

CUMBERLAND

Monaghan

Fairview

Carroll

Newberry

Franklin

Warrington

Conewago

East Manchester

Washington

Dover

Manchester

Springettsbury

Hellam

Paradise

West Manchester

Spring Garden

Lower Windsor

LANCASTER

Jackson

York

Windsor

Chanceford

ADAMS

North Codorus

Springfield

North Hopewell

Lower Chanceford

Heidelberg

East Hopewell

Penn

Codorus

Shrewsbury

Hopewell

Fawn

Peach Bottom

West Manheim

Manheim

MARYLAND

Chapter 3
BIBLIOGRAPHY

The following is a list of general sources which may aid in the research of York and Adams counties. For information on sources relating to a specific topic, see that topic.

GENERAL

"A Genealogist's Guide to Pennsylvania Records (A Guide to the hidden sources in the collections of the Genealogical Society of Pennsylvania) [York County]," by Helen Hutchinson Woodroofe, *PGM* 35 (2) 154-166.

German for Genealogy: A Translator's Handbook. By John W. Heisey. Reviewed in ONTG 11 (4) 3.

Handbook for Genealogical Research in Pennsylvania. By John W. Heisey. York: The author.

"More on Names - and Their Changes," ONTG May 1977 3-4

"Our Keystone Families," by Schuyler Brossman. Genealogy Column, pub. in [Middletown] *The Press and Journal,* Journal Building, 20 S. Union Street, Middletown, PA, 17057. Mentioned ONTG 11 (11) 1, and 15 (3) 2-3.

Pennsylvania Family Histories and Genealogies. By Donald Odell Virdin. St. Michaels, MD: Raymond B. Clark, Jr., 1984.

Pennsylvania Genealogical Library Guide. By John W. Heisey. Elverson [PA]: Olde Springfield Shoppe. Reviewed in ONTG 19 (9) 3.

REGIONAL HISTORIES

A Brief History of York County, Pennsylvania. By George R. Prowell. York: N.p., 1906.

Genealogical Reports for the Historical Society of York County. By Henry James Young, et al. [19--]

History and Topography of Lancaster and York Counties, from 1719 to 1745. By Israel Rupp. Lancaster: G. Hills, 1845.

History of York County...to the Present Time (1729 1834). By W. C. Carter. York: A. J. Glossbrenner, (1834). Repr. Baltimore: Gen. Pub. County, 1975. Reviewed in NGSQ 64(1)76.

History of York County from the Earliest Period to the Present Time. By John Gibson. Chicago: F. A. Battey, 1886. [contains biographical sketches].

History of York County, Pennsylvania. 2 vols. Chicago: J. H. Beers & Co., 1907. [contains biographical sketches]

GUIDES

York County, Pennsylvania Area Key. By Florene Clint. c.r. 1974 by The Author. 2nd ed., 1976.

BUSINESS RECORDS

Friederich Heinrich Gelwichs, Shoemaker and Distiller, Accounts, 1760-1763, Manheim Twp., York County, PA. Breinigsville: The Pennsylvania German Society, 1979.

Records of Anstein's Mill, Windsor Twp., at HSYC.

COMMUNITY HISTORIES

ABBOTTSTOWN: *A History of Abbottstown* [Adams County]. by Wilkes S. Eisenhart. S.l., s.n., 1953.

CODORUS: *Skinny Dipping in the Codorus: the Boyhood Recollections of Raymond Jacob Sechrist.* By Raymond Jacob Sechrist. York: Publications Committee of the Historical Society of York County. Mentioned in ONTG 17 (1) 3.

DALLASTOWN: *100 Years of Growth, 1866-1966, Dallastown, Pennsylvania.* S.l., s.n., c.1966.

DOVER: *Greater Dover Bicentennial Celebration, 1764-1964.* 1964 Greater Dover Bicentennial [Committee?].

A History of Dover Township, York County, Pennsylvania, 1740s-1990s. Dover Township Board of Supervisors. 1994.

GOLDSBORO: *The Life and Times of* .... By the Goldsboro Historical Association. S.l., s.n., n.d.

JACOBUS [Originally called New Paradise]: *Commemorating the 100th Year of the Founding of the Borough of Jacobus , York County, Pennsylvania, 1837-1987.* By John Geiselman et al. York: Mehl-Ad Associates, n.d.

NEW FREEDOM: *Commemorating the 100th Year of the Incorporation of ... , Pennsylvania, 1873-1973.* York: Mehl-Ad Associates, n.d.

NORTH CODORUS: *The Flowering of the Codorus Palatinate: A History of ... Twp.* York: Mehl-Ad Associates, n.d.

RED LION: *The Borough of ... Pictorial Souvenir (Golden Jubilee, 1880-1930).* S.l., s.n., n.d.

WELLSVILLE: *Remembrances for Tomorrow, 1892-1992.* By Joan S. Clippinger. S.l., s.n., n.d.

YORK: *Made in York.* By George R. Sheets. ONTG 16 (9) 2.

York City: 250 Years. ONTG 16 (9) 2.

York Since 1741. By Jim Rudisill. Noted in ONTG 16 (9) 2 and 17 (1) 2.

COUNTY HISTORIES

Adams County, Creation of, CC 4(1)33, (2)21. (3)33, (4)17.

A Brief History of York County, Pennsylvania. By George R. Prowell. York: N.p., 1906.

History and Topography of Lancaster and York counties, from 1719 to 1745. By Israel Rupp. Lancaster: G. Hills, 1845.

History of Adams County, Pennsylvania. By Robert L. Bloom. Mentioned in ONTG 17 (8) 2, (11) 2.

History of Adams County, Pennsylvania. By H. C. Bradsby, with Aaron Sheely. 1886. Repr.: Westminster: Family Line Publications, 1995.

History of York County, Pennsylvania. By George R. Prowell. 2 vols. Chicago: J. H. Beers & Co., 1907. [contains biographical sketches]

History of York County...to the Present Time (1729-1834). By W. C. Carter. York: A. J. Glossbrenner, 1834 (reprinted several times).

History of York County from the Earliest Period to the Present Time. By John Gibson. Chicago: F. A. Battey, 1886. [contains biographical sketches].

Susquehanna Saga: Early Chronicles of Historic York County and South Central Pennsylvania. By Lewis L. Doolittle. c.r. 1971 by The Author.

York County, Hist. of, CC 1(2)21.

ETHNIC GROUPS

Mennonite Family History Surname Index. Pub. by Mennonite Family History, P. O. Box 171, Elverson, PA 195220-0171. Reviewed in ONTG 11 (5) 1.

HOUSES AND STRUCTURES

The Bard-Hiestand Hotel Below York, CC 1 (1) 26.

The Bigler House, CC 4 (3) 17.

"The Bonham House, York, Pennsylvania, 'A Valuable Town Property.'" By Gloria O. Becker, Ph. D. Typescript, HSYC. 1987.

The Cookes House at York, CC 3 (3) 30.

The Crull Hotel Below Goldsboro, CC 5 (4) 31.

The Dritt House at Long Level, A Visit to, CC 4 (1) 18.

The Etter Hotel at Middletown Ferry, CC 5 (5) 31.

The Schultz House Near Stony Brook, CC 4 (2) 14.

The Baltzer Spangler House at York, CC 3 (4) 39.

The Waters Hotel at York Haven, CC 5 (3) 32.

The John Wright House at Wrightsville, CC 1 (3) 24.

MIGRATION OF YORK COUNTIANS

Gone to Ohio... Ashland, Brown, Columbiana, Harrison, Jefferson and Richland counties, From Pennsylvania Counties: Adams, Cumberland, Dauphin, Franklin, Lancaster and York. Compiled by Gloria L. Aughenbaugh (1990). SCPGS Spec. Pub. # 43.

Gone to Ohio ... Champaign, Crawford and Wood Counties From Pennsylvania Counties: Adams, Cumberland, Dauphin, Franklin, Lancaster and York. Comp. by Gloria L. Aughenbaugh. (1993). SCPGS Spec. Pub. # 53.

The Journal of James L. Purdy: Hopewell Township, York County, Pennsylvania and Mansfield, Richland County, Ohio... (1990) SCPGS Spec. Pub. # 42.

Some Adams County Families and Their Descendants in Bedford and Somerset Counties, CC 5 (4)12.

Some Carroll County, Ohio, Residents Whose Ancestors Came from York and Adams Counties, CC 2 (4) 36.

Some Harrison County, Ohio, Residents Whose Ancestors Came from York and Adams Counties, CC 4 (3) 21, (4) 33.

Some York County Families and Their Descendants in Somerset County, CC 5(3)18; 6 (2) 9, (3) 15.

They Went West Or More Precisely, Information Found in Newspapers of Astoria, Fulton Co., IL, 1886-1917, and Crawford County, OH, 1891-1938, Pertaining to Descendants of Families from South Central Pennsylvania and Adjacent Areas (July 1983). SCPGS Spec. Pub. # 23.

York County, PA, to Tuscarawas County, OH; ONTG 16 (5) 2.

OCCUPATIONS

Apprentices, Record of, 1860-1911 (SCPGS Spec. Pub. # 19, 1982).

Index to Tavern Licenses Allowed by York County, Pennsylvania, 1749-1806. By John R. McGrew. (SCPGS Special Publication # 48, 1985). Corrections in ONTG 19 (4) 2.

List of Constables, York County, 1785. (SCPGS Spec. Pub. # 52).

List of Retailers, 1866, CC 2 (2) 21.

Officers, York County, 1749-1800. Comp. by Kathryn M. Meals and Charles H. Glatfelter. Adams County Hist. Soc., 1982.

Chapter 4
CEMETERIES

CEMETERY RECORDS HELD BY HISTORICAL SOCIETY OF YORK COUNTY

There are a large number of cemetery records at HSYC for York and Adams counties. Following are two lists, one for York and one for Adams, in the following format: name of cemetery (township): file number.

YORK COUNTY CEMETERY RECORDS

Unidentified Cemetery near Lincoln Park (City of York): 726-5.

Adas Israel Cemetery adjacent to South Hills Hebrew (Spring Garden): 726-6.

Adamsville Cemetery, Arbor U. B. (York Township): 726-13.

Airville United Presbyterian Cemetery, Old Log, Shenk's (Lower Chanceford): 726-7.

(New) Airville Cemetery, United Presbyterian (Lower Chanceford): 726-8.

Albright's Cemetery, Salem Church of Evangelical Association (Warrington): 726-9.

Alt Burial Ground, Hanover (Penn Township): 726-10.

Altland's Meeting House Cemetery near Big Mount (Paradise): 726-11.

Andersontown Church of God Cemetery (Monaghan): 726-12.

Arbor United Brethren Cemetery, Adamsville (York Township): 726-13.

Asper Burial Ground, Louis Asper farm (Washington): 726-14.

Auchey Burial Ground (North Codorus): 726-15.

Aughenbaugh's Cemetery, between York and Zion's View (Manchester): 726-16.

Aughinbaugh Burial Ground, near E. Berlin (Washington): 726-17.

Baird Burial Ground (East Hopewell): 726-2.

Bair's Meeting House Cemetery, Menosimmon's (Heidelberg): 726-18.

Bair's Mennonite Meeting House Cemetery, Bair's Station (West Manchester): 726-191.

Bald Hill Cemetery, Parkville (Newberry): 726-230.

Barrens Cemetery, Salem's Evangelical Lutheran and Reformed, Salem Union Cemetery (Washington): 726-19.

Bat's Nest Burial Ground, Bat Pen, St. John's on the Hill (Newberry): 726-20.

Bear Burial Ground, Bare/Bar (Newberry): 726-21.

Beidler's Graveyard (Hellam Township): 726-22.

Bender Burial Ground, Jacob's, near Maytown (Warrington): 726-23.

Benedict's Church Cemetery, Mt. Olivet Church of God (Warrington): 726-24.

Bentz Burial Ground, now Zimmerman farm (Dover Township): 726-25.

Bentz Cemetery, Mt. Pleasant Methodist (Warrington): 726-362.

Bermudian Brethren Cemetery, German Baptist Meeting House (Washington): 726-26.

Bethany United Brethren, on Dover-Conewago Township line (Dover Township): 726-27.

Bethel Methodist Episcopal Cemetery (Chanceford): 726-28.

Bethlehem Cemetery, Stiltz, partly in MD and PA (Codorus): 726-29.

Bethlehem Evangelical Cemetery (Windsor): 726-30.

Black Rock Cemetery, Black Rock Brethren (Manheim): 726-31.

Blooming Grove U. E. Cemetery (Penn): 726-32.

Blymire's Cemetery, near Dallastown (York Township): 726-33.

Bott's Cemetery, Wolf's (West Manchester): 726-34.

Bowser's Cemetery, Dunkard Church Cemetery, near New Freedom (Shrewsbury): 726-35.

Boyer Burial Plot, near Parkville, near school (Newberry): 726-36.

Brenneman Burial Ground, 1/2 mile from Zion's, Shaffer's (Codorus): 726-37.

Brethren Church Cemetery, Church of the Brethren (North Codorus): 726-38.

Brethren Cemetery, Black Rock (Manheim): 726-31.

Brethren Cemetery, E. Codorus Church of the Brethren, near Loganville (Springfield): 726-39.

Brethren Church Cemetery, Chestnut Grove Brethren Church, 1 mile south of Jefferson (Codorus): 726-40.

Brethren in Christ Church Cemetery, on E. Prospect Road (Windsor Township): 726-41.

Brillhart's Cemetery, Stauffer's Schoolhouse Cemetery (North Codorus): 726-42.

Brown Cemetery (Fawn): 726-477.

Bryansville Cemetery, Evangelical (Peach Bottom): 726-43.

Bupp Burial Plot, Graff's farm, 1/2 mile from Meisenh. (Conewago Township): 726-44.

Bupp's Union Church Cemetery (Springfield): 726-45.

Burg Burial Ground, Hauser's Cemetery (Hellam Township): 726-46.

Canadochly Cemetery, Lutheran and Reformed Church (Lower Windsor): 726-47.

Cassel's Cemetery, near York Haven (Newberry): 726-48.

Cassel's Cemetery (Old) (Newberry): 726-48a.

Catholic Cemetery (German Catholic) (Spring Garden): 726-49.

Centre Presbyterian Church Cemetery (Fawn): 726-50.

Chanceford Presbyterian Church Cemetery (Lower Chanceford): 726-51.

Chapel Church Cemetery, near Cape Horn, York Boro. (York Township): 726-52.

Chestnut Grove (Brethren) Church Cemetery, near Jefferson (Codorus): 726-40.

Chestnut Grove U. B. Cemetery, several miles from Filey's (Carroll): 726-54.

Christ Lutheran Church Cemetery, Pidgeon Hill (Jackson): 726-55.

Christ Lutheran Churchyard (City of York): 726-56.

Church of the Brethren (Brethren Church) Cemetery (North Codorus): 726-38.

Church of the Brethren (East Codorus) Cemetery (Springfield): 726-39.

Church of God Cemetery, Holtzinger Church (Windsor Township): 726-136.

Confederate Grave, near Bigmount (Paradise): 726-57.

Confederate Grave, near Accomac (Hellam): 726-483.

Cooper Burial Ground (Peach Bottom): 726-58.

Coyle Burial Ground, at Accomac (Hellam Township): 726-59.

Crone's Cemetery, Emanuel's Church of Evangelical Association (Fairview): 726-60.

Cross Roads Cemetery, Cross Roads Boro. (East Hopewell): 726-61.

Cross Roads Cemetery, Frogtown (Fairview): 726-62.

Deardorff Burial Plot, near Markey's Fording (Dover Township): 726-63.

Deardorff's Cemetery (Gochenauer's) near Orts Mill (Washington): 726-64.

Dietz Burial Ground, near first Dietz home (Hellam Township): 726-65.

Dillsburg Cemetery, including Old Knaub Burial Ground (Carroll): 726-66.

Dosch Burial Ground (Kline, Shenberger) on S. Forry Laucks' farm (Lower Windsor): 726-67.

Downies Cemetery, between Brogue and Guinston (Chanceford): 726-68.

Dritt Burial Ground, Long Level (Lower Windsor): 726-69.

Druck Burial Ground, Druck Valley (Hellam Township): 726-70.

Dub's Cemetery, St. Paul's, Reformed and Lutheran (Manheim): 726-71.

Dunkard Brethren Cemetery, Shrewsbury (Shrewsbury): 726-72.

Dunkard Church Cemetery, Bowser's, near New Freedom Boro. (Shrewsbury): 726-35.

Dunkard Burial Ground (Miller) on Stiffler farm (Codorus): 726-73.

Dunkard Meeting House Cemetery, Mummert's, Pleasant Hill (Jackson): 726-75.

Dunkard Cemetery, Pleasant Hill Dunkard (North Hopewell): 726-74.

East Codorus Church of the Brethren, near Loganville (Springfield): 726-39.

East Prospect Cemetery (Lower Windsor): 726-76.

Ebenezer Evangelical Cemetery (Lower Windsor): 726-77.

Emanuel Evangelical Church Cemetery, Immanuel (Shrewsbury): 726-147.

Emanuel's Reformed Burial Ground, Hanover (Penn): 726-78.

Emanuel's Church of Evangelical Association, Crone's (Fairview): 726-60.

Emanuel's Union Lutheran Burial Ground, Jefferson (Codorus): 726-79.

Emig Burial Ground, Emig farm (Hellam Township): 726-80.

Ensminger Farm Burial Ground, Hess Burial Ground (Springfield): 726-81.

Erb Burial Plot (Springettsbury): 726-82.

Emey, Bald Mill, Parkville (Newberry): 726-230.

Evangelical Burial Ground, Hoke's farm (Springettsbury): 726-124.

Evangelical Cemetery, Bryansville (Peach Bottom): 726-43.

Evangelical Cemetery, near Jacobus (Springfield): 726-83.

Evangelical Cemetery, Shrewsbury Boro. (Shrewsbury): 726-84.

Evangelical Chapel Cemetery, Shenberger Chapel (Chanceford): 726-85.

Eyster Burial Ground, near Jacob Eisenhart's (West Manchester): 726-86.

Fairview Cemetery, Wrightsville (Hellam Township): 726-87.

Fairview Church of the Brethren, New, Stump's Union (York Township): 726-88.

Fawn Grove Methodist Protestant Church, Whiteside's Chapel (Fawn): 726-89.

Fawn Grove Friends Cemetery (Fawn): 726-105.

Feigley Burial Ground, on Hartman farm, near Loganville (Springfield): 726-90.

Ferree (?) Cemetery, Forry (Hellam Township): 726-99.

Fetrow's Cemetery near Yocumtown (Newberry): 726-91.

Filey's Cemetery (Monaghan): 726-92.

Firestone Burial Ground, on old Leib farm (Washington): 726-93.

First Presbyterian Church, E. Market Street (City of York): 726-94.

Fissel's Cemetery, Jerusalem Church, near Railroad (Shrewsbury): 726-96.

Fisher Burial Ground, near Smoketown (Fairview): 726-95.

Fitz Burial Ground, near Jefferson (North Codorus): 726-97.

Flickinger's Cemetery (Mumma's) York Street, Hanover (Penn): 726-214.

Fockenroth Burial Ground, Vockenroth, Spring Grove (all German) (North Codorus): 726-98.

Forry Cemetery (Ferree?), w. of Wrightsville (Hellam Township): 726-99.

Franklin Church Cemetery, St. John's Reformed and Lutheran (Franklin): 726-100.

Franklintown Cemetery (Franklin): 726-101.

Frantz Burial Ground (Manchester): 726-4.

Freysville Evangelical Cemetery (Windsor): 726-102.

Freysville Reformed and Lutheran Cemetery (Windsor): 726-103.

Friedensaal Church Cemetery, s.w. of Loganville (Springfield): 726-104.

Friends' Cemetery, Old Quaker Cemetery, Newberrytown (Newberry): 726-217.

Friends' Meeting House, Fawn Grove Friends (Fawn): 726-105.

Friends' Meeting House, near Wellsville (Warrington): 726-106.

Friends' Meeting House, W. Philadelphia Street (City of York): 726-107.

Garber's Mennonite Church Cemetery near Menges Mills (Heidelberg): 726-108.

Gatchelville Cemetery (Fawn): 726-109.

Gehly Burial Ground, on old Hersh Farm (Windsor Township): 726-110.

Gerber's Graveyard, on McConkey farm (Hellam Township): 726-111.

German Baptist Meeting House, Bermudian Brethren (Washington): 726-26.

German Catholic Cemetery, Catholic Cemetery (Spring Garden): 726-49.

Gibson Burial Ground, between Red Lion and Winterstown (North Hopewell): 726-112.

Gipe Burial Ground, at Shenberger's Chapel, beyond New Bridgeville (Chanceford): 726-53.

Glatfelter Burial Ground, near Zion's, Shaffer's (Codorus): 726-113.

Glen Rock Lutheran and Reformed (Shrewsbury): 726-114.

Gochenauer Burial Ground, Deardorff's Cemetery (Washington): 726-64.

Good's Burial Plot, between Manchester and Susquehanna Trail (Manchester): 726-115.

Goodling, see Stine (Springfield Township).

Gordon Cemetery (Hopewell): 726-478.

Grace Evangelical, Trinity Evangelical (West Manheim): 726-325.

Greenmount Cemetery, on Carlisle Road (City of York): 726-116.

Greenmount U. B. Cemetery, s.e. of Jefferson (Codorus): 726-117.

Grissinger's Cemetery, St. John's Lutheran (Newberry): 726-118.

Groff Burial Ground, on Spahr farm (Washington): 726-119.

Gross Cemetery, Neiman/Shiloh/Weigel (West Manchester): 726-1.

Gross and Metzger Burial Ground, in Manchester Boro. (East Manchester): 726-120.

Guinston Presbyterian Church Cemetery (Chanceford): 726-121.

Ham Burial Plot, near Sinseim (North Codorus): 726-122.

Hametown, St. Paul's Lutheran (Shrewsbury): 726-284.

Hamme Burial Ground (Dover Township): 726-123.

Harbold (Old) Cemetery (Paradise): 726-222.

Hartman Burial Ground, near Manchester Boro (East Manchester): 726-125.

Hauser's Cemetery, Burg Burial Ground (Hellam Township): 726-46.

Hebrew Orthodox Cemetery, South Hill Cemetery (Spring Garden): 726-126.

Hebrew Reformed Congregation, S. George near Jackson (City of York): 726-127.

Heindel Burial Ground, on Snell farm, n.e. of York (Windsor): 726-128.

Heindel's Cemetery at Heindel's School, near Brillharts (North Codorus): 726-129.

Hendrix Burial Ground, now owned by Dr. Dunnick (Shrewsbury): 726-130.

Hershey Burial Ground, no longer in existence, on Hershey farm, near Martin's Station (Jackson): 726-131.

Hess Burial Ground, Ensminger Burial Ground (Springfield): 726-81.

Highmount Cemetery (Hellam Township): 726-132.

Hildebrand Cemetery, 1 mile n.e. of E. Berlin (Washington): 726-133.

Hill Burial Ground, near Jefferson (Codorus): 726-134.

Hoke Burial Ground, on Michael Hoke farm (West Manchester): 726-135.

Holtzinger Church Cemetery, Church of God (Windsor): 726-136.

Holy Saviour Cemetery, Catholic, on Susquehanna Trail (Manchester): 726-137.

Holzschwamm Cemetery, Paradise Lutheran and Reformed (Paradise): 726-138.

Home Cemetery, Dallastown (York Township): 726-139.

Hoover's Cemetery (Jerusalem U. B.) Starview Village (East Manchester): 726-140.

Hopewell Cemetery (Hopewell): 726-141.

Hopewell United Presbyterian Cemetery (East Hopewell): 726-142.

Hopewell United Presbyterian Cemetery, Old (East Hopewell): 726-143.

Houston Burial Ground, Druck Valley (Hellam Township): 726-144.

Huber Burial Ground, on Anna M. L. Huber's farm (Hellam Township): 726-145.

Hursh Burial Ground (Fairview): 726-146.

Immanuel Evangelical Cemetery (Emanuel) near Glen Rock (Shrewsbury): 726-147.

Jacobs Burial Ground, Bender Burial Ground, near Maytown (Warrington): 726-23.

Jameson's Cemetery, Union, non-existent, N. Penn Street (City of York): 726-327.

Jefferson Cemetery, Jefferson Boro. (Codorus): 726-148.

Jerusalem Church Cemetery, Fissel's (Shrewsbury): 726-96.

Jerusalem Cemetery, mile from Starview on Cod. Fur. Road (East Manchester): 726-149.

Jewish Cemetery on Black Rock Road Hanover (Penn): 726-150.

Johannis Kirche Cemetery, Saddler's (Hopewell): 726-264.

Keeney Cemetery (Shrewsbury): 726-480.

Keeny's Cemetery, Stone's (Shrewsbury): 726-309.

Kehr Burial Ground (Heidelberg): 726-151.

Keller Burial Ground, near Stiltz Church (Shrewsbury): 726-152.

Keller's Graveyard, near E. Prospect (Lower Windsor): 726-153.

Kindig Burial Ground, near Crandall Health School (Hellam Township): 726-154.

Kister Burial Ground, back of school, Goldsboro (Newberry Township): 726-155.

Kline Burial Ground, Dosch/Shenberger (Lower Windsor): 726-67.

Klinefelter Burial Ground, Seitz's, near Fissel Church (Shrewsbury): 726-156.

Knab Burial Plot (Manchester): 726-157.

Knaub (Old) Burial Ground, Dillsburg Cemetery (Carroll): 726-66.

Kreutz Creek Cemetery (Hellam Township): 726-158.

Kunkel Burial Ground, near The Glades (Springettsbury): 726-159.

Lebanon (colored) Cemetery, North York Boro. (Manchester): 726-160.

Lebanon Lutheran Cemetery (North Hopewell): 726-161.

Lebanon Reformed Cemetery (North Hopewell): 726-162.

Lehman's Cemetery, Starview Village (East Manchester): 726-163.

Lehman's Graveyard, on Marietta Wat. County land (Hellam Township): 726-164.

Lenharts and Gerbers, Salem Cemetery, opposite Strayers Salem (Dover Township): 726-288.

Lerew Cemetery, 2 miles from Clear Spring (Franklin): 726-165.

Libhart Burial Ground, near Walter Beards (Hellam Township): 726-166.

Lichtenberger Burial Ground, on old Lichtenberger farm (East Manchester): 726-167.

Lichtenberger Burial Ground, on old Lichtenberger farm (Fairview): 726-168.

Liebenknecht's Cemetery, opposite Strayers Salem (Dover): 726-169.

Linebaugh Burial Plot, on Spangler farm (East Manchester): 726-170.

Lischy's Cemetery (North Codorus): 726-171.

Lischy's Old Burial Ground, St. Peter's Reformed and Evangelical Lutheran (North Codorus): 726-172.

Locust Grove Cemetery, off Old Plank Road (Windsor): 726-173.

Loganville Evangelical Cemetery (Old) (Springfield): 726-223.

Loganville Lutheran Cemetery (Springfield): 726-176.

Longstown United Brethren Cemetery, Tilden U. B. (Springettsbury): 726-322.

Loucks Cemetery, Loucks Schoolhouse, formerly Wolf's (West Manchester): 726-174.

Lutheran Cemetery, Manchester Boro. (East Manchester): 726-175.

Lutheran Cemetery, Loganville (Springfield): 726-176.

Lutheran Cemetery, Boro. of Shrewsbury (Shrewsbury): 726-177.

Lutheran Cemetery, Seven Valleys, St. Paul's (Springfield): 726-295.

Lutheran Evangelical, Rossville Lutheran, Stone, St. Michael's (Warrington): 726-281.

Lutheran and Reformed Cemetery, Dubs (Manheim): 726-71.

Machpelah Cemetery, 1 miles n. of Yorkana (Lower Windsor): 726-178.

Manchester Lutheran Cemetery, Manchester Boro. (East Manchester): 726-175.

Manheim Union Burial Ground, Runkle's, Wildasin's (Manheim): 726-340.

Manifold Burial Ground, McPherson farm, Muddy Creed Fks. (Fawn): 726-179.

Markey Burial Ground, near Markey's Fording on Conewago Creek (Washington): 726-180.

Marks Burial Ground, near Longstown (York Township): 726-181.

Martin's Burial Ground, Hershey's, near Martin's Station (Jackson): 726-182.

Maul, Old Mt. Carmel Burial Ground (Heidelberg): 726-224.

May's Meeting House Cemetery, 2 miles s.w. of Dover (Dover Township): 726-183.

McAlister Burial Plot, McAlister farm woods (East Hopewell): 726-184.

McConkey Burial Ground (Peach Bottom): 726-185.

McKendree Cemetery (Lower Chanceford): 726-186.

Meisenhelder Burial Ground, near Dover-Conewago Line (Dover Township): 726-187.

Meisenhelter Burial Ground, East Berlin: 726-188.

Mennonite Cemetery, rear 216 E. Market Street (City of York): 726-353.

Mennonite Cemetery, near Manchester (East Manchester): 726-189.

Mennonite Cemetery, near Stony Brook (Springettsbury): 726-190.

Mennonite Church Cemetery, Garber's (Heidelberg): 726-108.

Mennonite Meeting House Burial Ground, Bairs, Station (West Manchester): 726-191.

Mennonite Meeting House Burial Ground, near Davidsburg (Dover Township): 726-192.

Menosimmon's Meeting House Cemetery, Bair's (Heidelberg): 726-18.

Methodist Church Cemetery, Moore's (Fairview): 726-201.

Methodist Church Cemetery, Lewisberry (Newberry): 726-193.

Methodist Episcopal Cemetery, Bethel M. E. (Chanceford): 726-28.

Methodist Episcopal Graveyard (City of York): 726-472.

Methodist Protestant Church Cemetery, Mt. Nebo (Peach Bottom): 726-204.

Methodist Cemetery, Mt. Olivet (Peach Bottom): 726-208.

Metzger and Gross Burial Ground, Manchester Boro. (East Manchester): 726-120.

Meyers Burial Ground, 2 1/2 miles e. of Loganville (Springfield): 726-194.

Miller Burial Ground, near Brodbecks (Manheim): 726-195.

Miller Burial Ground, near Smoketown (Newberry): 726-196.

Miller Burial Plot, n. of Newberrytown (Fairview): 726-197.

Miller Burial Ground (Dunkard), on Stiffler farm (Codorus): 726-73.

Mill's Burial Plot, near Yocumtown (Newberry): 726-198.

Monaghan Presbyterian Cemetery, Dillsburg (Carroll Township): 726-199.

Moore Cemetery (Washington): 726-200.

Moore's Methodist Church Cemetery (Fairview): 726-201.

Moser Burial Ground, 2 miles north of York (York Township): 726-202.

Mt. Airy E. U. B. (Fortney P.O. (Warrington): 726-345.

Mount Carmel Cemetery, near Jacobs Mills (Heidelberg): 726-203.

Mount Carmel (Old) Burial Ground, Maul (Heidelberg): 726-224.

Mount Nebo Cemetery, Methodist Protestant (Peach Bottom): 726-204.

Mount Olivet Church of God, Benedict's (Warrington): 726-24.

Mount Olivet Cemetery (Fairview): 726-205.

Mount Olivet Cemetery, Hanover (Penn): 726-206.

Mount Olivet Cemetery (Hopewell): 726-207.

Mount Olivet, Methodist, Cemetery (Peach Bottom): 726-208.

Mount Pleasant Bethel Church of God Cemetery (Monaghan): 726-209.

Mount Pleasant Methodist Cemetery, Bentz (Warrington): 726-362.

Mount Rose Cemetery (Spring Garden): 726-210.

Mount Zion Evangelical Cemetery (Springfield): 726-211.

Mt. Zion E. U. B. Church Cemetery (Warrington): 726-481.

Mount Zion Lutheran Cemetery (Fairview): 726-212.

Mount Zion Lutheran and Reformed Cemetery (Springettsbury): 726-213.

Mount Zion U. B. Cemetery, Wentz's Meeting House Cemetery (West Manheim): 726-338.

Mumma's Cemetery, Flickinger's Burial Ground, York Street, Hanover (Penn): 726-214.

Mummert's Meeting House, Pleasant Hill Dunkard (Jackson): 726-75.

Myers Cemetery (Monaghan): 726-3.

Nebinger Burial Plot, Lewisberry ((Newberry): 726-215.

Neiman's Cemetery, Gross, earlier Weigle's, Shiloh Union Church, Shiloh (West Manchester): 726-1.

Newberry Friends Burying Ground, Old Quaker Cemetery, Newberrytown (Newberry): 726-217.

Newberrytown Cemetery, Paddletown (Newberry): 726-229.

Newcomer's Burial Ground, near Jefferson (North Codorus): 726-218.

New Freedom Cemetery, New Freedom (Shrewsbury): 726-219.

New Harmony Presbyterian Church Cemetery, Brogueville (Chanceford): 726-220.

New Salem Cemetery, beyond Strayer's Salem Lutheran and Reformed (Dover): 726-221.

North Trinity Church Cemetery, Trinity Evangelical (Lower Windsor): 726-324.

Old Brick Cemetery, Old Rossville, St. John's Reformed (Warrington): 726-273.

Old Harbolt Burial Ground (Paradise): 726-222.

Old Log Cemetery, Airville, United Presbyterian, Shenks (Lower Chanceford): 726-7.

Old Loganville, Loganville Evangelical, Cemetery (Springfield): 726-223.

Old Mount Carmel Burial Ground, mile from Mt. C. Cemetery and Church (Heidelberg): 726-224.

Old Pleasant Hill Dunkard Cemetery (Jackson): 726-236.

Old Rossville, Old Brick, St. John's Reformed (Warrington): 726-273.

Old Round Hill Cemetery, Round Hill Presbyterian (North Hopewell): 726-225.

Old St. Matthews Lutheran, 1 mile n. of Hanover, Winebrenner (Penn): 726-280.

Old Union Lutheran and Reformed Burial Ground, Bat Pen, Lewisberry (Newberry): 726-20.

Old United Brethren Burial Ground, Dover Boro. (Dover): 726-226.

Olewiler Cemetery, near Craley (Lower Windsor): 726-227.

Otterbein Chapel Cemetery, Spry U. B. (York Township): 726-228.

Paddletown Cemetery, Newberrytown Cemetery, Erney Cemetery (Newberry): 726-229.

Paradise Lutheran and Reformed, Holzschwamm (Paradise): 726-138.

Parkville Cemetery, Bald Hill, now called Erney (Newberry): 726-230.

Pidgeon Hill Cemetery, Christ Lutheran (Jackson): 726-55.

Pine Grove Cemetery (Lower Chanceford): 726-231.

Pine Grove United Evangelical Church Cemetery (York Township): 726-232.

Pine Swamp Burial Ground, near Fairmount Evangelical Church (Hellam Township): 726-233.

Pleasant Grove Cemetery (Windsor): 726-234.

Pleasant Grove U. B. Cemetery (Newberry): 726-235.

Pleasant Hill Dunkard Cemetery (North Hopewell): 726-74.

Pleasant Hill Dunkard Burial Ground (Old), Pidgeon Hills (Jackson): 726-236.

Pleasant Hill Dunkard, Mummert's, n. of Spring Grove (Jackson): 726-75.

Pleasant View Cemetery (Dunkard), near Dillsburg (Carroll): 726-237.

Pleasureville Cemetery (Springettsbury): 726-238.

Porter's Cemetery, Zion Evangelical (Heidelberg): 726-359.

Potter's Field (Almshouse) in Windsor Park (Spring Garden): 726-239.

Presbyterian Church Cemetery, Chanceford (Lower Chanceford): 726-51.

Presbyterian Church Cemetery, Stewartstown (Hopewell): 726-240.

Presbyterian Church Cemetery, Centre Presbyterian (Fawn): 726-50.

Prospect Hill Cemetery, N. George Street (City of York): 726-241.

Prowell Burial Ground, above Newberrytown (Fairview): 726-242.

Quaker Cemetery (Old), Friends, Newberrytown (Newberry): 726-217.

Quickel's Cemetery, Zion Lutheran and Reformed, near Zions View (Conewago): 726-243.

Redland Friends Cemetery (Newberry): 726-244.

Red Lion Cemetery, Red Lion, PA (York Township): 726-245.

Red Mount Cemetery, near Kralltown (Washington): 726-246.

Red Run Cemetery, Sower's, St. Paul's Lutheran Church (Washington): 726-247.

Reformed Cemetery, Shrewsbury Reformed, Boro. of Shrewsbury: 726-248.

Reformed and Lutheran Cemetery, Dub's, St. Paul's (Manheim): 726-71.

Rennoll Burial Plot, mile from Spring Grove (North Codorus): 726-249.

Rest Haven Cemetery, out of Hanover (Penn): 726-250.

Richcreek Burial Ground (Fairview): 726-251.

Rider Cemetery, on Linebaugh farm (Washington?): 726-252.

Riverview, East Prospect (Lower Windsor): 726-76.

Rock Chap Cemetery, in field out from Shrewsbury (Shrewsbury): 726-253.

Rockey Burial Ground, near Parkville (Newberry): 726-254.

Rodes Cemetery, near Conewago (East Manchester Township): 726-255.

Rodes (Roth's) Trinity Reformed, Pidgeon Hills (Jackson): 726-256.

Rohler's Mountain View Lutheran Cemetery (Dover): 726-257.

Rohler's U. B. Cemetery (Dover): 726-258.

Rossville Lutheran, Lutheran Evangelical, Stone Church, St. Michael's (Warrington): 726-281.

Roth Burial Ground (Hellam Township): 726-259.

Roth's Cemetery (Rodes) Trinity Reformed (Jackson): 726-256.

Round Hill Cemetery (East Hopewell): 726-260.

Round Hill Cemetery (Old) Round Hill Presbyterian (North Hopewell): 726-225.

Rubel's Burial Ground, near Jefferson (North Codorus): 726-261.

Ruby Burial Ground, near Trinity Evangelical Church (Lower Windsor): 726-262.

Rudy's Burial Ground, east of Hellam (Hellam Township): 726-263.

Runkle's Graveyard, Manheim Union Burial Ground, Wildasin's (Manheim): 726-340.

Saddler's Cemetery, Johannis Kirche, on Sadler's Church Road (Hopewell): 726-264.

Saginaw Cemetery, Union Cemetery, in New Holland (East Manchester): 726-265.

St. Bartholomew Cemetery, near Adams County Line (West Manheim): 726-266.

St. David's Cemetery, Sherman(s), on Hanover-Baltimore Pike (West Manheim): 726-267.

St. Jacob's Evangelical Lutheran Cemetery, York New Salem Boro. (North Codorus): 726-268.

St. Jacob's Union Cemetery, York New Salem Boro (North Codorus): 726-269.

St. James Cemetery (Chanceford): 726-270.

St. John's on the Hill, Bats Nest, Bat Pen, Union Lutheran and Reformed (Newberry): 726-20.

St. John's Catholic Cemetery, New Freedom Boro. (Shrewsbury): 726-271.

St. John's Lutheran Cemetery, Grissinger's (Newberry): 726-118.

St. John's Protestant Episcopal, N. Beaver Street (City of York): 726-272.

St. John's Reformed Church, Old Brick, Old Rossville, Cemetery (Warrington): 726-273.

St. John's Reformed and Lutheran, Franklin, near Clear Spring (Franklin): 726-100.

St. Joseph's Catholic Cemetery, Dallastown (York Township): 726-274.

St. Joseph's Catholic Cemetery, adjacent St. Olivet, Hanover (Penn): 726-275.

St. Luke' Cemetery (Chanceford): 726-276.

St. Mary's Catholic Cemetery (Paradise): 726-277.

St. Mary's Catholic Cemetery, in Wrightsville (Hellam Township): 726-278.

St. Matthew's Cemetery, Hanover (Penn): 726-279.

St. Matthew's Lutheran Cemetery, on Carlisle Pike (Penn): 726-280.

St. Michael's, Rossville, Lutheran, Stone Church (Lutheran Evangelical Church (Warrington): 726-281.

St. Paul's Cemetery, Dubs, Lutheran and Reformed (Manheim): 726-71.

St. Paul's Cemetery, Old and New Parks, Zieglers (North Codorus): 726-282.

St. Paul's Lutheran Cemetery (North Hopewell): 726-283.

St. Paul's Lutheran Cemetery, Hametown (Shrewsbury): 726-284.

St. Paul's Lutheran, Sowers, Red Run (Washington): 726-247.

St. Paul's Lutheran, Seven Valleys (Springfield): 726-295.

St. Paul's Lutheran and Reformed, Wolf's (West Manchester): 726-349.

St. Paul's United Evangelical Cemetery, Craley (Lower Windsor): 726-285.

St. Peter's Cemetery, 1 1/2 miles s.w. of Loganville (Springfield): 726-286.

St. Peter's and Paul's Cemetery, near Larue (Codorus): 726-287.

St. Peter's Reformed and Evangelical Lutheran, Lischy's Old Burial Ground (North Codorus): 726-172.

Salem Cemetery, Lenharts and Gerbers, opposite Strayers Salem Lutheran and Reformed Church (Dover): 726-288.

Salem Cemetery (Lower Chanceford): 726-289.

Salem Cemetery (Lower Windsor): 726-290.

Salem Cemetery, Salem Church of the Brethren in Christ, north of Newberrytown (Fairview): 726-291.

Salem Church Cemetery, Lutheran and Reformed, Jacobus (Springfield): 726-292.

Salem Church of Evangelical Association, Albrights (Warrington): 726-9.

Salem Union Cemetery, Barrens (Washington): 726-19.

Schneider Burial Ground, off road Starview-Pleasureville (East Manchester): 726-293.

Seiffert (Scivert) Burial Ground (Washington): 726-294.

Seitz Burial Ground, Klinefelter (Shrewsbury): 726-156.

Seven Valleys Lutheran, Lutheran Cemetery, St. Paul's (Springfield): 726-295.

Shaffer's Cemetery, Zion's, near Neiman (Brenneman) (Codorus): 726-296.

Sheffer's Cemetery (North Hopewell): 726-297.

Shenberger's, Kline/Dosch, Cemetery (Lower Windsor): 726-67.

Shenberger Chapel, Evangelical Chapel, Cemetery (Chanceford): 726-85.

Shenk's Cemetery, Airville, United Presbyterian (Old Log) (Lower Chanceford): 726-7.

Sherman's, St. David's (West Manheim): 726-267.

Shiloh Cemetery, Neimans/Gross/Weigels (West Manchester): 726-1.

Shoff's Burial Ground, near St. Luke's Lutheran Church (Chanceford): 726-298.

Shrewsbury Lutheran, Lutheran Cemetery, Shrewsbury Boro. (Shrewsbury): 726-177.

Shrewsbury Reformed Cemetery, Boro of Shrewsbury (Shrewsbury): 726-248.

Slate Ridge Cemetery (Peach Bottom): 726-299.

Slateville Presbyterian Cemetery (Peach Bottom): 726-300.

Smith Burial Ground, beyond Bermudian Brethren Church (Washington): 726-301.

Smoketown Cemetery, near Goldsboro (Newberry): 726-302.

Snyder Burial Ground, on Martin Druck farm (Hellam Township): 726-303.

South Hill Cemetery, Hebrew Orthodox (Spring Garden): 726-126.

Sowers Cemetery, St. Paul's Lutheran, Red Run (Washington): 726-246.

Spohnhauer Burial Plot, Welsh Cemetery (North Codorus): 726-304.

Spring Grove Cemetery (Jackson): 726-305.

Springville Cemetery (Lower Windsor): 726-306.

Spry U. B. Cemetery, Otterbein Chapel, U. B. in Christ (York Township): 726-228.

Starview Cemetery, Lehman's, at Starview (East Manchester): 726-163.

Stauffer's, Brillhart's, Cemetery, near Jefferson (North Codorus): 726-42.

Stewart Burial Ground (Spring Garden): 726-307.

Stewartstown Cemetery (Hopewell): 726-308.

Stiltz Cemetery, Bethlehem, astride Mason-Dixon PA-MD Line (Codorus): 726-29.

Stine's Cemetery, Keeny's, Goodling (Springfield): 726-309.

Stone Church Cemetery, Rossville Lutheran, Lutheran Evangelical, St. Michael's (Warrington): 726-281.

Stone Church Cemetery, St. Jacobs Lutheran and Reformed, near Brodbecks, s. of Jefferson Boro. (Codorus): 726-310.

Stone Church (colored), Wrightsville, near river (Hellam Township): 726-311.

Stoner Cemetery, along US 30 east, Lincoln Highway (Hellam Township): 726-312.

Stough's Burial Ground, Dover Boro. (Dover): 726-313.

Stoverstown Cemetery (North Codorus): 726-314.

Strayer's, Salem Lutheran and Reformed, mile w. of Dover (Dover): 726-315.

Strickler's Cemetery (Springettsbury): 726-316.

Strickler Cemetery, off Lincoln Highway, 2 miles west of Wrightsville (Hellam Township): 726-317.

Strickler's Cemetery, on Mahlon Haines farm (Springettsbury): 726-318.

Strinestown Cemetery (Conewago): 726-319.

Strong Burial Ground, on McKinley farm, near Glades (Hellam Township): 726-320.

Stump's Union, New Fairview Church of Brethren (York Township): 726-88.

Thorley Burial Ground (Fairview): 726-321.

Tilden U. B. Cemetery, Longstown U. B. (Springettsbury): 726-322.

Trinity Church Cemetery (Chanceford): 726-323.

Trinity Evangelical Cemetery, Grace Evangelical, at Pleasant Hill (West Manheim): 726-325.

Trinity Evangelical, North Trinity, between Wrights Long Lev. (Lower Windsor): 726-324.

Trinity Reformed Cemetery, Rodes/Roth's (Jackson): 726-356.

Tucker Burial Ground (Jackson): 726-326.

Union Cemetery, Saginaw (East Manchester): 726-265.

Union Cemetery, Jameson's,) non-existent, N. Penn St. (City of York): 726-327.

Union Cemetery, Dallastown (York Township): 726-328.

Union Cemetery, Boro. of Manchester (East Manchester): 726-329.

Union Chapel Cemetery (Lower Chanceford): 726-330.

Union Lutheran and Reformed, Bats Nest, Bat Pen, St. John's on the Hill (Newberry): 726-20.

United Brethren Cemetery Gay Street, perhaps same as Union Cemetery (City of York): 726-331.

United Brethren Cemetery, Bethany (Dover): 726-27.

United Brethren Cemetery, Winterstown (North Hopewell): 726-332.

United Brethren Cemetery, Zion (Windsor): 726-216.

United Brethren Cemetery, Jefferson (Codorus): 726-333.

United Brethren Cemetery (Old) Boro. of Dover (Dover): 726-226.

United Evangelical Cemetery (North Hopewell): 726-334.

United Presbyterian Cemetery, Old Log-Airville-Shenks (Lower Chanceford): 726-7 and 8.

Vockenroth Burial Ground, Fockenroth (North Codorus): 726-98.

Walgemuth's German Baptist Meeting House, near Dillsburg (Carroll): 726-335.

Wallace Burial Plot (East Hopewell): 726-336.

Walter's Union Cemetery (York Township): 726-337.

Warrington Friends Cemetery, Friends Meeting House Cemetery (Warrington): 726-106.

Weigel's Cemetery, Neiman/Shiloh/Gross, Cemetery (West Manchester): 726-1.

Welsh Cemetery, Sponhauer (North Codorus): 726-304.

Wentz's Meeting House, Mt. Zion U. B., near St. Bartholomew's Church (West Manheim): 726-338.

Westhofer Burial Ground, in woods near Emigsville (Manchester): 726-339.

Whitesides Chapel Cemetery, Fawn Grove Methodist Protestant (Fawn): 726-89.

Wildasin's Graveyard, near Dubbs' German Reformed 8 miles s.e. of Hanover, Manheim Union Burial, Runkle's Graveyard (Manheim): 726-340.

Wildasin Meeting House (Penn): 726-341.

Williams Burial Ground, Dunkard Valley (York Township): 726-342.

Wilson Burial Plot, on old Wilson farm (East Hopewell): 726-343.

Windsor Cemetery (Windsor): 726-344.

Winebrenner's Burial Ground, Old St. Matthews, 1 mile north of Hanover (Penn): 726-280.

Wintermyer, Bupp's (Conewago): 726-44.

Wise Burial Ground, near Chanceford Presbyterian Church (Lower Chanceford): 726-346.

Witman Burial Ground, near St. Luke's Lutheran Church (Chanceford): 726-347.

Wogan Burial Ground, Saginaw, near railroad and river (East Manchester): 726-348.

Wolf's Cemetery, also known as Butts (West Manchester): 726-34.

Wolf's Cemetery, St. Paul's Lutheran and Reformed (West Manchester): 726-349.

Wolf's, Loucks Schoolhouse (West Manchester): 726-174.

Wrightsville Presbyterian (Old), Wrightsville (Hellam Township): 726-350.

Yocumtown Church of God (Newberry): 726-351.

York Cemetery (York Township): 726-352.

York Friends Meeting House Cemetery, W. Philadelphia Street (City of York): 726-107.

York Mennonite Cemetery, Mennonite, originally in rear of 216 E. Market Street (City of York): 726-353.

York Road Cemetery (Heidelberg): 726-355.

Yorkana Cemetery, 7 miles east of York (Lower Windsor): 726-354.

Yost Cemetery, on Yost farm, R. D. 4, Dillsburg (Carroll or Washington): 726-356. 1992 - Tombstones beside barn on Faust Road, Pinehurst Farm (Washington Township).

Young Burial Ground, near Glatfelter's Station (Springfield): 726-357.

Yount Cemetery (Hopewell): 726-479.

Zerger Burial Plot, Old Passmore place, near Goldsboro (Newberry): 726-358.

Zieglers, St. Paul's (North Codorus): 726-282.

Zion Evangelical Cemetery, Porter's (Heidelberg): 726-359.

Zion Lutheran Cemetery, rear 36 S. Duke Street (City of York): 726-360.

Zion M. E. Cemetery (Hopewell): 726-361.

Zion U. B. Cemetery, U. B. in Christ (Windsor): 726-216.

Zions View Lutheran and Reformed, Quickel's (Conewago): 726-243.

Zions Cemetery, Shaffers (Codorus): 726-296.

ADAMS COUNTY CEMETERY RECORDS (Held at HSYC)
* Denotes cemetery no longer in existence.

Abbott Grave (Berwick Township): 726-363.

Arendtsville Cemetery (Butler Township): 726-364.*

Baker Burial Ground (Hamiltonban Township): 726-365.*

Bart's U. B. Cemetery (Union Township): 726-366.

Beamer's Burial Ground, Mosely (Menallen Township): 726-367.*

Benders Lutheran Church Cemetery (Butler Township): 726-368.

Bendersville Cemetery (Menallen Township): 726-369.

Bendersville Evangelical Churchyard (Menallen Township): 726-485.*

Bermudian (Lower) Lutheran Cemetery, Christ Evangelical Lutheran (Latimore Township): 726-370.

Bermudian Mount Olivet, Christ Evangelical, Cemetery (Latimore Township): 726-371.

Bethlehem U. B. Cemetery, aka Center Mills (Butler Township): 726-372.

Biglerville Cemetery (Butler Township): 726-373.

Bishop's U. B. Family Burial Ground (Germany Township): 726-486.*

Black's Graveyard, aka Old Marsh Creek Presbyterian Churchyard (Cumberland Township): 726-374.

Bosserman Burial Ground (Reading Township): 726-375.

Brethren Cemetery, aka "Latimore's" (Latimore Township): 726-376.

Brinkerhoff Slave Burial Ground (Straban Township): 726-499.*

Bucher Burial Ground, aka Hostetters (Berwick Township): 726-377.

Bushey's Cemetery, aka Lobach's (Latimore Township): 726-418.

Bushman Cemetery (Cumberland Township): 726-378.*

Butt's Graveyard (Cumberland Township): 726-488.*

Byer Burial Ground (Highland Township): 726-379.*

Carrollsburg Cemetery, aka Zimmerman's (Liberty Township): 726-470.

Center Mills Cemetery, aka Bethlehem U. B. (Butler Township): 726-372.

Chamberlin Cemetery (Franklin Township): 726-380.

Chestnut Grove (Old) Burial Ground, aka Harbolds and Zieglers (Latimore Township): 726-469.

Chestnut Grove Lutheran Cemetery (Latimore Township): 726-381.

Chestnut Hill Cemetery (Tyrone Township): 726-489.*

Christ Chapel Churchyard, Episcopal (Huntington Township): 726-490.

Christ Reformed Church Cemetery (Union Township): 726-382.

Clapsaddle's Cemetery, aka Scotsman Graveyard (Franklin Township): 726-476.

Cline's Cemetery (Menallen Township): 726-383.

Cochran-Annan Burial Ground, aka Zimmermans (Liberty Township): 726-470.

Cold Springs Cemetery, aka Strang's Cemetery (Hamiltonban Township): 726-384.

Conewago Chapel Cemetery, Sacred Heart R. C. (Conewago Township): 726-385.

Conewago Lutheran Churchyard, aka St. Michaels (Conewago Township): 726-491.*

Conewago Presbyterian Cemetery (Straban Township): 726-386.

Coulson's Graveyard, aka Days and Funts (Huntington Township): 726-387.

Days Graveyard, aka Coulsons and Funt (Huntington Township): 726-387.

Diehl Family Burial Ground (Butler Township): 726-492.

East Berlin Cemetery (Hamilton Township): 726-388.

Emanuel Reformed Cemetery, Hamilton Township (Abbottstown): 726-389.

Episcopalian Cemetery, Old White (Huntington Township): 726-390.

Evergreen Cemetery (Cumberland Township, Gettysburg): 726-391.

Fairfield Cemetery (Hamiltonban Township): 726-392.

Fairfield Methodist Churchyard (Hamiltonban Township): 726-493.*

Fairfield Presbyterian Churchyard (Hamiltonban Township): 726-494.*

Fairview Cemetery (Franklin Township, Arendtsville): 726-393.

Flohr's Lutheran Cemetery (Franklin Township): 726-394.

Fountaindale Lutheran Churchyard, aka St. Johns (Liberty Township): 726-495.

Fountaindale Union Cemetery, aka Methodist or Wesleyan (Liberty Township): 726-427.

Friends Cemetery (Menallen Township): 726-395.

Friends Grove Cemetery (Butler Township): 726-396.

Funts Burial Ground, aka Coulson and Day (Huntington Township): 726-387.

Gardner's Cemetery, Church of U. B. in Christ (Latimore Township): 726-397.

Gettysburg Catholic Cemetery, aka St. Francis Xavier (Cumberland Township): 726-398.

Gettysburg Colored Cemetery, aka Lincoln (Cumberland Township): 726-399.

Gettysburg Lutheran and Reformed Churchyard, aka St. James (Cumberland Township): 726-471.*

Gettysburg Presbyterian Churchyard (Cumberland Township): 726-484.*

Greenmount Cemetery (Franklin Township, Arendtsville): 726-400.

Griest Burial Ground No. 1 (Latimore Township): 726-401.

Griest Burial Ground No. 2 (Latimore Township): 726-402.

Ground Oak Cemetery, aka Upper Bermudian Lutheran (Huntington Township): 726-465.

Hampton Brethren Cemetery (Reading Township): 726-403.

Hampton Lutheran and Reformed Cemetery, aka Hampton Union (Reading Township): 726-404.

Hampton Union Cemetery, aka Hampton Lutheran and Reformed (Reading Township): 726-404.

Harbold's Cemetery, aka Ziegler and Old Chestnut Grove Cemetery (Latimore Township): 726-469.

Jacob Harbaugh's Reformed Church Cemetery (Liberty Township): 726-405.

Hawks Private Burial Ground, Haughs (Hamiltonban Township): 726-475.*

Heidlersburg Cemetery (Tyrone Township): 726-406.

Hill Cemetery (Freedom Township): 726-407.*

Hohf's Burial Ground (Butler Township): 726-408.*

Hostetter Burial Ground, aka Buchers (Berwick Township): 726-377.

Hostetter's Meeting House Cemetery, aka Manosimon Meeting House (Union Township): 726-409.

Huntington Friends Meeting House Cemetery (Latimore Township): 726-410.

Idaville Cemetery (Huntington Township): 726-411.

Jacobs Burial Ground (Paradise Township, York County): 726-412.

Jacobs Burial Ground (Hamilton Township): 726-413.

Keagy Cemetery (Conewago Township): 726-414.

Latimore Brethren Churchyard, aka Brethren (Latimore Township): 726-376.

Leas Burial Ground (Reading Township): 726-415.

Leer's Farm Cemetery, aka Robinette and Moorehead (Huntington Township): 726-416.

Littlestown Catholic Cemetery, aka St. Aloysius (Germany Township): 726-417.

Lobach Cemetery, aka Busheys (Latimore Township): 726-418.

Low Dutch Cemetery, aka Youngs (Mount Pleasant Township): 726-419.

Low Dutch Cemetery, aka Osbornes (Straban Township): 726-420.

Lower Marsh Creek Presbyterian Cemetery, aka Sanders (Highland Township): 726-421.

Manosimon Meeting House Cemetery, aka Hostetters (Union Township): 726-409.

Marsh Creek (Old) Cemetery, aka McClellans (Cumberland Township): 726-422.

Marsh Creek Brethren Cemetery, aka Pfoutz Mennonite Cemetery (Highland Township): 726-423.

Martins Burial Ground, aka Zimmermans (Liberty Township): 726-470.

McKnightstown Cemetery (Franklin Township): 726-424.

McClellan's Cemetery, aka Old Marsh Creek (Cumberland Township): 726-422.

McTaggart Cemetery (Berwick Township): 726-496.*

Mennonite Burial Ground (Franklin Township): 726-425.

Methodist Cemetery (Old) (Cumberland Township): 726-426.

Methodist or Wesleyan Cemetery, aka Fountaindale Union Cemetery (Liberty Township): 726-427.

Moorehead Cemetery, aka Leers and Robinette (Huntington Township): 726-416.

Mount Carmel Cemetery (Franklin Township): 726-428.

Mount Carmel Cemetery (Germany Township, Littlestown): 726-429.

Mount Joy Lutheran Church Cemetery (Mt. Joy Township): 726-430.

Mount Olive Cemetery (Hamilton Township, Abbottstown): 726-431.

Mount Olivet Cemetery, aka Bermudian Mt. Olivet (Latimore Township): 726-371.

Mount Hope Church Cemetery (Hamiltonban Township): 726-432.

Mount Tabor Cemetery (Menallen Township): 726-433.

Mount Zion U. B. Cemetery (Mt. Joy Township): 726-474.*

Mummasburg Mennonite Cemetery (Franklin Township): 726-434.

Mummert's German Baptist Meeting House Cemetery (Hamilton Township): 726-435.

National Cemetery, Gettysburg (Cumberland Township): 726-436.

New Oxford Catholic Cemetery (Oxford Township): 726-437.

New Oxford Cemetery (Oxford Township): 726-438.

New Oxford Reformed Graveyard (Oxford Township): 726-444.*

Oak Lawn Cemetery (Cumberland Township): 726-487.

Old Alms House Cemetery, aka Potter's Field (Cumberland Township): 726-441.

Osborne's Cemetery, aka Low Dutch Cemetery (Straban Township): 726-420.

Pine Bank, "The Pines", Cemetery, aka Rock Creek Cemetery (Mt. Joy Township): 726-439.

Pine Cemetery, Lutheran (Straban Township): 726-440.

Potter's Field, aka Old Alms House Cemetery (Cumberland Township): 726-441.

Presbyterian Cemetery, York Springs (Huntington Township): 726-442.

Prim Family Burial Ground (Tyrone Township): 726-497.*

Pfoutz Mennonite Cemetery, aka Marsh Creek Brethren Cemetery (Highland Township): 726-423.

Quaker (Old White) Cemetery, aka Huntington Friends Meeting House (Latimore Township): 726-410.

Quaker Cemetery (Butler Township): 726-443.

Rife (Reiff) Burial Ground (Union Township): 726-445.

Robinette Burial Ground, aka Leers and Moorehead (Huntington Township): 726-416.

Rock Chapel (Methodist) Cemetery (Huntington Township): 726-446.

Rock Creek Cemetery, aka Pine Bank Cemetery (Mt. Joy Township): 726-439.

Round Hill (Old) Cemetery (Reading Township): 726-447.
Sander's Cemetery, aka Lower Marsh Creek Presbyterian Cemetery (Highland Township): 726-421.

St. Aloysius R. C. Cemetery, aka Littlestown Catholic Cemetery (Germany Township): 726-417.

St. Francis Xavier R. C. Cemetery, aka Gettysburg Catholic (Cumberland Township): 726-398.

St. Ignatius R. C. Church Cemetery, Buchanan Valley (Franklin Township): 726-448.

St. James (Reformed) Cemetery, aka Sunnyside Cemetery (Mt. Joy Township): 726-449.

St. John's Evangelical Lutheran Cemetery (Germany Township, Littlestown): 726-450.

St. John's Lutheran Cemetery, Abbottstown (Hamilton Township): 726-451.

St. John's Reformed Cemetery, New Chester (Straban Township): 726-452.

St. Joseph's R. C. Cemetery, Bonneauville (Mt. Pleasant Township): 726-453.

St. Luke's Union Church Cemetery (Mt. Pleasant Township): 726-454.

St. Mark's Reformed Church Cemetery (Mt. Joy Township): 726-455.

St. Mary's R. C. Cemetery, Fairfield (Hamiltonban Township): 726-456.

St. Mary's R. C. Cemetery, McSherrystown (Conewago Township): 726-457.

St. Michael's Lutheran Cemetery, aka Conewago Lutheran Churchyard (Conewago Township): 726-491.*

St. Pauls African Methodist Zion Churchyard, Gettysburg (Cumberland Township): 726-498.*

Salem U. B. Cemetery (Mt. Pleasant Township): 726-458.

Sheely's Cemetery, Calvary U. B. in Christ Church (Franklin Township): 726-459.

Slaves Graveyard (Highland Township): 726-460.*

Slyder Burial Ground (Hamilton Township): 726-461.*

Snyder Family Burial Ground (Hamiltonban Township): 726-473.

Strang's Cemetery, aka Cold Springs Cemetery (Hamiltonban Township): 726-384.

Sunnyside Cemetery, York Springs (Latimore Township): 726-462.

Sunnyside Cemetery, aka St. James Reformed Cemetery (Mt. Joy Township): 726-449.

Tract Cemetery, aka Zimmermans Cemetery (Liberty Township): 726-470.

Trostle Meeting House Cemetery (Huntington Township): 726-463.

Two Taverns Cemetery at Grace Reformed Church (Mt. Joy Township): 726-464.

Upper Bermudian Lutheran Cemetery, aka Ground Oak Church (Huntington Township): 726-465.

Wenksville Cemetery (Menallen Township): 726-466.

Yellow Hill (Colored) Cemetery (Butler Township): 726-467.*

York Springs Lutheran Cemetery (Huntington Township): 726-468.

Young's Cemetery, aka Low Dutch Cemetery (Mt. Pleasant Township): 726-419.

Ziegler Burial Ground (Old), aka Old Chestnut Grove Burial Ground and Harbold's Burial Ground (Latimore Township): 726-469.

Zimmerman Burial Ground, aka Carrollsburg, Cochran-Annan, Martins and Tract Burial Ground (Liberty Township): 726-470.

Note: There are approximately twenty (20) additional burial sites listed for Adams County in various sources. Many of these Burial Grounds are listed as Indian, slave or "Unknown" Burial Grounds with little or no information to substantiate their existence and in most cases residents in the area where these Burial Grounds were to have been located have no knowledge of their existence.

OTHER COPIES OF TOMBSTONE RECORDS

YORK COUNTY

Colonial Burial Places (transcripts): GSP; pub. in *Genealogical Notes*, 13:225

Gravestone Inscriptions. York County (with other counties. See Gearhart and Gerberich Collections, GSP

Gravestone Inscriptions, Society of Friends in York (and Adams) Co. (transcripts): GSP

List of Cemeteries. York Co. (By townships) GSP

Codorus Township (York Co.)

Chestnut Grove Ch. of the Brethren Cemetery, Codorus Twp., YC;SCPGS Spec. Pub. # 7.

Hellam Township (York Co.)

Fairview Cem. Wrightsville, CC 1 (2) 32.

Newberry Township (York Co.)

"Bare Family Cemetery," *Mennonite Family History* 3:165.

Paradise Township (York Co.)

Altland's Meeting House Cemetery, Plot Map and Coded Information (SCPGS Spec. Pub. # 10).

Peach Bottom Township (York Co.)

Slate Ridge Cemetery, Peach Bottom Twp., Tombstone Inscriptions. (SCPGS Spec. Pub. # 52).

Slateville Presbyterian Cemetery, Peach Bottom Twp., Tombstone Inscriptions. (SCPGS Spec. Pub. # 52).

Warrington Township (York Co.)

Warrington (Friends) Meeting House Cemetery, Warrington Township...: Entries in the Grave Diggers Account Book, 1822-1847, Compared with Inscriptions on Tombstones, 1822-1847, existing in 1934. (SCPGS Spec. Pub. # 34, 1987).

Warrington Friends Meeting Cemetery, 726-106 in CVR

Washington Township (York Co.)

Bermudian Church of the Brethren Cemetery, Plot Map and Coded Information (SCPGS Spec. Pub. # 4).

West Manchester Township (York Co.)

Shiloh Cemetery, West Manchester Twp., Record of Burials, 1930-1975. (SCPGS Spec. Pub. # 52).

Shiloh Cemetery, Routes 74 and 238: records inscribed, ONTG 1 (4) 1, (5) 1.

York Township (York Co.)

Walter's Union Cemetery, York Twp., York Co. Notes on condition in ONTG 15 (11) 2.

ADAMS COUNTY

Old Cemeteries of Adams County, Pennsylvania, mentioned in ONTG 19 (5) 3.

Zimmerman Cemetery, Adams Co. Note on condition, ONTG 18 (1) 2.

Cumberland Township (Adams Co.)

"Conewago, or Low Dutch Graveyard, About Four Miles from Gettysburg," by Alfred R. Justice, from PGM 9:173-182; repr. in PVR 3:215-217.

Baltimore County (Maryland)

Zion United Methodist Church Cemetery, Freeland, Baltimore Co., MD, Alphabetical listing by Surname, of Information Given on Grave Markers and Tombstones (SCPGS Spec. Pub. # 3, 1973).

Carroll County (Maryland)

Pipe Creek (Friends) Meeting House Cemetery, Carroll County, MD: Graves Identified in the 1882 *History of Western Maryland,* by Scharf, compared with Inscriptions on Tombstones Existing in 1934. (SCPGS Spec. Pub. # 34, 1987)

St. Mary's Cemetery (Old Section) Silver Run, Maryland, Tombstone Inscriptions from. Compiled by Wendy Bish and Larry Bolin. (SCPGS Spec. Pub. # 50, 1992).

Chapter 5
CENSUSES, DIRECTORIES AND TAX LISTS

The compiler is indebted to Richard Konkel for the listing of original tax lists which follow.

Tax lists are an invaluable source for locating hard to find ancestors. They list all free men over 21 years of age on a yearly basis. Single men are listed separately, so when an individual shows up on the list of married men, an approximate year of marriage can be estimated. When a person disappears from the tax lists, it may indicate he has died or moved away. The tax lists also show value of real estate, livestock, and an individual's occupation.

Surviving tax lists and their location are as follows:

1762: A typed transcript of the tax list for the entire county is at HSYC. The original is at the HSP.

c1767-1799: Nearly complete records for these years are on microfilm at HSYC, which also holds the original manuscripts, but the latter are not to be used. They are arranged in books with returns from the several townships for a given year.

1800-1849: Nearly a complete run are on microfilm at the HSYC, which also holds the original manuscripts, but the latter are not to be used. These lists contain lists of poor children, taverns, etc., arranged by township, with the returns for several years in each book.

1850-1900: The originals, which have not been microfilmed, are at HSYC.

1900-Present: These are at the York County Archives.

Tax Lists By Township

Surviving Early Records of York County, PA - Collector's Warrants: County Tax of 1762 (for '63), Hellam Twp.; County Tax of 1767 (for '68): Cumberland and Newberry (Fragment) Twp.; Provincial Tax of 1767 (for '68): Germany, Hamiltonban and Newberry Twp. (1979). SCPGS Spec. Pub. # 8.

Surviving Early Records of York County, PA - Constable's Returns: Newberry Twp., 1765; Paradise Twp., 1769; York Twp., 1769 (1979). SCPGS Spec. Pub. # 9.

Chanceford Twp. Tax List, 1846-1847, CC 5(3)10.

Codorus Twp. Tax List, 1830-31, CC 1(4)22.

Fairview Twp. Triennial Tax, 1834-1835, CC 3(1)25, (40)34.

Index to the Taxables of Hanover and Heidelberg Township, York County, Pennsylvania, 1750-1817. By John R. McGrew. 1993) SCPGS Spec. Pub. # 51.

Heidelberg Twp. Tax List, 1818-1819, CC 2(3)27, (4)23.

Heidelberg Twp.: Hanover: Index of Taxables, 1750-1813; SCPGS Spec. Pub. # 51.

Menallen Twp. (Adams County) Federal Census, 1800, CC 2(4)44; 3(1)43, (3)43,(4)42; 4(1)41, (2)41, (4)41.

Newberry Twp., List of Taxables, 1765 (transcripts) GSP.

Paradise Twp. Tax List, 1849, CC 5(5)19; 6(1)25, (2)14.

Spring Garden Twp. Tax List, 1848, CC 1(1)34, (2)35.

Warington Twp. Tax List, 1800, CC 5(4)18.

Warrington Twp. Federal Census, 1840, CC 1(1)42, (2)43, (3)43, (4)43; 2(2)43, (3)43, (4)43.

Tax Lists By County

Alphabetical List of Taxables on Collector's Warrants, for 1771, SCPGS Spec. Pub. # 11.

An Alphabetical Listing of Heads of Households (with age and sex of all members of households) Included in the 1800 Census of York County, PA (Book I (of Two) - Surnames A-L (1981). Book II (of Two) - Surnames M-Z (1981). SCPGS Spec. Pubs. # 15, 16).

An Alphabetical Listing of Heads of Households (with age and sex of all members of households). Included in the 1800 Census of Adams County, PA (1982). SCPGS Spec. Pub. # 18.

An Alphabetical Listing of Heads of Households ... Included in the 1800 Federal Census of Cumberland Co, PA (1984-1985). SCPGS Spec. Pub. # 29.

Assessed Inhabitants of York County..., For Townships now in York County, 1762, Book 1 (1978), SCPGS Spec. Pub. # 5.

Assessed Inhabitants of York County..., For Townships now in Adams County, 1762, Book 2 (1978), SCPGS Spec. Pub. # 6.

"Delinquent" Taxables, 1758-1768, York County, PA. SCPGS Spec. Pub. # 26.

"Poor" Children Named on the Tax Lists, 1811-1844, York County, Pennsylvania. (1987-1988). SCPGS Spec. Pub. # 35.

Return of Taxables for the County of York, 1779-1783. Pennsylvania Archives, ser. 3, vol. 21. Harrisburg: 1898.

Tax List of York County, 1779. Westminster: Family Line, 1989. [Extracted from the *Pennsylvania Archives*]. It includes present day Adams County

York County Federal Census, 1790, CC 4 (3) 41, (4) 41; 5 (2) 41, (3) 41, (4) 41. (5) 42; 6 (1) 42, (3) 42.

Directories and Lists

"Clock Petition," in SCPGS Spec. Pub. # 37. Additions and Corrections, by Henry James Young, in ONTG 15 (7) 2-3.

Directory of Adams County, Pennsylvania, 1915, mentioned in ONTG 19 (2) 3.

Farm Journal Illustrated Farmers' Directory of York County (1915) was published with a road map of the county, mentioned ONTG 7 (5) 1.

"The Glass Tax (Federal Direct Tax of 1798)," ONTG 2 (3) Supp.

List of Subscribers for German Bible, Published in 1819, Lancaster, Pennsylvania, SCPGS Spec. Pub. # 37.

Chapter 6
CHURCHES

This is a listing of records of churches and pastors found at the Historical Society of York County, even if the churches are outside the present boundaries of York and Adams counties. Most churches are listed under their township. There are a few records of churches that cannot be placed, and these are listed by denomination in the notes that follow. Records found at the Historical Society of Pennsylvania are so noted.

COMPILED CHURCH RECORDS AND GUIDES

General

Abstracts and Identifications of Entries Giving European Origins in Church Records. By the South Central Pennsylvania Genealogical Society. c.r. 1990 by The Society.

Adams County Church Records of the 18th Century. By F. Edward Wright. Westminster: Family Line, n.d.

Baptismal Record for the Christian Protestant Congregation. By Charles T. Zahn. S.l., n.p., 1976.

Church and Pastoral Records in the Archives of the United Church of Christ and the Evangelical and Reformed Historical Society, Lancaster, Pa. By Florence M. Bricker. The Evangelical and Reformed Historical Society, 1982.

"Continental European Origins in Local Church Records," 14439 in CVR.

"A Genealogist's Guide to Pennsylvania Records (A Guide to the hidden sources in the collections of the Genealogical Society of Pennsylvania) [York County]," By Helen Hutchinson Woodroofe, *PGM* 35 (2) 154-166.

German Church Records: Beyond the Basics. By Kenneth L. Smith. Camden, ME: Picton Press. Mentioned in ONTG 15 (4) 2.

History of Churches, York County, Pa., in Chronological Sequence, 1700-1799. By Franklin W. Zarfoss. S.l., s.n., 1988. Mr. Zarfoss has recently compiled a series of volumes giving information on York County churches and pastors of the Lutheran, Reformed, United Methodist, and other denominations. These unpublished source books are at the HSYC.

Pastors and People: Volume I: Pastors and Congregations. By Charles H. Glatfelter. Breinigsville: The Pennsylvania German Society, 1980.

Pennsylvania German Church Records. 3 vols. Baltimore: Genealogical Publishing Co., 1983. (Reprints from the PA German Society).

Pennsylvania German Marriages. By Donna R. Irish. Baltimore: Genealogical Publishing Co., Inc., 1982.

York County, Pennsylvania Church Records of the 18th Century. By Marlene S. Bates, and F. Edward Wright. 3 vols. Westminster: Family Line Publications, 1991.

Christian Protestant

Baptismal Record for the Christian Protestant Congregation. Trans. by Charles T. Zahn. S.l., n.p., 1976.

Church of the Brethren

Light in the Valley: A History of the Codorus Church of the Brethren. By William L. Gould. Loganville: Codorus Church of the Brethren, 1976.

Lutheran

Early Lutheran Baptisms and Marriages In Southeastern Pennsylvania. 1896. Repr. Baltimore: Genealogical Publishing Co., Inc., 1988. (Pastoral records of Rev. John Casper Stoever).

York County Pennsylvania Lutherans (A Lutheran Legacy: Past Present and Future. By Dr. Charles H. Glatfelter. Mentioned in ONTG 19 (10) 1.

Mennonite

History of the Mennonite Brethren Church. By John A. Toews. Fresno [CA]. General Conference of the Mennonite and Brethren Churches, 1975.

Open Doors: The History of the General Conference Mennonite Church. By Samuel Floyd Pennabacker. Newton [KS]: Faith and Life Press, 1975.

Reformed

Genealogical Abstracts from Newspapers of the German Reformed Church, 1830-1839. Mentioned in ONTG 18 (7) 4.

Roman Catholic

"Catholic Records," ONTG, June 1977, pp. 3-4 (includes a list of basic sources).

Notes on the History of Catholics in York County. By Anna Dill Gamble. S.l., s.n., n.d.

Society of Friends

"The Friends," CC 4 (4) 26.

Pennsylvania Quaker Records. By Willard Heiss. Fort Wayne: Public Library of Fort Wayne, Ind., 1976 [includes Warrington Meeting, York County]

"The Seven Friends Meeting Houses Built in the 18th century in York County," CC 5 (2) 31

United Brethren in Christ

For a fuller description of these records, see "Hively's Genealogical Notes," ONTG 16 (7) 1.

United Methodist

Methodists in York County, 1781-1878, mentioned in ONTG 19 (2) 3.

Pleasant Grove (East End) United Methodist Church, 1890-1990, mentioned, ONTG 16 (2)

Trinity United Methodist Church; 614 in CVR

Yorkers Circuit of the Evangelical Association, YC; A-526 in CVR

Yorkshire United Methodist. See *Yorkshire United Methodist Church, 1879-1992.* By Doris L. Emenheiser. York: Shuman Heritage Printing Co., 1992.

ORIGINAL CHURCH RECORDS OF YORK AND ADAMS COUNTIES

At HSYC each township in York County is assigned a letter, which is used in numbering the volumes of church records from that township. If there is no CVR number, the records of that church have not been carded in the Vital Statistics Card File. If there is no number (preceded by the letter of that township), the church exists, but the records have not been copied or deposited at HSYC.

CARROLL TOWNSHIP

St. Paul's Lutheran Church, Dillsburg, Carroll Twp., YC; 377 in CVR; Vol. 1, 1855-1982, Vol. 2, 1913-1955, A1, A1a at HSYC.

CHANCEFORD TOWNSHIP

Chanceford Presbyterian Church 229 in CVR; B4 at HSYC.

Guinston (Muddy Creek) United Presbyterian Church, 252 in CVR; Vol. 1, 1772-1846, B1, Vol. 2, 1964-1970, at HSYC; Guinston Cong. Hist., CC 2 (2) 30, (3) 34.

New Harmony Presbyterian Church Records, 1849-1941; 33 in CVR; B7 at HSYC. See also Notes on History, in ONTG 19 (4) 1.

St. James Lutheran Church, Records, 1878-1976; 371 in CVR; B6 at HSYC.

St. Luke's Evangelical Lutheran Church Records, 1887-1961, 372 in CVR; B2 at HSYC.

St. Luke's Lutheran Church Records, 1839-1962; 372 in CVR; B2b at HSYC.

Staley's (Stehli's or St. Luke's) Lutheran/ Reformed Union Church, Chanceford Twp., York Co.; 372 in CVR; Vol. 1773-1835, B2, B3 at HSYC; Records, 1773-1835, at HSP. See *A 200th Anniversary History of St. Luke's Lutheran Church.* By Florence M. Gipe. S.l., s.n., n.d.

United Presbyterian Cong. of Guinston, 252 in CVR; B5 at HSYC.

CODORUS TOWNSHIP

Christ (St. Emanuel's) Reformed Church Jefferson Boro, Records, 1828-1928, 263 in CVR; C1 at HSYC.

Jefferson-Paradise Circuit, Register, 1853-1913; HSYC.

Shaffer's (Zion) Lutheran and Reformed Church, Seven Valleys, Records, 1861-1882, 387 in CVR; C4 at HSYC.

Steltz Union (Bethlehem) Union Church, New Freedom, Records, 1794-1842, 320-384 in CVR; C3 at HSYC.

Steltz (Bethlehem Reformed) Church, Records, 1839-1906, 320-384 in CVR; C3a at HSYC.

Stone (St. Jacob's) Union Church, Codorus Twp., YC; 262-385 in CVR; C2 at HSYC. See Bricker, p. 47. Marriages 1756-1858 pub. Irish, p. 57.

Records, 1756-1884 are also at HSP.

Baptisms and Burials at St. Jacob's (Stone) Union Church: Brodbecks, 1756 to 1936. By Don Yoder. S.l., s.n., c.1936. Transcription by Pastor Weiser contains names of baptismal sponsors and communicants and confirmands, 1784-1803.

A History of St. Jacob's (Stone) Church, 1756-1956, 200th Anniversary. By Charles H. Glatfelter. 1956. ----, Volume 2, 1956-1990. By Charles H. Glatfelter. Brodbecks, PA: 1990.

CONEWAGO TOWNSHIP

Quickel's (Zion) Lutheran and Reformed Church Records, 1765-1858, 310-404 in CVR; D1, (Quickel's Church Index: D1a) at HSYC; See Bricker, p. 47; Marriages 1765-1842 pub. in Irish, p. 57; See "Baptisms, 1765-1775," translated and copied by Henry Seiffert, in *Penn Pal,* beginning vol. 2, no. 4; Records, 1765-1833 at HSP. Lutheran Records, 1858-1905, at HSP.

DOVER TOWNSHIP

Strayer's (Salem) Lutheran Church, Dover Twp., Original Register, 411 in CVR; E1 at YCHS.

Strayer's (Salem) Lutheran Church Records, 1753-1873, 411 in CVR; E1b at HSYC.

Strayer's (Salem) Reformed Church Records, 1745-1921, 305 in CVR; E2 at HSYC. See Bricker, p. 47 which describes this as a Union Church Marriages 1745-1893 pub. in Irish, p. 58. Records for 1745, 1762-1873 are also at HSP.

EAST HOPEWELL TOWNSHIP

Cross Roads United Methodist Church, Cross Roads Boro, Births and Baptisms, 1931-1865, 31117 in CVR; F1 at HSYC.

EAST MANCHESTER TOWNSHIP

Hoover's (Christ Union) Lutheran and Reformed Church, Starview, 311-420 in CVR.

Manchester-Liverpool United Brethren Circuit, Class Lists, 1859-1879; Records are at HSYC.

FAIRVIEW TOWNSHIP

Mt. Zion Lutheran Church, Goldsboro, Cedar Point, Records, 1868-1938, 380 in CVR; H1 at HSYC.

New Cumberland Station United Brethren in Christ Church Records, 1868-1902, 616 in CVR; H2 at HSYC.

FAWN TOWNSHIP

Centre Presbyterian Church, New Park, Fawn Twp., YC; 228 in CVR.
Baptisms, 1904-1924, Marr., 1905-1923, (missing) I1 at HSYC.
Baptisms, 1851-1920, Marr., 1900-1918, I1a at HSYC.
Baptisms, 1851-1900, Marr., 1800-1898, Deaths, 1881-1890, (missing), I1b at HSYC.
Deaths, 1921-1936, I1c at HSYC.
List (of members?), undated, I1d at HSYC.
See Emory, Mary Helen, comp. *A List of People Who Have Been Members of or Connected With Centre Presbyterian Church, New Park, Pennsylvania...* S. l., s.n., 1980. See ALSO *History of Centre Presbyterian Church, New Park, Pennsylvania, 1780-1980.* Ed. by William F. Emery. S.l., s.n., n.d.

Cross Roads Circuit & Gatchelville Prospect United Methodist, Baptisms, 1903-1912, Marr., 1905-1923, A885 in CVR, I3 at HSYC.

Fawn Grove Circuit, Fawn/Olivet/Norrisville/St. Paul. Records, 1892-1920, I2 at HSYC. Records, 1920-1939, I2a at HSYC.

First Methodist Church, Fawn Grove Boro, 816 in CVR.

Prospect Methodist Church Records, 1927-1961, 30034 in CVR; I4a at HSYC.

Historical Record of Prospect Methodist Church, Baptisms, 1931-1955, Marr., 18937-1960, and Deaths, 1938-1943; 31211 in CVR; I5 at HSYC.

FRANKLIN TOWNSHIP

Emanuel Lutheran Church, Franklintown Boro, 374 in CVR; J1 at HSYC.

St. John's Evang. Lutheran Church Records, 1866-1967, 376 in CVR; J2, J3 at HSYC.

St. John's Reformed Church Records, 1852-1888, 376 in CVR, J3 at HSYC.

HEIDELBERG TOWNSHIP

Mt. Carmel Lutheran Church Records, 1886-1970, 355 in CVR; K1 at HSYC.

HELLAM TOWNSHIP

Kreutz Creek (St. James') Lutheran Church Records, 1757-1854; 383 in CVR; L1 at HSYC.

Kreutz Creek (Trinity) Reformed Church Records, 1757-1854, YC 299 in CVR; L2 at HSYC; Marriages 1757-1855 pub. in Irish, pp. 145-146; See ALSO Garrett, Walter E. *History of the Kreutz Creek Charge of the Reformed Church.* Philadelphia: 1924. See Kruetz Creek Charge, Hist. of, CC 6(1)14.

Methodist Episcopal Church, Wrightsville, 552 in CVR.

St. James Lutheran Church, Hellam Boro, 383 in CVR; L3 at HSYC.

Trinity Lutheran Church, Wrightsville Boro, Records, 1853-1954, 427 in CVR; L4 at HSYC.

HOPEWELL TOWNSHIP

Blimyer's United Reformed and Lutheran Church Register. See under York Township.

Hopewell United Presb. Church, Cross Roads Boro, 230 in CVR. Records, 1892-1930, M3a at HSYC. Records, 1834-1861, M3b at HSYC. Minutes, 1871-1919, M3d at MHSC.

Saddler's (St. John's) Reformed Church Records, 1791-1861, 321-389 in CVR; M1 at HSYC.

Saddler's Reformed/Presb Church (St. John's) Records, Births, 1876-1909, and Deaths, 1877-1907, 321-389 in CVR; M3 at HSYC; See Sadler's Lutheran Church Register, 1789-1989.

Sadler's Lutheran Church Register, 1789-1989. [Hopewell Twp.] By Elmer W. Orwig. Baltimore: Gateway Press, 1989.

Stewartstown Presbyterian Church Roll and Register, 237 in CVR; M2 at HSYC.
    Births/ Baptisms, 1872-1901, Marr., 1873-1888, Deaths, 1881-1890, 237 in CVR, M2a at HSYC.
    Stewartstown Presb. Church, Records, 1888-1931, 237 in CVR, M5 at HSYC.

United Presbyterian Church 1910-1965, 258 in CVR; M4 at HSYC.

United Presbyterian Church Records, 1910-1965, 253 in CVR; M6 at YCHS.

JACKSON TOWNSHIP

Roth's (Pigeon Hill or Trinity) Reformed Church, Records, 1818-1900, 304 in CVR; N1 at HSYC.

LOWER CHANCEFORD TOWNSHIP

Airville Associate Reformed Presbyterian Church Records, Baptisms, 1894-1920, Marr. 1894-1920, 17594 in CVR, O3 at HSYC. See also SCPGS Spec. Pub. # 13, 1981.

Bethel & Trinity Methodist Episcopal Church Records, 1898-1902, 627 in CVR; O2 at HSYC.

Castle Finn Circuit Methodist Church, 18208 in CVR.
    Records, 1841-1877, O1 at HSYC.
    Records, 1877-1885, O1a at HSYC
    Records, 1846-1903, O1b at HSYC
    Baptisms, 1857-58, Marr. 1899-1903, Preachers 1846 (missing) O1c at HSYC.
    Records, 1877-1882, O1d at HSYC.

Methodist Episcopal Church, Baptisms, 1882-1895, Marr., 1882-1895, and Deaths, 1882-1892, 17594 in CVR, O4 at HSYC.

Pine Grove United Presbyterian Church, Lower Chanceford Twp., York Co.; 234 in CVR.

LOWER WINDSOR TOWNSHIP

Canadochly Union (Reformed and Lutheran) Church, Register, 1755-1874, 300-382 in CVR; P2 at HSYC.
    See also: Bricker, p. 47.
    Marriages 1755-1819 pub. in Irish, pp. 294-297.

St. Luke Lutheran Church, Yorkana Boro, Register, 1895-1941, 10807 in CVR; P1 at HSYC.

MANCHESTER TOWNSHIP

Manchester-United Brethren Liverpool Circuit Class Lists, 1859-1862, 525 in CVR, Q1 at HSYC.

MANHEIM TOWNSHIP

Black Rock Church of the Brethren.

See: *History and Families of the Black Rock Church of the Brethren, 1738-1988.* By Elmer Q. Glenn. S.l., s.n., n.d.

Dub's (St. Paul's) Reformed Church Register, 1855-1877, 258 in CVR; R1 at HSYC.

MONOGHAN TOWNSHIP

NEWBERRY TOWNSHIP

Hay Run (St. Peter's Lutheran Church Register, 1867-1874, T1 at HSYC.

NORTH CODORUS TOWNSHIP

Lischy's (St. Peter's) Lutheran Church, 278-397 in CVR.
Register, 1773-1901, U1 at HSYC.
Register, 1798-1863, U4 at HSYC.
Register, 1893-1962, U5 at HSYC.
Marriages 1773-1902 published in Irish, p.327.

St. Jacob's Lutheran Church, York New Salem, 280 in CVR, U6 at HSYC.

Ziegler's (St. Paul's) Lutheran and Reformed Church, Seven Valleys, 331-414 in CVR;
Register of Union Church, 1771-1838, U2 at HSYC.
Register of Lutheran and Reformed Church, U3 at HSYC.
Early Interments in SCPGS Spec. Pub. # 25.

NORTH HOPEWELL TOWNSHIP

Lebanon Lutheran Church Register, 1877-1977, 388 in CVR; V2 at HSYC.

St. Paul's Lutheran Church, Felton Boro, Register, 1889-1977, 390 in CVR; V3 at HSYC.

Stabley's Reformed Church Register, 1841-1878, A-890 in CVR; V1 at YCHS.

PARADISE TOWNSHIP

Holtzscwamm (Paradise) Reformed Church Register, 1833-1935, 302 in CVR; W1 at HSYC.

Immaculate Heart of Mary Roman Catholic Church
(Brandt's Chapel), 1841-1945; 465 in CVR; W2 at HSYC.
1830-1900' 465 in CVR; W2a at HSYC.
Baptisms, marriages, and burials, 1830-1900; 465 in CVR; W2b at HSYC.

Paradise Mission, U. B. in Christ; Records, 1859-1913; A580 in CVR; W3 at HSYC.

PEACH BOTTOM TOWNSHIP

Slateville Presbyterian Church; 236 in CVR; X1 at HSYC.

PENN TOWNSHIP

Emanuel Reformed Church, Hanover, Penn Twp., YC; 271-82 in CVR; Y1, Y1a at HSYC;
See Bricker, p. 47; Marriages 1770-1856 pub. in Irish, pp. 133-135.

St. Joseph's Roman Catholic Church, Hanover Boro, 458 in CVR; Y6 at HSYC.

St. Matthew's Lutheran Church, Hanover Boro, 349 in CVR.
Register, 1743-1829, Y2 at HSYC.
Register, 1828-1851, Y2a at HSYC.
Register, 1743-1865, Y2b at HSYC.
Register, 1865-1893, Y3 at HSYC.
Burial Register, 1790-1865, Y4 at HSYC.
See also *Records Book, St. Matthews Lutheran Church, Hanover, York County, Pa., 1837-1848.*
Typescript, DAR Library. See also *The Lutheran Church on the Conewago at Hanovertown: A History of Saint Matthew Evangelical Lutheran Church, Hanover, Pennsylvania, 1735-1810.* By Pastor Frederick S. Weiser. Mentioned in ONTG 19 (5) 1.

St. Paul's Lutheran Church, Hanover Boro, Records, 1898-1970, 350 in CVR; Y5 at YCHS.

SHREWSBURY TOWNSHIP

Christ (Solomon's) Lutheran Church, 416 in CVR; Book 1, 1843-1875, Book 2, 1875-1890, Z11 at HSYC.

Fissell's (Jerusalem) Union Church Register, 1780-1840, 316-398 in CVR; Z1 at HSYC.

Fissell's Reformed Church, Register, 1845-1895, 316-398 in CVR, Z2 at HSYC.

New Freedom Reformed Church, 886 in CVR; Z4 at HSYC.

St. John the Baptist Roman Catholic Church, New Freedom, 462 in CVR. Baptisms, 1841-1955, Z14a at HSYC.
　Baptisms, Marriages, and Deaths, 1841-1955, Z14b at HSYC.
　See *From Planting to Perpetual Harvest: The History of St. John the Baptist Roman Catholic Church, New Freedom, Pennsylvania, 1841-1988.* By Sharon A. Dalton. c.r. 1989 by the author.

St. Paul's Lutheran Church, 1881-1963, 378 in CVR; Z13 at HSYC.

Shrewsbury Charge Reformed Church, A-887 in CVR; Z5, Z6 at YCHS.

Shrewsbury Circuit of the Evangelical Association, YC; A-527 in CVR.

Shrewsbury Circuit of the M. E. Church, including: Shrewsbury. Rock Chapel, Glen Rock, New freedom, 1866-1907; 32467 in CVR; Z15 at HSYC.

Solomon's (St. Paul's) Reformed Church, 322 in CVR; Z7 at HSYC.

Zion Lutheran Church, Glen Rock, Register, 1863-1935, 379 in CVR; Z10 at HSYC.
　See also *Zion Stands with Hills Surrounded: A History of Zion Evangelical Lutheran Church, Glen Rock, Pennsylvania.* By Charles H. Glatfelter. Glen Rock, PA: 1974.

Zion Shrewsbury (United Methodist) Circuit, 497 in CVR.

SPRINGETTSBURY TOWNSHIP

Mt. Zion Lutheran Church (formerly in Spring Garden Twp.) 403 in CVR.
　Register, 1921-1993, AA1 at HSYC.
　Register, 1895-1921, AA1a at HSYC.
　Register, 1940-1992, AA1 at HSYC.

SPRINGFIELD TOWNSHIP

Friedensaal (Schuster's, White) Lutheran Church, Records, 1755-1827, 413 in CVR; BB1 at HSYC; Early Interments in SCPGS Spec. Pub. # 25 This register is bound as Part 1 in the same volume as St. Peter's, below).

Salem Evang. Lutheran and Germ. Reformed Church Register, 1870-1949, 312-424 in CVR; BB4 at HSYC.

St. Peter's (Yellow) Reformed Church, 317 in CVR; BB1 at HSYC. This register is bound as Part 2 in the same volume as Friedensaal, above.

See Bricker, p. 47.

Peter and Paul Roman Catholic Church, Larue (near Seven Valleys). Records are on MF at HSYC.

Trinity Lutheran Church, 1865-1965, 415 in CVR; BB5 at HSYC.

SPRING GARDEN TOWNSHIP

No entries.

WARRINGTON TOWNSHIP

St. John's (Brick, now St. Michael's) Lutheran Church, Rossville, Register, 1823-1889, 409 in CVR; DD1 at HSYC.

Warrington Monthly Meeting, Register, 1788-1859, 603 in CVR; YY2a at HSYC.
    See: Heiss, *Pennsylvania Quaker Records*.
    Walmer, Margaret B. *100 Years at Warrington: York County, Penn. Quaker Marriages, Removals, Births & Deaths*. Bowie: Heritage Books, 1989.

WASHINGTON TOWNSHIP

Red Run (St. Paul's, or Sower's) Church Records, 1845-1886, 276-412 in CVR; EE3 at HSYC.

Salem Lutheran (Barrens) Church, Dillsburg, 375 in CVR.
    Register, 1865-1907, EE1 at HSYC.
    Register, 1922-1966 (Evangelical Lutheran), EE1a at HSYC.

Salem Reformed Church, Register, 1812-1934, 375 in CVR, EE2 at HSYC.

Salem (Barrens) Union Church, Rules and Regulations, in German, EE4ms at HSYC.

WEST MANCHESTER TOWNSHIP

Neiman's (Shiloh) Reformed Church, 306 in CVR.

Neiman's (Shiloh) Lutheran Church, 402 in CVR.

Shiloh Union Church, 726-1 in CVR.

Wolf's (St. Paul's) Lutheran Church Register, 1847-1901, 425 in CVR; FF1 at HSYC; Marriages 1764-1894 pub. in Irish, p. 463.

Wolf's (St. Paul's) Reformed Church Register, 1764-1936, 303 in CVR; FF1 at HSYC.

See Bricker, p. 48.

WEST MANHEIM TOWNSHIP

Mt. Zion U. B. (Wentz Meeting House), West Manheim Twp., YC; A-584 in CVR.

St. Bartholomew's Church, Lutheran and Reformed, Register, 1843-1977, 261-364 in CVR, GG2 at HSYC.

Sherman's (St. David's) Lutheran and Reformed Church 260-365 in CVR.
    Register, 1763-1770; GG1 at HSYC.
    Register, Vol. 2, 1783-1870, GG2 at HSYC.
    See Bricker, p. 48.

WINDSOR TOWNSHIP

Cross Roads Circuit and Gatchelville Prospect Methodist Episcopal Church, 885 in CVR; HH3, HH4 at HSYC.

Frey's Union Church, Freysville, Register, 1809-1832, 1861-1862, 314-405 in CVR; HH1 at HSYC.

Zion United Brethren "Class Book," 24 Jan 1846, 726-216 in CVR, HH2 at HSYC.

YORK TOWNSHIP

Asbury (First) United Methodist Church, 553 in CVR.
    See *Children of the Circuit Riders: the History of Asbury United Methodist Church, York, Pennsylvania, 1781-1985*. By George R. Sheets. Mentioned in ONTG 11 (6) 2.

Blymire's (St. John's) Union Lutheran and Reformed Church, 308-370 in CVR; II1 at HSYC;
    See also: Bricker, p. 47.
    Marriages 1767-1834 pub. in Irish, p.58.
    Pennsylvania German Church Records. Vol. 2, pp. 1-42. Baltimore: Genealogical Publishing Co., Inc., 1983.

Christ Lutheran Church, Dallastown Boro. Register, 1871-1939, 373 in CVR, II2 at HSYC.

St. Joseph's Roman Catholic Church, Dallastown Boro. Records, 1850-c1957 are on MF and in book form at HSYC, 463 in CVR.
    Baptisms, 1850-1949, II3a at HSYC.
    Marr. and Deaths, 1856-1957, II3b at HSYC.

United Brethren Church, Spry, York Twp., 528 in CVR.

YORK CITY

Christ Lutheran Church, transcribed by Weiser, "W," 430 in CVR.
    Vol. 1, 1733-1794, JJ1 at HSYC.
    Vol. 1a, 1730-1744, JJ1aa at HSYC.
    Vol. 2, 1795-1826, JJ1a at HSYC.
    Vol. 3, 1826-1856, JJ1b at HSYC.
    Vol. 4, 1735-1848, JJ1c at HSYC.
    Vol. 5, 1848-1882, JJ1d at HSYC.
    Becker Notes, JJ1f at HSYC.

Christ Lutheran Church, transcribed by Young, "Y."
    Index Vol. 1, A-K, and Vol. 2, L-Z.
    Vol. 1, Baptisms, 1733-1776, JJ1 at HSYC.
    Vol. 1a, 1730-1744, JJ1aa at HSYC.
    Vol. 2, Baptisms, 1766-1810, JJ1a at HSYC.
    Vol. 3, Baptisms, 1810-1832, JJ1b at HSYC.
    Vol. 4, Baptisms, 1832-1856, JJ1c at HSYC.
    Vol. 5, Marriages, 1735-1848, Burials, 1748-1794, JJ1d at HSYC.
    Vol. 6, Baptisms, 1858-1882, JJ1e at HSYC.
    Vol. 7, Burials, 1801, Marriages, 1801-1848, Confirmations, 1770-1799, JJ1f at HSYC.
    Vol. 8, Burials, 1839-1856, JJ1g at HSYC.

English Episcopal Church of Yorktown (Samuel Johnson), 624 in CVR.
    Vol. 1, 1769, JJ5a at HSYC.
    Vol. 2, JJ5b at HSYC.

First Moravian Church, Register, 1751-1899, 590 in CVR; JJ2 at HSYC.

First Moravian Church, York (transcripts): GSP; HSP.

See: "The Moravian Congregation at York," by Rev. S. C. Albright, CC 5 (1) 1, (2) 23,(3) 21, (4) 17.

First Presbyterian Church, 241 in CVR.
    Vol. 1, 1835-1859, JJ7 at HSYC.
    Vol. 2, 1835-1891, JJ7a at HSYC.
    Vol. 3, 1836-1902, JJ7b at HSYC
    Vol. 4, 1865-1890, JJ7c at HSYC.

    See also Cathcart, Rev. Robert, under section KK.

First Reformed and Trinity First Reformed Church, York; 291 in CVR.
    Vol. 1, 1745-1817, JJ3 at HSYC.
    Vol. 2, 1817-1877, JJ3a at HSYC.
    Vol. 3, 1765-1885, JJ3b at HSYC.
    Vol. 4, 1839-1877, JJ3c at HSYC.
    See Bricker, p. 48.
    Marriages 1744-1853 pub. in Irish, pp. 472-508.
    The Americanization of a Congregation: A History of Trinity United Church of Christ, York, PA.
By Benjamin T. Griffin. York: 1994.

First United Brethren, York Circuit, 518 in CVR.

Memorial United Church of Christ, Register, 1898-1973, 295 in CVR, JJ13 at HSYC.

St. John (the Baptist) Protestant Episcopal Church, York, YC; 444 in CVR; JJ5 at YCHS.

St. John's Lutheran (Missouri Synod), York, organized 1874; immigrant families mentioned in ONTG 18 (5) 3.

St. Joseph's Roman Catholic Church Records are on MF and in book form at HSYC.

St. Mary's (Church of the Immaculate Conception) Roman Catholic Church (German speaking). Records are on MF and in book form at HSYC.
St. Matthew's Lutheran Church, Baptisms 1889-1912, Marriages, 1891-1912, Burials, 1892-1912, 436 in CVR, JJ12 at HSYC.

St. Patrick's Roman Catholic Church, Register, 1810-1895 (English speaking), 3 vols. Records are on MF and in book form at HSYC. JJ11 at HSYC.

St. Paul's (First English) Lutheran Church, 437 in CVR; JJ8 at HSYC.

St. Rose of Lima Roman Catholic Church Records are on MF at HSYC.

Trinity Evangelical Church (York Mission Central PA Conference), 1871-1901, 1917-1948, 484 in CVR; JJ10 at HSYC.

Zion (Second English) Lutheran Church, 441 in CVR; JJ9 at YCHS.

Zion Reformed Church and German Branch of First Reformed Church, 290 in CVR; JJ4 at HSYC.

York Monthly Meeting Removals, 1788-1851, 602 in CVR; JJ6 at HSYC.

PASTORAL REGISTERS

Barton, Rev. Thomas, Marriages 1755-1759, 15215 in CVR, KK1 at HSYC. See also SCPGS Spec. Pub. # 34.

Cathcart, Rev. Robert, Presbyterian minister at York and Hopewell, 1793-1837, 230 in CVR, KK2 at HSYC.

Craumer, Rev. William H., Baptisms, Marriages, and Deaths, c.1870; at HSP.

Cuthbertson, Rev. John, (Presbyterian) Reg. of Marriages and Baptisms, Adams and York County; KK3 at HSYC. Transcript by Helen S. Fields at the HSP. See Also *Register of Marriages and Baptisms... of... John Cuthbertson*. Transcribed by Helen S. Fields. Washington: 1934. His diary, 1783-1791 at HSP.

Deininger, Rev. Constintine J., (Lutheran) Private Register; 12587 in CVR; KK4 at YCHS; Register, 1854-1885 at HSP.

Faust, Jacob N., Register, 1898-1937, 30023 in CVR; KK5 at HSYC.

Goering, Rev. Jacob, Pastoral records, Hagerstown, MD and York, PA; 13529 in CVR; KK8 at HSYC; Pastoral records, 1788-1789, at HSP.

Gring, Rev. Daniel, Reformed Minister of Southern York County, Private Register of Pastoral Acts; 14059 in CVR.

Illing, Rev. Traugott Frederick. (Protestant Episcopal) *Register of Marriages and Baptisms, 1780-1798.* Harrisburg Pub. Co., 1891. (Contains some Northern York County records).

Ketterman, Rev., Private register, Jefferson Lutheran Church, YC; 22797 in CVR; KK9 at HSYC.

Historical Record of Prospect Methodist Church; KK13 at HSYC.

Lehman, Daniel, Notebook; 12021 in CVR.

Lischy, Rev. Jacob, (Reformed) Baptismal Records, 1744-1769 (transcripts) at HSP. Lischy's Private Register; 11387 in CVR; KK6, KK6a at HSYC (This contains the oldest German

Reformed Church Records). Surname Index of Lischy Register, 11387 in CVR; KK6a at HSYC.

Martz, Rev. George Jacob, Private Records, 1869-1878; SCPGS Spec. Pub. # 2.

Methodist Register in York County, 1781-1878; KK12 at HSYC.

Morris, John, Notarial Dockets, YC; 19635 in CVR.

Newcomer, Bishop Christian; Abstracts from Journal, 1795-1830; 16158 in CVR.

Pearson, Dr. Isano William (1824-1900), of York Springs Account Book; 19245 in CVR.

Shaffner, Henry B., Reformed, Registers for 1808-1835, (available at the Lancaster County, PA, Historical Society; Call No. LC310.3/285.8/S525), contains some material on York County families.

Smith, Rev. Jacob C., [United Brethren in Christ] Marriages, 1846-1886, for York County et al; HSP; HSYC.

Stoever, John Casper, Register of Baptisms and Marriages; 15542 in CVR; K11, K11a at HSYC; Unpublished Baptisms in SCPGS Spec. Pub. # 31.

Strine, Rev. John Jacob; Marriages in Lancaster County, 1822-1870; SCPGS Spec. Pub. # 25.

Walker, Benjamin, Diary; 15360 in CVR.

Walker, John, Diary; 14750 in CVR.

Weisz, Rev. Dr. Israel, [Reformed Minister], Private Register, 1873-1893; Strayer's (Salem) Church; KK14 at HSYC.

Welsh, Rev. G. W., Records; 11858 in CVR; KK10 at HSYC.

Yagle, Dr. George, Balto., MD, Record Book; 22919 in CVR.

Zehring, Rev. Jacob D., Baptisms and Sermons, YC; 22908 in CVR.

ORIGINAL CHURCH RECORDS OF ADAMS COUNTY

BERWICK BORO

Abbotstown (Emanuel) Reformed Church, Adams County; Register, 1768-1800, 268 in CVR, LL1 at HSYC; Records before 1800 pub. in *Adams County Church Records.*
   See Bricker, p. 10.

St. John's Lutheran Church, Abbotstown, 336 in CVR. The Church built c.1770, but no 18th century records have been found.
   Register, 1837-1850, LL2 at HSYC.
   Register, 1850-1877, LL2a at HSYC.
   Register, 1884-1920, LL3 at HSYC

BUTLER TOWNSHIP

Bender's Lutheran Church(or Union?), Biglersville, 343 in CVR;
   Records, 1786-1860, MM1 at HSYC.
   Records, 1860-1898, MM1a at HSYC
   Records before 1800 pub. in Adams County; See Bricker, p. 10.

Biglerville (Trinity) Church Records, 1912-1950; See Bricker, p. 10

(Biglerville) St. Paul's Lutheran Church Records, 1881-1934, 344 in CVR, MM2 at HSYC.

CONEWAGO TOWNSHIP

Conewago Church, near Littlestown, Adams County, 450 in CVR; Marriages 1791-1835, Baptisms 1791-1815, Deaths 1791-1833, NN1 at HSYC.
   Marriages 1747-1871 pub. in Irish, p. 286.

Conewago Chapel (Sacred Heart of Jesus Cath. Church. 450 in CVR.
   Baptisms, 1790-1890, NN1a at HSYC.
   Marriages, 1796-1883, NN1b at HSYC.
   Deaths, 1752-1799, NN1c at HSYC.
   Records before 1800 pub. in *Adams County Church Records.*
   See Notes on, ONTG 11 (4) 1.

St. Aloysius Roman Catholic Church, Littlestown, Adams County; church begun about 1791; records begin c1840.

CUMBERLAND TOWNSHIP (GETTYSBURG)

Christ Lutheran (College) Church, Gettysburg, 1819-1974; 347 in CVR; 001 at HSYC.

Marsh Creek (Hill) United Presbyterian Church, Gettysburg, 1814-1832; 249 in CVR; 002 at HSYC.

Rock Creek Reformed Presbyterian Church, 249 in CVR, OO3 at HSYC; Records before 1800 pub. in *Adams County Church Records.*

St. Mark's (Mark's or White) Reformed Church, Gettysburg, 289 in CVR; OO4 at HSYC.
   See Bricker, p. 10.

Trinity Reformed Church, Gettysburg, 272 in CVR; OO5 at HSYC.
   See Bricker, p. 10.

Upper Marsh Creek Presbyterian Church, Gettysburg, Adams County; 243, 249 in CVR; OO2, OO3 at HSYC; Records before 1800 pub. in *Adams County Church Records.*

FRANKLIN TOWNSHIP

Arendt's Evangelical Lutheran and German Reformed, Register, 1785-1873, 269-339 in CVR; RR1 at HSYC.
   Records before 1800 pub. in *Adams County Church Records;* See Bricker, p. 10.

Flohr's Lutheran Church, 338 in CVR.

GERMANY TOWNSHIP

Christ Reformed Church, Germany (or Union) Twp., near Littlestown, Register, 1747-1811, 266 in CVR: RR2 at HSYC; Records before 1800 pub. in *Adams County Church Records.*
   See Bricker, p. 11.

St. John's Lutheran Church, Littlestown, 352 in CVR.
   Vol. 1, 1762-1858, RR3 at HSYC.
   Vol. 2, 1763-1900, RR4 at HSYC.
   Records before 1800 pub. in *Adams County Church Records.*

HAMILTON TOWNSHIP

Trinity Lutheran Church, East Berlin Boro, Register, 1822-1884, 337 in CVR; CCC1 at HSYC.

HUNTINGTON TOWNSHIP

Christ Church, York Springs Boro, Protestant Episcopal Church, 445 in CVR; VV1 at HSYC.
   Records before 1800 pub. in *Adams County Church Records.*

Upper Bermudian (Ground Oak) Lutheran Church, 363 in CVR.
   Register, 1791-1874, VV2 at HSYC.
   Register, 1868-1905, VV2a at HSYC.

York Springs Lutheran Charge, York Springs, Register, 1840-1867, 367 in CVR; VV3 at HSYC.

York Springs Circuit of the Methodist Epis. Church, Adams County; 556 in CVR.

York Springs (formerly Franklin Circuit), United Brethren, Class Lists, 1849-1854. HSYC.

LATIMORE TOWNSHIP

Chestnut Grove Lutheran Church, Register, 1868-1967, 368 in CVR; WW1 at HSYC.

Huntington Monthly Meeting, Latimore Twp., Adams County,; established c1745, but no records for 18th century are available.

Lower Bermudian (Mt. Olivet) Union Church, 274-369 in CVR.
    Register, 1745-1864; WW2, WW2a at HSYC.
    Records before 1800 pub. in *Adams County Church Records*.
    See also Bricker, p.10-11.

Lower Bermudian (Christ Evang. Lutheran) Church, 369 in CVR;
    Register, 1865-1909, WW3 at HSYC.
    Register, 1909-1965, WW4 at HSYC.
    Marriages 1745-1864 pub. in Irish, pp. 247-248.

Upper Bermudian (Ground Oak) Union Church Records before 1800 pub. in *Adams County Church Records*.

MENALLEN TOWNSHIP

Bethlehem Lutheran Church, Bendersville, 1870-1966; 340 in CVR; YY1 at HSYC.

Menallen Monthly Meeting, 606 in CVR; YY2 at HSYC.
    Records before 1800 pub. in Adams County Church Records.
    See Births and Deaths, 1748, CC 2(4)28; 3(1)13.
    Menallen Minutes, Marriages and Miscellany. Quaker Records, 1780-1890. By Margaret B. Walmer. Bowie: Heritage Books, 1992.

St. James (Wenks) Lutheran Church, Wenksville, Register, 1902-1965; 342 in CVR; YY3 at HSYC.

MOUNT JOY TOWNSHIP

Grace Lutheran Church, The Taverns, 1888-1959; 351 in CVR; ZZ1 at HSYC.

Mt. Joy Lutheran Church, 1824-1943; 357 in CVR; ZZ2 at HSYC.

MOUNT PLEASANT TOWNSHIP

St. Luke's Lutheran Church, near Bonneauville, 1883-1959, 353 in CVR; AAA1 at HSYC.

OXFORD TOWNSHIP

New Oxford (St. Paul's) Reformed Church, 267 in CVR; BBB1 at HSYC.

STRABAN (and OTHER) TOWNSHIPS

Annunciation of the Blessed Mary (St. Mary's) McSherrystown; DDD12a, d at HSYC.

Church of the Immaculate Conception of the Blessed Virgin Mary, Fairfield, 31589 in CVR.
    Baptisms, 1864-1956; DDD9a at HSYC.
    Marriages, 1864-1956; DDD9b at HSYC.
    Deaths and Confirmations, 1898-1927; DDD9b at HSYC.

Great Conewago Presbyterian Church, near Hunterstown, Straban Twp.; 244 in CVR; DDD1 at HSYC.(See also Dutch Reformed, Conewago Twp., below.)

Dutch Reformed, Conewago Twp.; Records, 1769-1800, at HSP. (See also Great Conewago Presbyterian Church, near Hunterstown, above).

Immaculate Conception Roman Catholic Church (St. Mary's), New Oxford, Baptisms and Burials, 1891-1990; 459 in CVR; DDD11 at HSYC.

Low Dutch (Reformed) Settlement of Conewago, Straban Twp., Adams County; 335 in CVR; NN2, NN2a, NN2b at HSYC; Records before 1800 pub. in *Adams Co Church Records.*

St. Aloysius Roman Catholic Church, Littlestown, 460 in CVR.
Baptisms, 1865-1949; DDD10a at HSYC.
Baptisms, 1950-1956; DDD10b at HSYC.
Baptisms, 1844-1900; DDD10c at HSYC.
Marriages and Burials, 1844-1900; DDD10d at HSYC.

St. Francis Xavier Church, Gettysburg.
Registers, 1831-1988; 457 in CVR, DDD4 at HSYC.
Register of Baptisms, 1849-1943; 457 in CVR; DDD4b at HSYC.
Register of Baptisms, 1944-1956; 457 in CVR; DDD4d at HSYC.
Register of Marriages, 1899-1943; 457 in CVR; DDD4c at HSYC.

St. Ignatius Roman Catholic Church, Buchanan Valley, Franklin Twp., 456 in CVR; DDD5 at HSYC.
Baptisms, 1864-1987; DDD5b at HSYC.
Marriages and Burials, 1864-1987; DDD5c at HSYC.

St. John's Lutheran Church, Fairfield, Hamiltonban Twp., c1853-c1951; 31995 in CVR; DDD6 at HSYC.

St. Joseph's Roman Catholic Church, Bonneauville, Marriages and Baptisms; 461 in CVR.

Part I, 1859-1935; DDD8a at HSYC.

Part II, 1859-1935; DDD8b at HSYC.

St. Paul's Lutheran Church (the Pines, Salem), New Chester, Straban Twp.; 1862-1960; 360 in CVR; DDD2 at HSYC.

York Springs Circuit M. E. Church, Baptisms and Marriages, 1864-1906; 556 in CVR; DDD7 at HSYC.

York Springs United Brethren in Christ Class Lists, 1849-1854; 550 in CVR; DD3 at HSYC.

CHURCH RECORDS OUTSIDE YORK AND ADAMS COUNTIES

Berks County
Church and Burial Grounds, Plow Church, Robeson Twp., 41647 in CVR; III1 at HSYC.

Bucks County
Lower Milford (Swamp) Reformed Church, Trumbauersville, 1769-1843; 16610 in CVR.

Center County
Center Meeting, Society of Friends, Halfmoon Twp., Center County, PA; 14047 in CVR.

Cumberland County
Shippensburg Reformed Church, Cumberland County, Records, 1770-1842 (SCPGS Spec. Pub. # 17).

Dauphin County
Salem Evang. and Reformed Church, Harrisburg; 16621 in CVR.

Zion Lutheran Church, Harrisburg, Baptisms, 1795-1816; 14900 in CVR; JJJ1 at HSYC.

Franklin County
Besore's Salem Reformed Church, Washington Twp.; 19564 in CVR; HHH1 at YCHS.

Jacob's Lutheran Church, Waynesboro; 19365 in CVR.

Elias Lutheran Church, Emmittsburg, MD; Records from Trinity Evang. Lutheran Church, 31931 in CVR; GGG8 at HSYC.

Harford County Methodist Episcopal Circuit, Harford County; 22641 in CVR.

Monocacy Church Records, c1777-c1872; 31107 in CVR; GGG9 at HSYC.

Moravian Community & Cong. at Graceham, 1759-1871; 14439 in CVR; GGG4 at HSYC.

Pipe Creek Meeting, Soc. of Friends; 15530 in CVR; Graves Identified in Scharf's *Western Maryland,* compared with those existing in 1934.

St. Benjamin's or Krider's Church, Pipe Creek, Evang. Lutheran and Reformed Church Record, 22976 in CVR.
    Lutheran, 1766-1837; GGG1 at HSYC.
    Reformed, 1763-1836; GGG1 at HSYC.

St. Mary's Lutheran Church, Silver Run, MD; 17436 in CVR; GGG2 at YCHS.

St. Mary's Lutheran and Reformed Church, Silver Run, Carroll County, MD; 17501 in CVR.
    Lutheran, 1766-1863; GGG2 at HSYC.
    Reformed, 1762-1866; GGG2 at HSYC.
    Tombstone Inscriptions, Old Section of Cemetery; 16611-25 in CVR; GGG2a ar HSYC.

St. Paul Lutheran and Reformed Church, Clearspring, Wash. County, MD; 10332 in CVR.

Salem Reformed Church, west of Hagerstown, Washington County, Md; 10281 in CVR; GGG7 at HSYC.

Winter's (St. Luke's) Luthuran Church, Uniontown, Frederick County, 1784-1874; 227-12 in CVR.

Zion Lutheran Church, near Frederick; 1779-1827; 227-11 in CVR; GGG5 at HSYC.

Zion (Kroh's) Lutheran and Reformed Congregation, Manchester, Carroll County, MD; 227-10 in CVR:
    Volume 1, 1760-1836; GGG3 at HSYC.
    Volume 2, 1784-1853; GGG3a at HSYC.

Delaware Church Records at HSYC.

Newark Monthly Meeting, Soc. of Friends; 14464 in CVR.

Chapter 7
FAMILY HISTORIES

COLLECTIONS OF FAMILY HISTORIES

Amish and Amish Mennonite Genealogies. By Hugh G. Gingerich. Gardenville: Pequea Publishers, 1986.

A Biographical History of York County, Pennsylvania. Originally published as Part 2 of Gibson's 1886 History of York County, Pennsylvania. Ed. by John Gibson. repr.: Baltimore: Genealogical Pub. Co., 1975.

Biographical and Portrait Cyclopedia of Cumberland, York, and Adams Counties. Edited by Samuel T. Wiley. (1897) Repr.: Southwest Pennsylvania Genealogical Services, 1986.

Early Families of York County, Pennsylvania, Vol. 1. By Keith Dull. Westminster: Family Line Publications, 1995.

Early Families of York County, Pennsylvania, Vol. 2. By Keith A. Dull. Westminster: Family Line Publications.

Family Records From Bibles, Volume 1 (1988). SCPGS Spec. Pub. # 36.

Founding Catholic Families of Conewago. By Barbara Brady O'Keefe. Miami: The Author. Mentioned in ONTG 11 (8) 2.

Genealogical Information Regarding the Families of Hornberger and Yingling, And Related Families of Eckeret, Lenhart, Steffy, Gerwig and Rahn. By Claude J. Rahn. Vero Beach, FL: The Author, 1951. (Reviewed in NGSQ 41 (1) 28).

Genealogy of the Conewago Valley, mentioned in ONTG 19 (8) 3.

Index to Selected Amish Genealogies. By Harold E. Cross. Baltimore: The Johns Hopkins University School of Medicine, 1970.

INDIVIDUAL FAMILY HISTORIES

(Includes Autobiographies and Diaries)

The book titles included here were taken chiefly from Donald Virdin's *Bibliography of Pennsylvania Families,* if the family had known connections to York County, or if the book had York County as part of the title. A number of titles were also taken from "Hively's Genealogical Notes," which appears regularly in *Our Name's the Game.* Many families are shown as included in Dull's *Early Families of York County, Pennsylvania* (2 vols.) See above.

ABBOTT: *The ...-Adlum-Green Families.* By Willis W. Eisenhart. 1957.

ADAMS: *... of the Alleghenies.* McSherrystown: John Timon Reily Historical Society.

ADLUM: See ABBOTT.

ALBRIGHT: "Genealogical Records of George ...." By May Albright Seitz. Typescript, HSYC, 1943.

... (Albrecht) Family of York Co., PA, 1743 to 1800. Mentioned in ONTG 20 (6) 4.

A Genealogical History of Bernard ... and His Descendants in America. By Clayton M. Albright. Privately Printed. 1958.

AMOS: *The Children of Mt. Soma.* By Gertrude J. Stephens, and Maurine C. Schmitz. Mentioned in ONTG 17 (6) 2.

ANDERSON: "James ... York County, Penna." PMHB XXXI (1907), 507

[Anderson, Binkele] "York County, Penna., Genealogical Notes." PMHB XXXI (1907), 243

ARECHTLER: See *Early Families of York Co., Vol. 2*, by Dull.

ARMSTRONG: "Notes on Andrew ..., 1782," SCPGS Spec. Pub. # 7.

ARNOLD: *Some Descendants of Peter ...* ,

AULT: *The ... Family Heritage (History, Portraits, Biographies, and Stories)*. By Mary Ruth Wright. Mentioned in ONTG 18 (2) 2.

AUMEND: *The ... Family.* Mentioned ONTG 17 (11) 3.

BAEHLI: See *Early Families of York Co., Vol. 1*, by Dull.

BAEHLIE: See *Early Families of York Co., Vol. 2*, by Dull.

BAHN: See *Early Families of York Co., Vol. 1*, by Dull.
... Family. Mentioned, ONTG 11 (1) 4

BAIRD: *... and Beard Families*. By Fermine Baird Catchings. 1918.

BAKER: "The ... Estate Scheme," ONTG 20 (11) 3-5.

BARNHART: *The Descendants of John and Mariah (Hively)....* ONTG 16 (9) 3.

BARTON: Rev. Thomas, Biog. Data, SCPGS Spec. Pub. # 34.

BEALE: Here Comes Tomorrow. By Mary Beale Hitchins. 1958.

BEARD: See BAIRD.

BEARDSLEY: *Records of the Families of Brothers, Swan, Bonar, Reeves and ...* . Mentioned, ONTG 16 (2) 2.

BECKER: Family mentioned, ONTG 11 (1) 3-4.

BEDINGER: Family data in ONTG 20 (5) 2.

BEHLER: *... Families of York Co., PA, and Surrounding Areas*, mentioned in ONTG 19 (10) 5.

BEHR: "... Family," *Mennonite Family History* 3:165

BEIDLER: John Stoner ... Diary, 1865, at HSYC.
... Family, mentioned, ONTG 16 (1) 3.

BENTZ: *... Family.* Mentioned in ONTG 18 (3) 2.

BERRY ... *Family History.* By William Beery and Judith B. Garber. Elgin, IL: 1957. (Rev. NGSQ 45(4)230).

BIEHLMAJER: See *Early Families of York Co., Vol. 1*, by Dull.

BIERI: See *Early Families of York Co., Vol. 2*, by Dull.

BIXLER: *John ... Pioneer Immigrant*, mentioned in ONTG 19 (2) 3.

BLACK: *The History of Adam ... I Family*, mentioned in ONTG 18 (5) 4.
... Family, mentioned in ONTG 11 (11) 2.

BOBB: *The ... Family.* By Luella May Waggoner. 1963.

BOHN, Jacob, Chart of Descendants. Mentioned in ONTG 11 (11) 1.

BOMBERGER: See BRUBAKER.

BONAR: *Records of the Families of Brothers, Swan, ... , Reeves and Beardsley*, mentioned, ONTG 16 (2) 2.

BORTNER: *... Families of York Co., PA.* Mentioned in ONTG 19 (7) 3.

See also *Early Families of York Co., Vol. 1*, by Dull.

BOUDREAU: *The Descendants of Exzelia Elizabeth Boudreau's Paternal and Maternal Grandparents.* mentioned, ONTG 17 (2) 2.

BOWSER: *...* Family History. By Addison Bartholomew Bowser. repr. 1976.

BOYER: See *Early Families of York Co., Vol. 2*, by Dull.

BRINER: *... Family History.* Mentioned in ONTG 18 (5) 4.

BROOKS: Obituary of Elmer Ellsworth ..., (1901), SCPGS Spec. Pub. # 7.

BROTHERS: *Records of the Families of ..., Swan, Bonar, Reeves and Beardsley.* Mentioned, ONTG 16 (2) 2.

The Brua Family and Bruaw, Bruah, Brewer Genealogy. By Lynn Austin Brua. 1989. ONTG 16 (1) 2, 16 (5) 1.

BRUBAKER: *...,* BOMBERGER, and FOGLESANGER. By B. Elizabeth Shearer Rahn and Claude J. Rahn. 1952.

CALLEN: *The ... Chronicles*, mentioned in ONTG 16 (5) 1-2

CAMPBELL: "The ... Families of York County. Pennsylvania." 1951. Typescript.

CARRIER: ... Family, mentioned in ONTG 17 (5) 2.

CLEMMER: *Henrich and Maria ... of Franconia, Pennsylvania,* mentioned in ONTG 18 (7) 4.

CLINTON: ... *Family Research,* mentioned in ONTG 18 (6) 4.

CLOTFELTER. See GLATTFELTER.

COFFMAN: See KAUFFMAN.

COMER: *The Family of Ada Rose ...,* mentioned in ONTG 17 (2) 2.

CONRAD: Court Case Described, ONTG 16 (11) 3.

COON: ... - Gohn Descendants from Chanceford Township, York County, Pennsylvania. By Frances Davis McTeer. Holiday, FL: 1979.

CRONBAUGH: ... of York County, Pennsylvania, 1807-1977, and Many Cousins, Jacob..., John ..., Nicholas .... By Lois E. Wilson Cronbaugh. Cedar rapids, Iowa: 1977.

CRUMRINE. See Krumrein.

CUNNINGHAM : *Arthur ... , About 1755-1829; Pennsylvania, Maryland, Virginia & Ohio; And Some of His Descendants,* mentioned, ONTG 16 (4) 2.

CURRAN: mentioned, ONTG 16 (3) 2.

DALE: See DIEHL.

DANNER: ... *Families of York Co., PA; Fulton Co., Ill.,* mentioned in ONTG 19 (8) 2.
   Family mentioned in ONTG 16 (10) 2.

DEAL: See DIEHL.

DECKARD: *Genealogy of the ... Family.* By Percy Edward Deckard. 1932.

DELLINGER: *The Chronicles and Genealogy of the Jacob ... Family of York County, PA.* By Donald F. Billet. Hilton Head [SC]: The Author. Mentioned in ONTG 19 (11) 2.

DELLONE: mentioned in *Der Kurrier* (Sept. 1990).

DEMOSS: Hazel Zellers Blasser ms., mentioned in ONTG 16 (4) 2.

DEVENY: ... *Families of York Co., PA, and Surrounding Areas,* mentioned in ONTG 20 (1) 3.

Genealogical Reports on the Four ... Brothers in York County, PA, mentioned in ONTG 20 (8) 5.

DICK: Jacob ... , Rev. War Pension Application W-9407. ONTG 15 (8) 3-5.

DIEHL: ... -Deal-Dill-Dale Families of America; *Vol. I; Diehl Families of York and Adams Co.,*

PA. By Harry A. Diehl. Wilmington, DE: the Author. Mentioned in ONTG 15 (3) 2.
See also *Early Families of York Co., Vol. 2,* by Dull.

DILL: See DIEHL.

DORLAND: See RUSSLER.

DRAPER: *Paternal and Maternal Lineal Genealogy Through the Great-Great-Great-Grandparents of Barbara Jayne ...,* mentioned ONTG 17 (11) 3.

DUBBS: See *Early Families of York Co., Vol. 1,* by Dull.

DUBS: ... *Families of York County, PA, and Surrounding Areas,* mentioned in ONTG 18 (9) 3.

EARHART: Genealogy of the ... and Thomas Families. By Ronald E. Earhart. Kettering, OH: The Author, 1981.

EBAUGH: *History of the John ... Branch of the ... Family,* mentioned in ONTG 18 (9) 3.

EBERLY: The ... Family. By Levi E. Martin. 1896.

ECKENRODE. See ECKROTH.

ECKENROTH. See ECKROTH.

ECKERT: See HORNBERGER.

ECKROTH: ... - *Eckenroth-Eckenrode Family,* mentioned in ONTG 18 (1) 3.

EDIE: Hazel Zellers Blasser ms., mentioned, ONTG 16 (2) 2.

EHRHARDT: See *Early Families of York Co., Vol. 2,* by Dull.

EHRHART: *The Ehrhart Family,* mentioned, ONTG 16 (2) 2.

EICHELBERGER: Family Data, mentioned in ONTG 19 (5) 2.

EISENHART: Descendants of Peter .... By Ruth M. Eisenhart. 1971.

ELLIOTT: Data given in ONTG 20 (1) 2.

ENSMINGER: The ... Family of Cocalico, Lancaster County, and Elsewhere.. By Raymond Martin Bell. 1971.

ERB: ... Family History. By Gladys E. G. Lichtenwalter. 1961.

EYSTER: Obituary of Sarah Anne ... (1907), SCPGS Spec. Pub. # 7.

FAUST: .../*Foust Manuscript.* By Thelma Berkey Walsmith. Mentioned in ONTG 18 ((5)

2.
Genealogy of Heinrich ... and Related .../Foust Families, mentioned in ONTG 18 (6) 4.

FEW: *Some Descendants of Richard ...* , mentioned in ONTG 18 (1) 3.

FIRESTONE: "... Family of Frederick County, Maryland," by George Ely Russell, *Western Maryland Genealogy* 9 (1), and 9 (2) [The family has York Co., PA, Connections].

FISCHEL: "The ... Family of York County, Pennsylvania. and North Carolina." Penna. Mag. of Hist. and Biog. XXXI (1907), 508.

FISHBURNES: *The ...* , mentioned in ONTG 18 (6) 4.

FISHEL: "... Buried at the Roth Church." Frank l. Crone. Penna. Mag. of Hist. and Biog. XLIV (1920) 287-188.

FISHER: The ...-Stombaugh Families and Allied Lineages of Maryland and Pennsylvania. By Florence Hepp Petersen. 1950.

Notes Concerning the ... Family of Fishing Creek Valley, Newberry and Fairview Townships, York County, Pennsylvania. By Donald F. Lybarger. Cleveland: 1966.

Descendants of Christian ... and Other Amish-Mennonite Pioneer Families. By Janice A. Egeland. Baltimore: Moore Clinic, Johns Hopkins Hospital, 1972.
Mentioned, ONTG 16 (2) 3.

FLESHMAN: See SCHUCK.

FOGLESANGER: See BRUBAKER.

FORNEY: *The ... Family of Hanover, Pennsylvania, 1690-1893.* By Lucy Forney Bittinger. Pittsburgh: 1893.

Sketches of the ... Family. By Howard O. Folker. Philadelphia: 1911.

Sketches and Genealogy of the ... Family from Lancaster County, Pennsylvania, in Part. By John K. Forney. Abilene: 1926.

FORTINET: See FORTINEUX.

FORTINEUX: *The ... - Fortinet family in America.* By Philip G. Goff. Tucker, GA: The Author.

FOUST. See FAUST.

FOX: *History of the ... Family,* mentioned, ONTG 16 (5) 1-2.

FREELAND: ... *and Allied Families.* By Barney F. Freeland. Delmar., CA.

FREINDSCHAAFT: *The David and Ella Markey ...,* mentioned, ONTG 17 (5) 2.

FREM: *The Descendants of Johan Carl ...,* mentioned ONTG 17 (11) 3.

FRENCH: *John and Maria Barbara ... Research,* mentioned in ONTG 18 (7) 4.

FREY: *Ancestry and Posterity (in Part) of Gottfried ..., 1605-1913.* By Samuel Clarence Frey. York: 1914.

FRIESNER: See *Early Families of York Co., Vol. 2,* by Dull.

GAERTNER: See *Early Families of York Co., Vol. 1,* by Dull.

GANS: See *Early Families of York Co., Vol. 1,* by Dull.

GENTZLER: ... *Families of York County, PA, and Surrounding Areas,* mentioned, ONTG 17 (5) 2.

GERBERICH. *The ... History.* By Albert H. Gerberich. 1925.

See also *Early Families of York Co., Vol. 1,* by Dull.

GERWIG: See HORNBERGER.

GIBBS; Hazel Zellers Blasser ms., mentioned, ONTG 16 (2) 2.

GILBERT: *The ... of Conajohela Valley.* By Melvin Gilbert. 1980. See Notes in ONTG 11 (3) 3.

GLATTFELTER: *The Descendants of Adam ..., Vol. 1 & Vol. 2,* mentioned in ONTG 18 (9) 3.
The ... in America. Mentioned in ONTG 19 (1) 3.

A Family History Tracing Casper ... of Glattfelden, Switzerland, ... By Janet L. Zemanek and Ruth Clotfelter Camenisch,, mentioned in ONTG 20 (2) 2.

GOHN: See COON.

GOOD: *History and Genealogical Record of the ...-Hileman Families.* By Rev. P. G. Bell. 1907.

GRASS. See GROSS.

GREEN: See ABBOTT.

GRIEST: mentioned, ONTG 16 (11) 2.

GRIMM: See *Early Families of York Co., Vol. 2,* by Dull.

GROFF: *The Groff Book.* Pub. by Groff History Associates, 151 Cherryhill Rd., Ronks, PA 17572

GROSS: *The Family of William Henry..., and Mary Ann Stare,* mentioned, ONTG 16 (7) 2.

... - *Grass Families of York County,* mentioned in ONTG 18 (1) 3.

GROTE: *Descendants of Charles John Henry ... & Johanna (Ziegler) ... ,* mentioned in ONTG 18 (5) 4.

GUISE: *The Nicholas ... Family Tree.* By H. W. Weidner. 1940.

GULL: ... Family, mentioned, ONTG 17 (5) 2.

GUTHRIE: ... *& Allied Families,* mentioned, ONTG 17 (5) 2.

HACKER: *A German-American ...-Hocker Genealogy,* mentioned in ONTG 18 (9) 3.

HADDOCK: *Legends of the ... Family,* mentioned, ONTG 17 (5) 2.

HAKES: *The ... of Chanceford Township.*

HAMANN: See *Early Families of York Co., Vol. 2,* by Dull.

HAMILTON: *The ... Family.* By James Alexander Hamilton. 1921.

HAMMER: "Discovering the Place of Origin of Johann Frantz ... ," in *The Palatine Immigrant,* Sept. 1994, issue.

HANNIGAN: ... Family History, mentioned, ONTG 17 (2) 2.

HARMAN: *The Descendants of John Henry ..., 1724-1783, and John Jonas Rupp, 1729-1801, Revolutionary War Soldiers.* By Vashti Seaman. 1963.

HARVEY: ... *Family.* By Mrs. Flora H. Kittle. 1927.

HEIDELBAUGH: ... *Families of America.* By James E. Heidelbaugh. Rev. ONTG 16 (3) 1.

HEILMAN: Family data, mentioned in ONTG 19 (5) 2.

HEIMLICH: ... *(Himelick) Family Tree & Allied Lines,* mentioned in ONTG 18 (1) 3.

HENDERSHOTT: ... *Ancestors,* mentioned, ONTG 17 (5) 2.

HENRY: ... *Families of York County [PA],* mentioned in ONTG 18 (7) 4.

See also RUSSLER.

HERR: "Ancestry of John ... of Hellam Township, York County," ONTG 17 (4) 2.

HERRING: See *Early Families of York Co., Vol. 2,* by Dull.

HILDEBRAND: See *Early Families of York Co., Vol. 2,* by Dull.

HILEMAN: See GOOD.

HIMELICK. See HEIMLICH.

HINKLE: ... *Heritage,* mentioned ONTG 17 (11) 3.

HOCKER. See HACKER.

HOFFMAN: See *Early Families of York Co., Vol. 1,* by Dull.

HOFFMASTER: See Peters.

HOLLOPETER: *The ... Brothers and their Edmond Wives,* mentioned ONTG 17 (11) 3.

HOOVER: ...-*Thompson: A Genealogical Study.* By Marjorie H. Diedrich. Sarasota: Genealogical Enterprises.

HORNBERGER: ... *and Yingling: Genealogical Information Regarding These and Related Families of Eckert, Lenhart, Steffy, Gerwig and Rahn.* By Claude J. Rahn. 1951.

HOSTLER: *The ... Family.* By John Dwight Kilbourne. Privately Printed: 1976.

HOUSER: Family, mentioned, ONTG 17 (8) 1.

HURSH: *Henry and Susanna Rudisill Hursh-- Their Ancestors and Descendants.* Pub. by the Hursh/Horst/Hurst Family Association, rev. in ONTG 20 (11) 2.

HUSTON: *The Descendants of Captain John... of Cumberland, York & Westmoreland Counties, Pennsylvania,* mentioned, ONTG 16 (7) 2.

HYSON: *Descendants of Archibald....,* Book may be updated by Archibald Hyson. ONTG 11 (4) 1-2.

JAULER: See *Early Families of York Co., Vol. 2,* by Dull.

JOHNSON: *The Descendants of Anthony Morris...,* 3 vols.

JUNG: See YOUNG.

KAGARISE: *Ancestors and Descendants of John Calvin and Mary Clapper ...,* mentioned, ONTG 17 (5) 2.

KAIN: Genealogical Records of George Hay ..., mentioned, ONTG 16 (4) 2.

KALTREIDER: *Some Descendants of Heinrich and Gertrude ... of Kersens, Switzerland,* mentioned in ONTG 17 (5) 2.

KAUFFMAN: *The ... -Coffman Families of North America, 1584-1937, A Genealogy and History of.* By Charles Fahs Kauffman. York: 1940. Mentioned in ONTG 16 (11) 2.

KELLENBERGER: *... and Shearers of Pennsylvania, Maryland, and Points West.* By Ralph and Star Rowland. Fairfax, VA: (c.1985).

KELLER: Descendants of Henry ... of York County, Pennsylvania, and Fairfield County, Ohio. By Edward Seitz Shumaker. Indianapolis: 1924.
Some Data on the ... Families of York County, Pennsylvania. By Rev. Edward C. Ruby. Typescript, HSYC.
Hazel Zellers Blasser ms., mentioned, ONTG 16 (4) 2.
See also *Early Families of York Co., Vols. 1 and 2,* by Dull.

KERN: See *Early Families of York Co., Vol. 2,* by Dull.

KESSLER: See *Early Families of York Co., Vol. 2,* by Dull.

KIEHLE: *... Family History,* mentioned, ONTG 17 (5) 2.

KING: *From Deutschland to Pennsylvania, U.S.A.,* [... of York Co., PA], mentioned in ONTG 19 (7) 2.

See also McILHENNY.

KIRKWOOD: Hazel Zellers Blasser ms., mentioned, ONTG 16 (2) 2.

KITZMILLER: *From the Danube to the Susquehanna.* ONTG 16 (10) 2.

KLINEDINST: Family data, mentioned in ONTG 19 (5) 2.

KLINEFELTER: Hazel Zellers Blasser ms., mentioned, ONTG 16 (4) 2.

See also *Early Families of York Co., Vol. 1,* by Dull.

KNISELY: *... Family.* By George W. Knisely. 1978.

KOCH: Family, mentioned, ONTG 16 (2) 3.

KOONTZ: The ... Family and Its relatives. By Mrs. Azariah H. Koontz. 1963.

KOPP: *... Families of York County, PA, and Surrounding Areas,* mentioned in ONTG 18 (9) 3.

KRAMER: See *Early Families of York Co., Vol. 1,* by Dull.

KRAMM: David .... By Alfreda Patton., York: 1978.

KROELLER: See *Early Families of York Co., Vol. 2,* by Dull.

KRUMREIN-KRUMRINE-CRUMRINE Genealogical Collection donated to HSYC by Dolores Crumrine Rutherford. ONTG 15 (11) 1.

KRUMRINE. See KRUMREIN.

KULL: See *Early Families of York Co., Vol. 2,* by Dull.

KUNCKEL: See *Early Families of York Co., Vol. 1,* 1, by Dull.

KURTZ: Hazel Zellers Blasser ms., mentioned, ONTG 16 (5) 1-2

LANDES: "The Christian ... Family of York County, Pennsylvania," by Dr. Emmert F. Bittinger, in *Mennonite Family History,* Oct. 1994.

LANIUS: See *Early Families of York Co., Vol. 1,* by Dull.

LAU: *The Descendants of Christian ....* By Michael W. Lau, mentioned, ONTG 17 (3) 1.

LEAMERS: ...: A Family History. By Laurence E. Leamer. 1976.

LEESE: *... Families of York County, PA, and Surrounding Areas,* mentioned in ONTG 18 (9) 3.

LEMASTER: ... Family, mentioned, ONTG 17 (5) 2.

LENHART: See HORNBERGER.

LENTZ: Gen., mentioned, ONTG 16 (7) 2.

LEONHARD: See *Early Families of York Co., Vol. 2,* by Dull.

LIEBHART. *George ... , His Two Wives and Twenty Children.*

LIGHTFOOT: See *Early Families of York Co., Vol. 1,* by Dull.

LIVINGSTON. See MYERS.

LOHR: See *Early Families of York Co., Vol. 2,* by Dull.

LONG: *Descendants of Philip Leopold ...,* mentioned, ONTG 16 (6) 2

LONGACRE: The ... Longaker-Longenecker Family. By A. B. Longaker. 1899.

LONGAKER: See LONGACRE.

LONGENECKER: *Pitchforks and Pitchpipes,* mentioned in ONTG 18 (5) 4.

See also LONGACRE.

LOUGHRY: A Brief Genealogy. By Julia A. Jewett. 1923.

LUCKENBAUGH: ... *Families of York Co., PA, and Surrounding Areas,* mentioned in ONTG 19 (10) 5.

MANIFOLD: ... Family Bible, CC 3 (1) 21

Hazel Zellers Blasser ms., mentioned, ONTG 16 (5) 1-2.

McADAMS: *The Sons of Adam.* Pub. by the McAdams Historical Society, 14018 Davana Terrace, Sherman Oaks, CA 91423. Mentioned in ONTG 11 (8) 2.

McALLISTER: Descendants of Archibald ... (c.1700-1768). By Mary Catherine McAllister. 1898.

McGAUGHEY: *Descendants of William and Margaret ...., 1740-1984.* By Polly Rachel Mc-Gaughey. Mentioned in ONTG 11 (11) 1. *Descendants of William and Margaret ....* By Mrs. Charles W. Sutton. -----: *Supplement, 1991.* Mentioned, ONTG 17 (9) 2-3.

McDONALD FAMILY. Hazel Zellers Blasser ms.,mentioned, ONTG 16 (10) 2.

McGAUGHEY: *Descendants of William and Margaret ...., 1740-1984.* By Polly Rachel Mc-Gaughey Sutton. Oklahoma City: the Author.

McILHENNY: *The ...-King History.* By J. A. Himes. n.d.

McMASTER: *The ... Family.* By Col. John P. Horan. 1960.

MEADS; Hazel Zellers Blasser ms., mentioned, ONTG 16 (2) 2.

MENGES: ... *Families of York County, PA, and Surrounding Areas,* mentioned, ONTG 17 (5) 2.

MICHAEL: Jacob ... 's Unprobated Will (1769, York Twp., York Co., PA). SCPGS Spec. Pub. # 26.

MILLER: See *Early Families of York Co., Vol. 1,* by Dull.

" Admin. Bond of John ...," SCPGS Spec. Pub. # 7.

MITCHELL: *Descendants of John ... of Drumore Township.*

MOHRING: *Condensed History of Johann Wolfgang ...,* mentioned in ONTG 18 (6) 4.

MOOMAW: ... *-Mumma-Mumaugh Genealogy,* mentioned, ONTG 16 (9) 3.

MORTON: *The Lookout Mountain Mortons and Their Descendants plus Ancestors and Relatives from York Co., Pennsylvania,...., 1731-1989.* By Donna Morton Mogan. Mentioned in ONTG 15 (4) 1.

MOSER: See *Early Families of York Co., Vol. 2,* by Dull.

MYERS: ... *and Livingston Families,* mentioned in ONTG 18 (1) 3.

NEFF: *A History of the Descendants of Henry ...,* mentioned in ONTG 18 (1) 3.

NELL: *Jacob ... and Descendants, 1780-1982;* mentioned, ONTG 16 (2) 2.

NESS: ... *Families of York County, Pennsylvania,* mentioned in ONTG 19 (2) 3.

Family, mentioned, ONTG 16 (2) 3.

NEWCOMER: *Descendants of Ulrich ...,* mentioned ONTG 17 (11) 3.

NISSLEY: "The Earliest Nissley families in America," by Philip Cassell Swarr. *Mennonite Family History* 1(3)15-19

OECHNER: See *Early Families of York Co., Vol. 2,* by Dull.

OLP: The ... Family of Shrewsbury Township, York Co., PA. By James Lloyd Knipe. Typescript. Lancaster, PA: 1952.

... Family, mentioned, ONTG 17 (5) 2.

ORWIG: *Descendants of Jacob ... & George ... .* By Elmer W. Orwig. Baltimore: Gateway Press, 1978.

OTSTOT: ... Family, mentioned in ONTG 18 (11) 3.

OTTERBEIN: *The Life Of Rev. Philip William ...* By Rev. A. W. Drury. 1898.

PAULUS: *The ... Family of York County, Pennsylvania.* By James F. McJohn. Mentioned in ONTG 17 (10) 2.

PENCE: Data given in ONTG 19 (8) 2.

PETERS: *Our ... - Hoffmaster Ancestry,* mentioned, ONTG 17 (5) 2.

PETERSHEIM: *Descendants and History of Georg ... Family,* mentioned in ONTG 18 (6) 4.

PFAUTZ: "Earliest ... /Fouts Families in America," by John Scott Davenport. NGSQ 63(4)243-263.

PORTER: "... Families of Chester County and York County, Pennsylvania." Porter Farquharson Cope. Penna. Mag. of Hist. and Biog. XXVI (1902),156-158.

RAGG: See *Early Families of York Co., Vol. 2,* by Dull.

RAHN: See HORNBERGER.

RAMSEY: *... of York Co., PA, Volumes I and II,* mentioned in ONTG 19 (7) 3.

REED: *A Brief History of the ... Family of Millcreek Twp., Erie Co.....* By John Elmer Reed. 1946.

REEVES: *Records of the Families of Brothers, Swan, Bonar, ..., and Beardsley,* mentioned, ONTG 16 (2) 2.

REIBER: *The ... Genealogy and Related Families (Descendants of Jacob Reiber, the Immigrant Ancestor of Sandhofen, Germany, 1727-1810, and Later of Lehigh County and York County, Pennsylvania.* By John R. Reiber. St. Petersburg: The Author. Mentioned in ONTG 17 (6) 1-2, 18 (2) 2.

REIFFSCHNEIDER: *... Family,* mentioned ONTG 17 (11) 3.

REIN: *The ... -Rhein-Reinau Ancestors of the Rhyne Family.* By Dr. Howard S. Rhyne, rev. in ONTG 20 (8) 4.

REINAU. See REIN.

REPLOGLE: *The ... Genealogy....* By Paul H. Replogle. 1963.

RHEIN. See REIN.

RHODES: *Elisah and Mary Ellen Kaylor ... Family History,* mentioned ONTG 17 (11) 3.

RHYNE. See REIN.

ROSS: *... Family,* mentioned, ONTG 17 (5) 2.

ROTHROCK: *The Heritage and the Legacy of John Ramsey ...,* Colorado Pioneer. By Mary Catherine Romer. Tucson, AZ: 1985. (rev. NGSQ 75(1)63).

"....," PMHB XXI (1897), 498-499

RUBI: *History of the ... Ruby Families of Switzerland and America.* By Jay W. Ruby and Ruth Ruby. Lakeland, FL: Thye Authors, 1983.

Descendants of Caspar ... By Edward O. Ruby. Typescript, HSYC. 1941.

RUBY: See RUBI.

RUDISILL: *The Worley F. Rudisill Family (Rudisill-Smyser Genealogy),* mentioned, ONTG 16 (5) 1-2

See also HURSH.

RUHL: See *Early Families of York Co., Vol. 1,* by Dull.

RUPP: See HARMAN.

RUSSLER: *... Family: History and Descendants (with Dorland Family 1652-1992 & Henry Family, 1771-1992).* By Helen Stambaugh Olson. Mentioned in ONTG 18 (7) 3.

RUTH: *Descendents [sic] of John George ... and Allied Families.* By Ruth Bailey Allen. Clayton [GA]: Allen's Books and Crafts, Inc. rev. ONTG 18 (9) 2.

SANDERS: *The ... Family,* mentioned in ONTG 18 (1) 3.

SCHAEFFER: *The ... /Shaeffer/Sheaffer Search.* By Carol M. Sheaffer, M. D., and Margaret E. Sheaffer. Mentioned in ONTG 17 (1) 3.

SCHAFFER: See *Early Families of York Co., Vol. 2,* by Dull.

SCHEFFER: *The John Adam ... Family History and Lineage, 1751-1958.* by Hazel Sheffer Crawford. Emlenton: 1958.

SCHENCK: See *Early Families of York Co., Vol. 1,* by Dull.

SCHERER: See *Early Families of York Co., Vol. 1,* by Dull.

SCHMALHORST: *A History of the ... , Smallhorst, Smallhurst & Weiberg, Weyberg, Whybark Families of America,* mentioned in ONTG 18 (9) 3.

SCHMIDT: See *Early Families of York Co., Vol. 1,* by Dull.

SCHMIEG: *Johann Andreas ... and Johann Simon ..., Father and Son Palatine Immigrants of 1753, and Their American Descendants.* By James Smee and Kevin Greenholt. Mentioned in ONTG 18 (7) 2.

SCHOLL: *...-Sholl-Shull Genealogy.* By John William Scholl. 1928.

SCHONHALER: See *Early Families of York Co., Vol. 2,* by Dull.

SCHUCK: *..., Fleshman, and Sydenstricker Families,* mentioned, ONTG 17 (5) 2.

SCHULTZ: See *Early Families of York Co., Vol. 1,* by Dull.

Abstract of the Journals of Jacob C. ... (Time Keeper for the Northern Central Railway Co., of MD and PA, 1856-1876). SCPGS Spec. Pub. # 26.

SEIBERT: *The ... Family,* mentioned, ONTG 17 (5) 2.

SEILER: *Ulrich...Descendants.* By Samuel J. Saylor, 547 Green Meadows Drive, Dallastown, PA 17313-9627. Mentioned in ONTG 15 (2) 2.

SEITZ: ... , *Stump and Related Families,* mentioned in ONTG 19 (2) 3. See also *Early Families of York Co., Vols. 1 and 2,* by Dull.

SENFT: *The Descendants of John Philip ... .* By Michael W. Lau. Mentioned in ONTG 19 (4) 1.

SHAEFFER: ... Family, mentioned, ONTG 16 (10) 2. See also Schaeffer.

SHAFFER: See *Early Families of York Co., Vol. 1,* by Dull.

SHEAFFER. See also Schaeffer.

SHEARER: ... *Families of York County, Pennsylvania,* mentioned in ONTG 18 (5) 4.

See also KELLENBERGER; see also mention in ONTG 16 (4) 3-4.

SHENBERGER: "Report" and supplementary text mentioned, ONTG 17 (10) 2.

SHENEFIELD: *The ... Family, 1733-1975,* mentioned in ONTG 18 (1) 3.

SHERK: The ... Family. By Thomas A. Sherk.

SHIRK: "Joseph Scherch, Immigrant of 1727, and His Descendants," by Thomas A. Sherk and James W. Sherrick, in *Pennsylvania Mennonite Heritage,* July 1990.

SHIVELY: *Descendants of Christian Shively of Warwick Twp., Lancaster County, and Later of York County, Pennsylvania.* By Arthur Geiger Black. Kansas City, MO: 1941.

SHOE: Zachariah ..., 1739-1812; Grave marked; ONTG 17 (10) 2.

SHOLL: See SCHOLL.

SHUE: *If the Shoe Fits... A History of the ... Family,* mentioned in ONTG 18 (10) 3.

Family data, mentioned in ONTG 19 (5) 2.

SHULL: See SCHOLL.

SHULTZ: *Early History of Dr. Martin ... and Juliana Stentz: A Trained Physician Who Came to East Tennessee in Late 1770s.* By Donald B. Reagan. Knoxville: The Author. Mentioned in ONTG 15 (6) 2.

SHUMAN: *The George ... Family.* By William C. Shuman. 1913.

SHUTE: ... *Roots,* mentioned, ONTG 17 (2) 2.

SIMON: See *Early Families of York Co., Vol. 2,* by Dull.

SIMONIS: See *Early Families of York Co., Vol. 2,* by Dull.

SMALLHORST: See SCHMALHORST.

SMALLHURST: See SCHMALHORST.

SMITH: "Descendants of James ... of York, Pennsylvania, A Signer of the Declaration of Independence." Robert M. Torrence. Penna. Gen. Magazine, XX:1 (1955) 29-33

Record of the ... Family of Washington Township, York County, Pennsylvania. by Michigan D.A.R. Gen. Records Committee. Typescript. 1934.

SMYSER: *History of the ... Family in America.* By Amanda Lydia Laucks-Xanders. York: 1931.

SMYSER: See Rudisill.

SNYDER: Family, mentioned, ONTG 16 (2) 3.

SOLINGER: Family, mentioned ONTG 17 (11) 3.

SPAAR: *The ... - Spahr Family.* By Max Curt Spahr. 1962.

SPAHR: See SPAAR.

SPANGLER: ... *Families of York Co., PA, and Surrounding Areas,* mentioned in ONTG 19 (10) 5.

SPENGLER: *The Annals of the Families of Caspar, Henry, Baltzer, and George ... Who Settled in York County Respectively in 1729, 1732, 1732 and 1751.* By Edward W. Spangler. York: 1896.

SPRENCKEL: See *Early Families of York Co., Vol. 1,* by Dull.

SPRENKLE: *A History of the ... Family in America.*

Ancestors and Descendants of ... Sprinkle, mentioned, ONTG 16 (5) 1-2

SPRINGER, George; Unrecorded will, in ONTG 17 (9) 1.

STABLER: See *Early Families of York Co., Vol. 2,* by Dull.

Family Data in ONTG 20 (1) 1.

STAMBAUGH: ... *Families of York County, Pennsylvania,* mentioned in ONTG 19 (2) 3.

STEFFY: See HORNBERGER.

STENTZ: See *Early Families of York Co., Vol. 2,* by Dull.

STEVENSON: "James ..., Senior, of Strabane Township, York County, Pennsylvania." By George Urie Stevenson. 1974. Typescript.

STEWART: *John ... 1740-1820, and His Wife...,* mentioned, ONTG 16 (7) 2.

STOMBAUGH: See FISHER.

STRALEY: *Genealogy of the ... Family.*

STRICKLER: Forerunners. By Harry M. Strickler. 1925.

Bible Record, mentioned, ONTG 15 (4) 2-3.

STROEHER: *An Interim Report on the Descendants of Johan Nicholas..., I, Resident of Germany, Chanceford Twp., York County, PA, and Shepherdstown, Berkeley County, WV.* By Glenda S. Strayer. Reviewed, ONTG 17 (1) 3.

STRONG: *Descendants of James ... of York Co., PA,* mentioned in ONTG 20 (6) 4.

STUBBS: *The ... of Little Britain,* mentioned in ONTG 18 (5) 4.

STUMP. See SEITZ.

SWAN: *Records of the Families of Brothers, ... , Bonar, Reeves and Beardsley,* mentioned, ONTG 16 (2) 2.

SWARTZ: See *Early Families of York Co., Vol. 2,* by Dull.

SWOPE: *The ... Family.* By H. E. Swope and C. W. Swope. 1946.

... Family, mentioned in ONTG 18 (5) 4.

SYDENSTRICKER: See SCHUCK.

TAYLOR: Family, mentioned, ONTG 16 (2) 3.

THOMAS: See EARHART.

THOMPSON: ... Family (Zellers manuscript), mentioned, ONTG 17 (5) 2. See also HOOVER.

THORNTON: *Thorntons of Brookhave, Youngstown, and York,* mentioned, ONTG 17 (2) 2.

TOME: ... *Descendants of York Co., PA,* mentioned in ONTG 18 (9) 3.

TROUT; *Wendell ... of Hopewell Center, York Co., Pennsylvania, and His Descendants,* mentioned in ONTG 18 (7) 4.

250 History of My ... Family. By George E. Trout. Mentioned in ONTG 17 (2) 2, (11) 2.

TURNER: ... *and Allied Families,* mentioned, ONTG 16 (7) 2.

Valentine: mentioned, ONTG 11 (11) 2.

VANCE: *Handel ... (Johann Diehl Wentz), the Immigrant, 1728-1797,* mentioned ONTG 17 (11) 3.

VAUTRIN: *The ...-Wotring-Woodring Family, 1640-1790.* By Raymond M. Bell and Mabel G. Granquist. 1953.

WALTERMYER: ... Family (Zellers manuscript), mentioned, ONTG 17 (5) 2.

WAGNER: ... *Families of York Co., PA, and Surrounding Areas,* mentioned in ONTG 20 (8) 5.

WANNERS: The ..., mentioned in ONTG 18 (9) 3.

WEBB: *John ... (c.1754-1824) and Elizabeth Montgomery: Ancestors and Descendants.* By William Brooke Fetters. Mentioned in ONTG 19 (3) 4.

The James ... Family of York Co., PA, 1700-1993, mentioned in ONTG 20 (1) 3.

WEIBERG: See SCHMALHORST.

WEIDNER: *Through Four Generations: Heinrich ..., 1717-1792 & Catharine Mull ..., 1733-1804,* mentioned in ONTG 18 (6) 4.

WEIRMAN. See WEYERMAN.

WELK: See *Early Families of York Co., Vol. 2,* by Dull.

WELLS: ... *Family Sketches,* mentioned in ONTG 18 (1) 3.

WENTZ. See VANCE.

WEYBERG: See SCHMALHORST.

WEYERMAN: *William ... (Weirman) of Adams County, and Allied Families,* mentioned ONTG 17 (11) 3.

WHISLER. See WISSLER.

WHISSLER. See WISSLER.

WHITEFORD: *The ... Family.* By A. W. Whiteford. S.l, s.n., n.d.

WHYBARK: See SCHMALHORST.

WILSON: *Robert ... of York Co.* By Charles Hellen Wilson and George Henry Wilson. n.d.

WISSLER: *Compilations of Early ..., Whisler, and Whissler Families,* mentioned ONTG 17 (11) 3.

WOLCOTT: Genealogy, mentioned, ONTG 16 (4) 2.

WOLF: ... *Families, York Co., PA,* mentioned, ONTG 17 (5) 2.

WOODMANSEE: *A Branch of the Family of Isaac ...,* mentioned in ONTG 18 (5) 4.

WOODRING: See VAUTRIN.

WOTRING: See VAUTRIN.

YINGLING: *The ... Genealogy.* By Claude J. Rahn. 1958.

See also HORNBERGER.

YOUNG: *Baltzer ... (1760-1845) and Mary Elizabeth Buss; Ancestors and Descendants.* By William B. Fetters, mentioned in ONTG 20 (8) 2.

Henry James ... . Obituary, in ONTG 20 (8) 1-2.

ZINN: Genealogy of the ... Family. By E. Maurice Gras. 1962.

ZULAUF: *Descendants of Johannes...,* mentioned in ONTG 17 (5) 2.

FAMILY REPORTS

One of the most important resources for family histories in York County are the Genealogical Reports found at HSYC. These reports contain items from church records, tombstones, probate, land, newspaper and other records. Copies of the reports may be found in the various family file folders, and are also bound in a series of volumes. The following list, made available to the compiler of this Guide by the staff of the Historical Society, shows the family names for which reports exist.

Alexander	Baublitz	Blymire	Chandlee
Altland	Bayer	Boeckel	Clapsaddle
Ament	Beals-Bails	Boone	Clemmer-Clemens
Anderson	Bear	Bosher	Cloninger
Anstine	Beard	Bossert	Coleman-Kohlman
Armor	Bechtel	Bott	Collins
Armstrong	Becker	Bowers	Comfort
Ayres	de Beelen	Brokow. See Bercaw.	Conn
Bahn	Beitzel	Brose	Cook-Koch
Baker	Bender	Bruce	Cooper
Baker-Becker	Benford-Benfer	Bruch	Copeland
Ballentine	Bentzel	Brungart	Copp
Bard	Bercaw-Brokow	Brown	Coppenhaffer
Barker	Berkheimer	Buchanan	Cormeny
Barnett	Bentz	Bushong	Cosine
Barnhart	Berkley-Berckle	Busser	Cramer-Craumer-Cremer
Barnitz. See Wirt.	Billmeyer	Bryan-O'Brien	Crawford
Barshinger	Binder	Caldwell	Creager
Bartlett-Bartley	Bishop	Campbell	Criswell
Bartmess	Black	Carpenter	Croft-Kraft
Barton	Blesing	Carson	Crone
Baumgardner	Blessing	Chambers	

Cronemiller
Croll-Crowell-Krail
Crow-Kroh
Crum
Cunningham
Cuppy-Cuppet
Davis
Decker
Dehoff
Dewald
Dickson-Dickenson
Diehl
Dinkle. See Dunckel
Dise
Dohm
Donnell
Douglas
Doudel
Dreichler
Dritt
Dubs
Dunckel-Dinkle
Dunlap
Dunn
Ebert
Edmundson
Ehrhart
Eichelberger
Eicholtz
Eirich
Eitell
Ellicker
Elliot
Emenheiser
Emig
Ensminger
Ennter
Epler
Eshbach
Everitt
Ewing

Eyler
Eyster
Fahs
Faris
Felty. See Vetty.
Fetg-Uelty
Fenstermacher
Ferree
Fetrow
Fickel-Fickle
Fickes
Finley
Fisher-Fischer
Fitz
Flinchbaugh
Fohl
Foltz-Fultz
Foreeman-Fuhrman-
    Fortney
Foy
Freed
Friedline (Fritzline,
    Friedly) Friedley
Fritzline
Fuhrman. See
Foreman.
Fulton
Galbreath
Gallentine
Ganshorn
Gantzert
Gardner
Garner
Garrett
Gates
Geesey-Giese
Gemilll
Gerselman
Getz
Gilliland
Gitt
Glass

Glatfelter
Glen
Gohn
Gordon
Gossler
Gotz
Graham-Grimes
Graybill
Griere
Grimes. See Graham.
Gross
Haas
Haffner
Hake-Houck-Koke
Hamacher
Hamilton
Hammer
Hantz
Harman-Herman
Harper
Hart
Hartman
Hartzell
Hartzler-Hertzell-
Hertzler
Hassler
Hausman
Hedick
Heilman
Hendricks-Henderson
Hengst
Herman-Harman
Hershberger
Hershner
Hess
Hetrick
Hewitt
Hickenbeber-
    Hickenlooper
Hill
Hipple
Hoff

Hoffheins
Holder
Holtzapple
Holtzinger
Hooghtelin
Hoover
Horn
Hose
Hossack
Houck. See Hake
Householder
Houts
How (Howe)
Howard
Hubley
Huntsicker
Hyde
Ickes
Ihloze
Irion-Irions
Irwin
Jacobs
Jameson
Jenkins
Jones
Julius
Kann
Keller
Kelly
Kenworthy
Kimmel
Kinard
King-Konig
Kister
Kitt-Gitt
Kitzmiller
Klein
Klinefelter
Kling
Knab
Knisely

Koch-Cook
Kohler
Kohlman-Coleman
Koke. See Hake.
Konig. See King.
Kopenhaffer
Kopp
Kraft-Croft
Krall. See Croll
Kroll-Croll-Crowell
Kreider
Kreiss
Kroh-Crow
Krout
Kruger
Kuhn
Kump
Kunkel
Landis
Lanius
Larue
Lau
Lauer
Laux. See Loucks.
Lawson
Lecrone
Lehman
Lehn-Leininger
Lenhgart
Lentz
Lilly
Linn
Little
Litton-Litten
Livingston
Lobach
Loucks-Laux
Love
Lutz
Maish
Manifold

Mansperger
Marbourg
Marlin
Marsh
Marshall
Maughlin
Mauss
Maxwell
McAdams
McChord
McClean
McClellan
McConaughy
McElwain
McCleary
McCurdy
McDonal
McGowan-McQuown
McGrew
McIntire
McJimsey
McKesson
McKinley
McNaghten
Meads
Melsheimer
Menges
Meredith
Miller
Minnich
Momeyer
Moore
Morrison
Mundorf
Musser
Myers
Nace-Nes-Ness
Naylor
Nebinger
Neiman
Neiswanger

Noel-Noell-Nell
Ness
O'Brian. See also Bryan
Olewiler
Opp
Overlander
Owings
Oyler
Palmer
Parker
Paxton
Pedan
Pentz
Peter-Peters
Pflegger
Picking
Powell
Pressel
Prowel
Purdy
Rankin
Ratz
Read-Reed-Reid
Rebert
Redsecker-Ricksecker
Reeser
Reiman
Reisinger
Resser
Rex
Richey
Ricksecker. See Redesecker.
Robinson
Rohrbaugh
Root-Ruth
Rothrock-Ruthrauff
Roudebush
Rouzer
Rowland
Rudy

Ruhl
Runk
Runle
Rupert
Ruth-Roth
Ruthrauff-Rothrock
Saltzgiver
Sample
Sands
Sauer
Schreimer
Schultz
Schwaab
Schwartz
Scott
Seiler-Sellers
Seiling
Sensing
Seyler. See Zoeller.
Shafer
Shanks
Sharp
Shaw
Shenberger
Sherman
Shetter
Shigley
Shive
Shively
Shoemaker-Schumaker
Shollas
Shrack
Shue
Shugart
Shuller
Siddon
Sinard
Sinclair
Sipe
Sitton
Slagle

Slaybaugh
Slaymaker
Smith
Smyser
Snyder
Somers-Summers
Souder
Spangler
Speer
Spitler
Sprenkle
Squibb
Stabley-Stabler
Stair
Stauffer
Stehly
Stein
Steiner-Stoner
Steinmetz
Stentz
Stoehr
Stoner. See Steiner
Stouch-Stough
Strack
Strawbridge
Strickler
Strohman
Strong
Studebaker
Summers. See Somers
Swan
Swoope
Tawswer
Taylor
Test
Thomas
Throne
Todd
Toomey
Treichler
Trexler. See Trostle.

Tronell. See Trostle.
Trostle-Tronell-
   Trexler
Trout-Traut
Tyson-Dise
Uelty. See Fetg.
Underwood
Updegraff
Upp
Valentine
Vetty-Welty-Felty
Vore-Voar
Wagner
Wahl-Wall
Wallace
Waltemeyer
Warren
Weaverline
Weidman
Weigel
Weisang
Weiser
Weitzell-Whitesell
Welsh
Welty-Felty-Velty
Wentz
Weyer-Wire
White. See Wise.
Whitesell. See
Weitzell.
Wiest
Wiley
Will-Wills
Williams
Wilson-Williams
Wilt
Winebrenner
Winebrenner
Wineholt
Winter
Winterode
Wirt-Barnitz

Wise-Weis-White
Witmeyer
Wohlgemuth
Wolf
Wolford
Young
Ziegler
Zoeller-Seyler
Zimmerman
Zinn
Zitger

Chapter 8

LAND

Pennsylvania Land Records: A History and Guide for Research. By Donna Bingham Munger. Wilmington: Scholarly Resources, 1991. Mentioned in ONTG 16 (7) 2.

"Adams County, PA, Historical Title Search Program," ONTG, 9 (8), supp. page.

The compiler is indebted to the Rev. Dr. Neal Otto Hively of Chambersburg, PA, for graciously compiling the summary of York County Land Records.

All of the primary source documents: warrants, surveys, patents, are on microfilm at the Pennsylvania Historical and Museum Commission, Harrisburg, PA. The Search Room at the Pennsylvania Archives is open Tuesday through Friday, 8:00 a.m. to 4:00 p.m.; Saturdays, 8:00 a.m. to 2:00 p.m. An identification, sign-in, and surveillance systems apply to anyone using the Archives and are in place to protect the records.

Copies of the primary documents are kept at the HSYC. The originals are not accessible to the public but the files are fully indexed and copies are available to the public.

The Adams County Historical Society, Gettysburg, PA, has duplicate documents, usually on microfilm, for most of the documents at the HSYC.

Warrant registers for all Pennsylvania counties are available on microfilm at the Archives.

Warrant Registers for Lancaster County, 1732-1750 (photocopies), are available at the HSYC.

West Side Applications (special land warrants issued between 1766 and August 1769) are available on microfilm.

Deed Books from 1749 to the present are available at the Court House (but as of the Fall of 1995 many early records will be moved to the York County Archives). Deed books from 1749 to c.1900 are available on microfilm at the HSYC.

Deed Books, 1749-1859 (transcripts); and Deed Index, 1749-1812 (transcripts) are available at the Genealogical Society of Pennsylvania.

Land Drafts (transcripts) are available at the Genealogical Society of Pennsylvania.

Abstracts from Case of Charles Cecil's [Calvert?] Claims to Lands in York County, 1681-1764. SCPGS Spec. Pub. # 25.

Alquire, Joan L. *York County, Pennsylvania Deeds.* 3 vols., 1749-1758, 1758-1761, and 1763. South Holland, IL: Alquire Abstracts.

Brackbill, Martin H. "Family Data in Some Pennsylvania Land Patents, 1760-1761," NGSQ 64 (4) 275-283.

-----. "-----, 1760-1763." NGSQ 66 (1) 61-64, (3) 205-210; 67 (2) 130-141.

-----. "-----, 1762-1764." NGSQ 68 (2) 83-ff.

Calendar of Transactions, Deed Book 3-B, 1793-1816, CC 4(1)1, (2)1, (3)1, (4)1; 5(2)1, (3)1, (4)1, (5)1; 1812-1817, 6(1)1; 1811-1817, 6(2)1; 1791-1817, 6(3)1.

Deed Abstracts, Book 3-B, 1796-1815, CC 1(1)1; 1813-1815, 1(2)1, (3)1; 1814-1815, 1(4)1; 1811-1815, 2(2)1; 1809-1816, 2(3)1; 1813-1816, 2(4)1; 1810-1812, 3(1)1 ; 1816, 3(3)1; 1811-1816, 3(4)1.

Genealogical Abstracts of Eighteenth Century Original and Mostly Unpublished Deeds Pertaining to Adams County, Pennsylvania. Surname Index (1988). SCPGS Spec. Pub. # 37.

Index to Draft Books, 1765-1875, Adams County, PA, mentioned in ONTG 20 (1) 3.

The Manor of Maske and Individual Properties. By Dr. Charles H. Glatfelter and Arthur Weaner. Gettysburg, Adams County Historical Society. Mentioned in ONTG 18 (7) 1.

The Manor of Springettsbury: Its History and Early Settlers. Neal Otto Hively. Pub. by the Author. This book describes the earliest settlers in the region, including the founding of York Town. *Springettsbury Map.* By Neal Otto Hively. Shows the 65,000 acre Proprietary Manor and 391 original tracts, York Town location, and earliest owners. See mention in ONTG 19 (3) 2-3.

Notes and Documents Concerning the Manorial History of the Town of York, York County, Pennsylvania. Compiled by Henry James Young (1992). SCPGS Spec. Pub. # 47.

Warrant Register of Lancaster County [PA], mentioned in ONTG 20 (1) 3.

Warrant Register of York County [PA], mentioned in ONTG 20 (1) 3.

York County, Pennsylvania, Land Appraisement Certificates issued by the County Commissioners, 1835-1859 (SCPGS Spec. Pub. # 38).

Neal O. Hively has compiled a number of books and connected draft warrant maps for York County, PA.

Each book contains the surveys arranged numerically, followed by the township and the book and page of the York Warrant Register. A typical entry for a survey gives the a) WARRANT: application number, date, acreage, and to whom issued; b) SURVEY: date land was laid out, acreage, for whom it was surveyed, and name of the tract (if any); and c) PATENT: date patent was granted, acreage, and to whom. Sometime several years elapsed between the issuance of the warrant and the granting of the patent, and the names of individuals given in these documents were different.

The value of the Draft Warrant Maps is that they show the actual boundaries of the surveys, with the name of the original owner given and the name of the tract (if there was one). The metes and bounds of the tract are shown on the boundaries, and the map also shows streams, township lines, survey lines, roads, and churches. For details on Hively's Draft Maps see page 13.

Chapter 9
MILITARY
"PA" refers to the Pennsylvania Archives (published series).

List of Pensioners, 1883, CC 1 (2) 39, (3) 36, (4) 37; 2 (2) 41, 2(3)23.

Militia Muster and Pay Rolls, 1790-1800, PA (6) V 829-835.

Militia Officer Returns, 1790-1817, PA (6) IV.

Militia Rolls, 1783-1790, PA 6 (III) 1413-1483.

Revolutionary War
Associators and Militia Muster Rolls, 1774-1780, PA (2) XIV 473-546; PA (6) II, 413-817.

Burials of Old Rev. War Soldiers, CC 1 (1) 23; 2 (3) 34; 2 (4) 32; 3 (1) 9.

Camp Security, Prisoners of War in York County, 1781-1783, mentioned, ONTG 16 (7) 2.

Compiled Military Records of York Countians in the Revolution at the HSYC. There are two series: a red and black series.

Lieutenants Accounts, 1777-1786, PA (3) VII 39-114.

Recruiting List of Lieut. Stephen Stephenson, York County, 1770. PMHB 25:420.

War of 1812
Burials of War of 1812 Veterans, CC 4 (4) 19; 5 (2) 27, (3) 27, (4) 27, (5) 27; 6 (1) 31, (2) 31, (3) 9.

War of 1812-1814, Returns of 5th division, PA (6) VII 311-368.

Civil War
An Abstract of the 1865 York County, Pennsylvania, Assessors Military Roll (1986-1987). SCPGS Spec. Pub. # 33.

The GAR: Its Organization and the Men of Post # 37 (1988-1989). SCPGS Spec. Pub. # 39.

History of Pennsylvania Volunteers. By Samuel Bates. Repr. in 10 volumes. Wilmington, [NC]: Broadfoot Pub. Co. Mentioned in ONTG 19 (1) 2.

The 1863 Letter of George W. Finlaw (pertains to Civil War incident in York County, Pennsylvania. (Feb. 1984). SCPGS Spec. Pub. # 4.

World War I
York County Soldiers of, CC 6 (1) 36, (2) 36, (3) 36.

Chapter 10
NATURALIZATION

Original Naturalization Papers for York County are kept at the new York County Archives.

Abstract of Pennsylvania Records of Naturalizations, 1695-1773, Found in *Colonial Records (Minutes of the Provincial Council),* Volumes 1, 2, 3, 4, 9, & 10; *The Statutes at Large of Pennsylvania,* Volumes II, III, IV, V, VI, VII & VIII; *Pennsylvania Archives,* Series 1, Volumes 1, 2, 3, & 4. (Oct. 1983). SCPGS Spec. Pub. # 24.

Adams County Naturalizations, mentioned in ONTG 19 (2) 3.

Colonial Maryland Naturalizations. By Jeffrey A. Wyand and Florence L. Wyand. Baltimore: Genealogical Publishing Co., 1986. (includes many settlers of York County who found it easier to get to Annapolis than to Philadelphia).

An Immigrant Nation: United States Regulation of Immigration. 1798-1991. Washington: United States Government Printing Office. Mentioned in ONTG 18 (1) 1.

Lancaster County Naturalizations, 1740-1750, CC 4 (1) 26.

Naturalization Records (Colonial), 1749-1773, CC 4 (2) 31, (3) 32.

Naturalization Records, (Federal) 1802, CC 1 (1) 18; 1798-1799, 1 (2) 20; 1800, 1 (3) 20; 1 (4) 21; 1805-1806, CC 2 (2) 20; 1806-08, 2 (3) 21; 1808-1809, 2 (4) 21; 1809-1820, 3 (1) 20; 1811-1812, 3 (3) 23; 1812-1814, 3 (4) 13; 1814, 4 (1) 11; 1814, 4 (2) 12; 1814-1816, 4 (3) 16; 1815, 4 (4) 14; 1815-1817, 5 (2) 9; 1817, 5 (3) 9; 1817-1818, 5 (4) 15; 1818, 5 (5) 11; 1818-1820, 6 (1) 12; 1820-1822, 6 (2) 13; 1821-1825, 6 (3) 14.

"Naturalizations in Pennsylvania (Prior to 1791)," ONTG 2 (1) Supp.

Naturalizations of Foreign Protestants in the American and West Indian Colonies. By M. S. Giuseppi. London: The Huguenot Society of London, 1921. Repr.: Baltimore: Genealogical Pub. Co., Inc., 1964. (contains a large number of PA naturalizations, 1740-1772).

Chapter 11
NEWSPAPERS

Published Abstracts and Indices

Abstracts of South Central Pennsylvania Newspapers. By Martha Reamy and F. Edward Wright. 3 vols., 1785-1800. Westminster: Family Line Publications, 1988. Vol. 1: 1785-1790. Vol. 2: 1791-1795. Vol. 3: 1796-1800.

Death Index, York County,...1789-1850 (copied from Old Newspapers). Typescript, 7 vols.

Deaths in Newspapers on File in Hanover Public Library,...1828-1900. 3 vols. Typescript, DAR Library.

Hanover Evening Sun Obituary Index, 1942-1967, 2 vols., mentioned in ONTG 20 (1) 3.

Marriage Index to York Newspapers, 1783-1850. Typescript, 8 vols.

Marriages and Deaths from the York Recorder, 1821-1830. [By F. Edward Wright]. Westminster: Family Line Publications, 1995.

Marriages in Newspapers on File Hanover Public Library..., 1828-1900. (1945).

Items from Old Adams County Newspapers, CC 1 (2) 29.

Items from Old County Newspapers, CC 1 (1) 19.

Items from Old York County Newspapers, CC 1 (3) 39, (4) 39; 3 (3) 34; 5 (2) 10.

Marriages and deaths (The York Press), 1865, CC 6 (2) 21; Oct. 1865-Feb. 1866, CC 6 (3) 25.

Marriages and Deaths from the "York Gazette,": April-May 1852, CC 6 (1) 21.

Marriage and Death Notices, 1851-52, CC 4 (1) 21; 1852, CC 4 (2) 29; 1851-52, CC 4 (3) 43; 1852, CC 4 (4) 23; 1873, CC 1 (1) 30; Feb. 1904, CC 3 (4) 27.

News Items from the York Springs Comet, 1880-1908; 1909-1914, mentioned in ONTG 19 (2) 3.

Pennsylvania Newspaper Project. See ONTG 11 (10) 2.

"Welsh Immigrant Information from the *Delta Herald and Times.*" (SCPGS Spec. Pub. # 52).

York County, Pennsylvania, Newspapers

We are indebted to Richard Konkel for generously sharing the following list of newspapers which he compiled.

All newspapers published in York unless otherwise noted. cop. = copies, b = bound, m = microfiche, u = unbound

ACTIVE CHRISTIAN - Monthly; July 1886-u

ADVERTISER - Monthly; June 1860-u

AGE - Daily; Feb 26 1883-u; July 1883-Jan 1884-b; Nov 7 1883-u; Nov 8 1883-u; Jan 1884-u; Jan 1 1884-July 1884-b; Years's address of the newsboy-u; July 1884-Jan 1885-b; July 26 1884-u; Nov 8 1884-u; Jan 1885-July 1885-b; July 1885-Jan 1886-b; Oct 3 1885-u; Jan 1886-July 1886-b; July 1886-Jan 1887-b; July 23 1886-u; Jan 1887-July 1887-b; July 1887-Jan 1888-b; Sept 23 1887 (2 cop.-u); Sept 24 1887-2 cop.-u; Nov 23 1887-u; Jan 1888-July 1888-b; Mar 13 1888-u; July 1888-Jan 1889-b; Jan 1889-July 1889; July 1889-Jan 1890-b; Jan 1890-July 1890-b; May 29 1890-u; July 1890-Jan 1891-b; Sept 18 1890-u; Sept 19 1890-u; Dec 4 1890-u; Jan 1891-July 1891-b; Apr 10 1891-u; July 1891-Jan 1892-b; July 9 1891-u; Sept 1 1891-u; Oct 22 1891-u; Jan 1892-July 1892-b; June 16 1892-u; June 18 1892-u; July 1892-Jan 1893-b; Nov 13 1892-u; Jan 1893-July 1893-b; July 1893-Jan 1894-b; Jan 1894-July 1894-b; Mar 8 1894-u; July 1894-Jan 1895-b; July 19 1894-u; Jan 1895-July 1895-b; July 1895-Jan 1896-b; Jan 1896-July 1896-b; July 1896-Jan 1897-b; Oct 6 1896-u; Nov 30 1896-u; Dec 1 1896-u; Jan 1897-July 1897-b; Jan 1897-carrier's address-u

AMERICAN PROTECTIONIST Oct 15 1860-u

AMERICAN LUTHERAN Aug 8 1874-u

AMERICAN EAGLE Jan 1 1855-u; Nov 3 1855-u

ART, INK, AND TYPE; Vol. 1 No 4-u; "1" 5-u (2 cop.) "2" 1-u

BANNER (official Organ Sons of Union Veterans of Civil War) 1902-1910-u; 1911-1919-u; Jan 1930-Oct 1939-u; 1940-1946-u

BEF (Bonus Expeditionary Forces)News - Weekly; July 9 1932-Vol. 1 No. 2-u; July 9 1932 Vol. 1 No. 3-u; July 16 1932-u; July 23 1932-u; July 30 1932-u; Aug 6 1932-u; Aug 213 1932-u; Aug 20 1932-u; Aug 27 1932-u; Sept 3 1932-u; Sept 10 1932-u; Sept 17 1932-u; Sept 24 1932-u; Oct 1 1932-u

BENEFACTOR Vol. 1, No. 21 (undated)-u

THE BLOWER; 1 undated issue-u

BOY COMPASS; April 1911-u

CARRIAGE BOX - Weekly; Mar 5 1864-July 1865-b-rare book room; Mar 5 1864-July 1865-m; Aug 6 1864-u; Aug 3 1864-u; Aug 20 1864-u; Nov 19 1864-u; Nov 26 1864-u; Dec 31 1864-u; Jan 28 1865-u; Mar 25 1865-u; Apr 1 1865-u; June 10 1865-u; July 8 1865-u

CHRISTIAN MESSENGER; April 1947-u; May 1947-u; Aug 1947-u; Sept 1947-u; Oct 1947-2 cop.; Nov 1947-u; Dec 1947-3 cop.-u; Jan 1948-u; Feb 1948-2 cop.; Mar 1948-cop.-u; Apr 1948; May 1948-4 cop.-u

COLUMBIA DAILY NEWS Lancaster Co. PA. Columbia; Aug 21 1909-u - Daily

COLUMBIA HERALD, Lancaster Co. PA. Columbia; June 3 1874-u

COMMON SENSE Mar 1948-2 cop.-u; Apr 1948-u; May 1948-2 cop.-u; June 1948-3 cop.-u; July 1948-4 cop.-u; Aug 1948-u; Sept 1948-u

DAILY (Supplement to Every Saturday); Dec 21 1889-u; Jan 11 1890-u

DAILY RECORD Hanover - Daily; Dec 29 1894-u; Sept 11 1895-u; Mar 21 1898-u

DAILY RECORDER - Daily; June 17 1861-Aug 20 1861-b

DALLASTOWN ADVOCATE Dallastown - Weekly; Aug 30 1902-u; Sept 6 1902-u; Sept 13 1902-u; Sept 20 1902-u; Sept 27 1902-u; Oct 4 1902-u; Oct 11 1902-u; Oct 18 1902-u; Oct 25 1902-u; Nov 1902-u; Nov 8 1902-u; Nov 15 1902-u; Nov 22 1902-u; Nov 29 1902-u; Dec 6 1902-u; Dec 13 1902-u; Dec 20 1902-u; Dec 27 1902-u

DELTA HERALD AND TIMES Delta; Mar 20 1901-supplement-m; Dec 13 1907-June 14 1912-m; June 28 1912-Feb 18 1916-m; Oct 2 1914-u; Feb 25 1916-April 2 1920-m; Mar 9 1917-u; Mar 7 1920-u; May 28 1926-u; Sept 10 1926-u; Feb 18 1927-u; Feb 23 1928-2 cop.-u; Oct 18 1928-u; Feb 14 1929-u; Feb 21 1929-u; Feb 28

1929-u; July 10 1930-u; June 30 1932-Aug 29 1935-m; Sept 5 1935-June 30 1938-m; July 7 1938-Dec 28 1939-m; Nov 30 1940-u; June 13 1941-u; July 10 1941-Jan 24 1946-m; Jan 31 1946-Dec 19 1946-m

DEMOCRAT AND FARMERS AND MECHANICS ADVOCATE Hanover; Jan 6 1843-u

DEMOCRAT ADVOCATE; Dec 21 1889-Supplement-u

DEMOCRATIC AGE; see The Age

DEMOCRATIC PRESS - Weekly; June 25 1845-June 15 1847-b; June 22 1847-June 12 1849-b; June 25 1851-June 28 1853-b; May 23 1873-u; July 18 1873-u

YORK DEMOCRATIC PRESS same as Democratic Press; Jul. 1 1839-Dec 31 1862-m; Feb 5 1864-u; May 6 1864-u; July 14 1865-May 27 1870-m; Aug 11 1865-u; Apr 5 1867-May 7 1901-m(misses a week between); Jan 1 1869-Carriers address to patrons-u; Dec 18 1866-u; Jan 11 1867-u

DIE DEUTCHE GAZETTE - Weekly; May 20 1796-July 18 1817-b; Mar 7 1828-Feb 26 1830-b; Mar 12 1830-May 27 1831-b; Mar 23 1832-Mar 7 1834-b

DILLSBURG NEW ERA Dillsburg; Dec 1 1875-u

DISPATCH AND RECORD see the Evening Dispatch

DOVER AREA REPORTER Dover; Oct 3 1963-3 cop.-u; Nov 7 1963-u; Dec 5 1963-u; Jan 2 1964-u; Feb 6 1964-2 cop.-u; May 7 1964-u; June 4 1964-2 cop.-u; July 2 1964-2 cop.-u; Aug 6 1964-3 cop.-u; Aug 13 1963-u; Sept 3 1964-2 cop.-u; Oct 1 1964-2 cop.-u; Oct 8 1964-u; Nov 12 1964-u; Dec 3 1964-u; Jan 6 1965-u; Feb 4 1965-u; Mar 4 1965-u; Apr 1 1965-u; Vol. 1-#5-undated-u; Vol. 1 #11-undated-u

DAS EVANGELISCHE MAGAZIN EV. LUTHERISCBEN KINCHE; Apr 1829-u; Jun. 1829-u; Jul. 1829-u; Aug 1829-u; Sep. 1829-u; Oct 1829-u; Nov 1829-u; Dec 1829-u; Jan 1830-u; Feb 1830-u; Mar 1830-u; Apr 1830-u; May 1830-u; Jun. 1830-u; Jul. 1830-u; Aug 1830-u; Sept 1830-u; Oct 1830-u; Nov 1830-u; Dec 1830-u; Jan 1831-u; Feb 1831-u; Mar 1831-u; Apr 18313-u; May 1831-u; Jun. 1831-u; Jul. 1831-u; Aug 18331-u; Sep. 18331-u; Oct 1831-u; Nov 18313-u; Dec 18331-u; Jan 1832-u; Feb 1832-u; Feb 1832-u; Mar 1832-u; Apr 1832-u; May 1832-u; Jun. 18323-u; Oct 1832-u; Dec 1832-u; Jan 1833-u; Mar 1833-u; Apr 1833-u

EVENING DISPATCH York - Daily; May 29 1876-Dec 21 1876-b; Jun. 9 1987-u; Jun. 10 1876-u; Jun. 13 1876-u; Jun. 14 1876-u; Jun. 15 1876-u; Jun. 17 1876-u; Jun. 19 1876-u; Jun. 20 1876-u; Jun. 21-1876-u; Jun. 22 18976-u; Jun. 23 1876-u; Jun. 24 1876-u; Jun. 27 1876-u; Jun. 29 1876-u; Jul. 1 1876-u; Jul. 14 1876-u; Jul. 17 1876-u; Jul. 18 1876-u; Jul. 19 1876-u; Jul. 20 1876-u; Jul. 21 1876-u; Jul. 22 1876-u; Jul. 24 1876-u; Jul. 25 1876-u; Jul. 26 1876-u; Jul. 27 1876-u; Jul. 28 1876-u; Jul. 29 1876-u; Jul. 31 1876-u; Aug 1 1876-u; Aug 2 1876-u; Aug 3 1876-u; Aug 4 1876-u; Aug 5 1876-u; Aug 7 1876-u; Aug 8 1876-u; Aug 9 1876-u; Aug 10 1876-u; Aug 12 1876-u; Aug 14 1876-u; Aug 15 1876-u; Aug 16 1876-u; Aug 17 1876-u; Aug 18 1876-u; Aug 19 1876-u; Aug 21 1876-u; Aug 22 1876-u; Aug 23 1876-u; Aug 24 1876-u; Aug 25 1876-u; Aug 26 1876-u; Aug 28 1876-u; Aug 29 1876-u; Aug 30 1876-u; Aug 31 1876-u; Sept 1 1876-u; Sep. 2 1876-u; Sep. 4 1876-u; Sep. 5 1876-u; Sep. 7 1876-u; Sep. 8 1876-u; Sep. 9 1876-u; Sep. 11 1876-u; Sep. 12 1876-u; Sep. 19 1876-u; Sep. 20 1876-u; Sep. 21 1876-u; Sep. 22 1876-u; Sep. 23 18876-u; Sep. 25 1876-u; Sep. 26 1876-u; Sep. 27 1876-u; Sep. 28 1876-u; Sep. 29 1876-u; Sep. 30 1876-u; Oct 2 1876-u; Oct 3 18786-u; Oct 4 1876-u; Oct 5 1876-u; Oct 7 1876-u; Oct 9 1876-u; Oct 11 1876-u; Oct 12 1876-u; Oct 13 1876-u; Oct 14 1876-u; Oct 17 1876-u; Oct 19 1876-u; Oct 18 1876-u; Oct 21 1876-u; Apr 25 1876-u; Jul. 2 1877-Dec 31 1877-b; Aug 7 1877-u; Sep. 3 1877-u; Sep. 4 1877-u; Jul. 1 1878-u; Jul. 2 1878-Jun. 27 1878-b; Nov 6 1878-u; Jan 1 1879-Jun. 30 1879-b; Apr 25 1879-u; Jul.1 1879-Dec 31 1879-b; Jan 1 1880-Jun. 30 1880-b; Jul. 1 1880-Dec 31-1880-b; Jan 1 1881-Jun. 30 1881-b; Jul. 1 1881-Dec 31 1881-b; Sep. 24 1881-u; Jan 2 1882-Jun. 30 1882-b; Jul. 1 1882-Dec 30 1882-b; Jan 1 1883-Jun. 30 1883-b; Jul. 2 1883-Nov 27 1883-b; May 20 1884-u; May 31 1884-u; Jun. 5 1884-Dec 31 1884-b; Jan 2 1885-Jun. 30 1885-b; Apr 10 1885-u; Jul. 1 1885-Nov 24 1885-b; Jan 3 1887-Jun. 30 1887-b

EVENING HERALD see Hanover Herald

EVENING SUN - Daily; Nov 11. 1918-u; Apr 16 1919-u; Jun. 9 1919-u; Feb 18 1932-u; Jun. 10 1932-u; Aug 24 1932-u; Oct 20 1932-u; Nov 23 1932-u; Dec 1 1932-u

EVENING TELEGRAM; See York Evening Telegram

EXPOSITOR Jun. 3 1813-u

FANCIER'S EXCHANGE BULLETIN - Weekly; Jan 12 1877-u; Jan. 30 1877-u; Mar 6 1877-u; Mar 13 1877-u; Mar 20 1877-u; Mar 27 1877-u; Apr 3 1877-u; Apr 24 1877-u; May 1 1877-u; May 8 1877-u; May 25 1877-u; May 22 1877-u;

May 29 1877-u; Jun. 5 1877-u; Jun. 12 1877-u; Jun. 19 1877-u; Jun. 26 1877-u; Jul 3 1877-u; Jul 24 1877-u; Jul. 31 1877-u; Aug 7 1877-u; Aug 14 1877-u; Aug 21 1877-u; Aug 28 1877-u; Sep. 4 1877-u; Sep. 11 1877-u; Sep. 18 1877-u; Sep. 25. 1877-u; Oct/ 2 1877-u; Oct 2 1877-u; Oct 16 1877-u; Oct 23 1877-u; Oct 30 1877-u; Nov 6 1877-u; Nov 21 1877-u; Dec 5 1877-u; Dec 18 1877-u; Feb 14 1878-u; Mar 20 1878-u; Apr 3 1878-u; Apr 17 1878-u; May 1 1878-u; May 15 1878-u; May 29 1878-u; Jun. 12 1878-u; Jul. 3 1878-u; Sep. 13 1878-u; Oct 7 1878-u; Nov 7 1878-u; Dec 2 1878-u

FATHER ABRAHAM Lancaster; June 26 1868-u; Aug 28 1868-u; Sept 4 1868-u

FIREMAN - Monthly; September 1875-u

FIVE STAR NEWS Manchester; December 7 1972-u

FRANK LESLIE'S ILLUSTRATED-New York, New York - Weekly; Nov 16 1861-u; Nov 30 1861-u; Dec 14 1861-u; Dec 28 1861-u; Jan 4 1862-u; Jan 11 1862-u; Jan 18 1862-u; Jan 25 1862-u; Feb 1 1862-u; Feb 15 1862-u; Mar 1 1862-u; Mar 29 1862-u; Apr 5 1862-u; Apr 12 1862-u; Apr 19 1862-u; Apr 26 1862-u; May 3 1862-u; May 3 1862-War supplement-u; May 10 1862-u; May 17 1862-u; May 17 1862-War Supplement-u; Feb 10 1872-u

FREE PRESS York; Sep. 7 1972-u; Sep. 28 1972-u; Oct 5 1972-u; Nov 23 1972-u; Jan 11 1973-u; Jan 18 1973-u; Feb 1 1973-u

FRIEND; See The Monthly Friend

GAZETTE York; Mar 17 1892-u; Jul. 22 1908-u; Sep. 8 1911-u; May 24 1915-4 cop.-u; May 29 1915-u

GAZETTE AND DAILY York - Daily; Sep-Dec 1918-b; Jan-Jun 1919-b; Aug-Dec 1919-b; Jan-Aug 1920-b; Oct-Dec 1920-b; Jan-Aug 1921-b; Oct-Dec 1921-b; Jan-Dec 1922-b; Jan-Dec 1923-b; Jan-Dec 1924-b; Jan-Dec 1925-b; Jan-Dec 1926-b; Oct 31 1926-u; Jan-Dec 1927-b; Oct 13 1927-u; Oct 14 1927-u; Mar-Dec 1928-b; Jan-Dec 1929-b; Jan-Dec 1930-b; Jan-Dec 19331-b; Jan-Dec 1932-b; Jan-Dec 1933-b; Aug 24 1933-incomplete 2 cop.-u; Aug 25 1933-incomplete-u; Aug 26 1933-incomplete-u; Aug 29 1933-incomplete-u; Jan-Dec 1934-b; Oct 4 1934-u; Oct 5 1934-u; Oct 6 1934-u; Oct 8 1934-u; Jan-Dec 1935-b; Jan-Dec 1936-b; Jan-Dec 1937-b; Jan-Dec 1938-b; Apr 21 1938-u; Jan-Dec 1939-b; Feb 3 1939-incomplete; Jan-Dec 1940-b; Apr 13 1940-u 2 cop.; Jan-Nov 1941-b; Jan-Dec 1942-b; Jan-Dec 1943-b; Jan-Dec 1944-b; Jan-Dec 1945-b; Aug 15 1945-2 cop.-u; Jan-Dec 1946-b; Jan-Dec 1947-b; Mar 21 1947-

u; Jan-Dec 1949-b; Aug 19 1949-2 cop.-u; Jan-Dec 1950-b; Jan-Dec 1951-b; Jan-Dec 1952-b; Jan-Dec 1953-b; Jan 2 1954-Dec 1967-m; Apr 16 1958-u; Sep 1960-b; Mar 1963-b; May-Jun 1963-b; Nov 27 1963-u; Jan-Dec 1968-b; Jan-Dec 1969-b; Jan-Dec 1970-b; Oct 9 1970-u; Jan. 1 1918-Dec 31 1970

GAZETTE PRESS York; Jan 6 1905-Feb 8 1906-b

GENERAL ADVERTISER - Weekly; Jan 1 1789-Dec 31 1793-m; Jan 7 1789-u; Jan 14 1789-u; Jan 21 1789-u; Jan 28 1789-u; Feb 4 1789-u; Feb 11 1789-u; Feb 18 1789-u; Feb 25 1789-u; Mar 4 1789-u; Mar 11 1789-u; Mar 25 1789-u; Apr 1 1789-u; Apr 8 1789-u; Apr 15 1789-u; Apr 22 1789-u; Apr 29 1789-u; May 6 1789-u; May 13 1789-u; May 20 1789-u; May 27 1789-u; June 13 1789-u; Jun 10 1789-u; Jun 17 1789-u; Jun 24 1789-u; Jul 1 1789-u; Jul 8 1789-u; Jul 15 1789-u; Jul 22 1789-u; Jul 29 1789-u; Aug 5 1789-u; Aug 12 1789-u; Aug 19 1789-u; Aug 26 1789-u; Mar 18 1789-u; Sep 2 1789-u; Sep 9 1789-u; Sep 16 1789-u; Sep 23 1789-u; Sep 30 1789-u; Oct 7 1789-u; Oct 14 1789-u; Oct 21 1789-u; Oct 28 1789-u; Nov 4 1789-u; Nov 11 1789-u; Nov 18 1789-u; Nov 25 1789-u; Dec 2 1789-u; Dec 9 1789-u; Dec 1789-u; Dec 23 1789-u; Dec 30 1789-u; Jan 16 1790-u; Jan 13 1790-u; Jan 20 1790-u; Jan 27 1790-u; Feb 3 1790-u; Feb 10 1790-u; Feb 17 1790-u; Feb 24 1790-u; Mar 3 1790-u; Mar 10 1790-u; Mar 17 1790-u; Mar 24 1790-u; Mar 31 1790-u; Apr 7 1790-u; Apr 14 1790-u; Apr 21 1790-u; Apr 28 1790-u; May 5 1790-u; May 11 or 12 1790-u; May 19 1790-u; May 26 1790-u; Jun 2 1790-u; Jun 9 1790-u; Jun 16 1790-u; Jun 23 1790-u; Jun 30 1790-u; Jul 7 1790-u; Jul 14 1790-u 2 cop.; Jul 21 1790-u 2 cop.; Jul 28 1790-u 2 cop.; Aug 4 1790-u 2 cop.; Aug 11 1790-u 2 cop.; Aug 18 1790-u 2 cop.; Aug 25 1790-u; Sep 1 1790-u; Sep 8 1790-u 2 cop.; Sep 15 1790-u 2 cop.; Sep 22 1790-u 2 cop.; Sep 29 1790-u 2 cop.; Oct 6 1790-u; Oct 13 1790-u; Oct 20 1790-u; Oct 27 1790-u 2 cop.; Nov 3 1790-u 2 cop.; Nov 10 1790-u 2 cop.; Nov 17 1790-u 2 cop.; Nov 24 1790-u 2 cop.; Dec 1 1790-u 2 cop.; Dec 8 1790-u; Dec 15 1790-u 2 cop.; Dec 22 1790-u 2 cop.; Dec 29 1790-u 2 cop.; Jan 5 1791-u; Jan 12 1791-u; Jan 19 1791-u; Jan 26 1791-u; Feb 2 1791-u; Feb 9 1791-u; Feb 16 1791-u; Mar 9 1791-u; Mar 16 1791-u; Mar 23 1791-u; Mar 30 1791-u; Apr 6 1791-u; Apr 13 1791-u; Apr 20 1791-u; Apr 27 1791-u; May 4 1791-u; May 11 1791-u; May 18 1791-u; May 25 1791-u; Jun 1 1791-u; June 8 1791-u; Jun 15 1791-u; Jun 22 1791-u; Jun 29 1791-u; Jul 6 1791-u; Jul 13 1791-u; Jul 20 1791-u; Jul 27 1791-u; Aug 3 1791-u; Aug 10 1791-u; Aug 17 1791-u; Aug 31 1791-u; Sep 7 1791-u; Sep 14 1791-u; Sep 21

1791-u; Sep 28 1791-u; Oct 12 1791-u; Oct 19 1791-u; Oct 26 1791-u; Nov 2 1791-u; Nov 9 1791-u; Nov 16 1791-u; Nov 23 1791-u; Nov 30 1791-u; Dec 14 1791-u; Dec 21 1791-u; Dec 28 1791-u; Jan 11 1792-u; Feb 1 1792-u; Feb 8 1792-u; Feb 29 1792-u; Mar 7 1792-u; Mar 14 1792-u; Mar 21 1792-u; Apr 4 1792-u; Apr 11 1792-u; Apr 18 1792-u; Apr 25 1792-u; May 2 1792-u; May 9 1792-u; May 16 1792-u; May 23 1792-u; May 30 1792-u; Jun 6 1792-u; Jun 13 1792-u; Jun 20 1792-u; Jun 27 1792-u; Jul 4 1792-u; Jul 11 1792-u; Jul 25 1792-u; Aug 8 1792-u; Aug 15 1792-u; Aug 22 1792-u; Aug 29 1792-u; Sep 5 1792-u; Sep 12 1792-u; Sep 19 1792-u; Sep 26 1792-u; Oct 3 1792-u; Oct 10 1792-u; Oct 17 1792-u; Oct 24 1792-u; Oct 31 1792-u; Nov 7 1792-u; Nov 14 1792-u; Nov 21 1792-u; Nov 28 1792-u; Dec 5 1792-u; Dec 12 1792-u; Dec 19 1792-u; Dec 26 1792-u; Jan 2 1793-u; Jan 9 1793-u; Jan 16 1793-u; Feb 6 1793-u; Feb 14 1793-u; Feb 20 1793-u; Feb 27 1793-u; Feb 23 1793-u; Mar 6 1793-u; Mar 13 1793-u; Mar 20 1793-u; Mar 27 1793-u; Apr 3 1793-u; Apr 10 1793-u; Apr 17 1793-u; Apr 24 1793-u; May 1 1793-u; May 8 1793-u; May 15 1793-u; May 29 1793-u; Jun 5 1793-u; Jun 12 1793-u; Jun 19 1793-u; Jun 26 1793-u; Jul 3 1793-u; Jul 17 1793-u; Jul 24 1793-u; Jul 31 1793-u; Aug 14 1793-u; Aug 21 1793-u; Aug 28 1793-u; Sep 11 1793-u; Sep 18 1793-u; Sep 25 1793-u; Oct 2 1793-u; Oct 9 1793-u; Oct 16 1793-u; Oct 23 1793-u; Oct 30 1793-u; Nov 6 1793-u; Nov 13 1793-u; Nov 20 1793-u; Nov 27 1793-u; Dec 25 1793-u; Jan 1 1794-Dec 31 1798-m; Feb 18 1795 photography-u; Feb 25 1795-photography-u; Mar 11 1795-photography-u; May 27 1795-photography-u; Jun 17 1795-photography-u; Jun 22 1795-photography-u; Aug 5 1795-photography-u; Nov 25 1795-photography-u; June 6 1796-photography-u; Sep 20 1797-u; Nov 29 1797-u; Feb 21 1798-u; Aug 29 1798-u; Dec 5 1798-u 2 cop.; Feb 27 1799-u; Sep 4 1799-u; Jan 1 1800-u

GETTYSBURG COMPILER-Adams Co., Gettysburg - Weekly; July 1 1961-u

GLEN ROCK ITEM Glen Rock; Jul. 2 1874-Dec 13 1878-m; Dec 20 1878-Aug 29 1869-m; Sep 5 1879-Feb 17 1882-m; Feb 3 1882-Dec 7 1883-m; Dec 14 1883-Nov 5 1886-m; Nov 12 1886-Jan 3 1890-m; Jan 10 1890-Jul 21 1893-m; Aug 4 1893-Feb 14 1896-m; Feb 21 1896-Dec 2 1898-m; Feb 4 1898-u; Dec 9 1898-Nov 29 1901-m; Dec 6 1901-Sep 9 1904-m; Sep 16 1904-Sep 27 1907-m; Oct 4 1907-Sep 29 1932-m; Jun 15 1932-2 cop.-u; Oct 6 1932-Aug 31 1939-m; Dec 8 1937-2 cop.-u; Sep 7 1939-Jul 30 1942-m; Nov 28 1940-u; Aug 4 1942-Jan 21 1943-m; Jan 21 1943-u

DER HANOVER CITIZEN UND YORK CO. DEMOKRAT Hanover; Sept 1863(?)-u

HANOVER DAILY RECORD Hanover - Daily; Jul-Dec 1897-b; Jan-Jun 1898-b; Mar 21 1898-u; Jul-Dec 1898-b; Jan-Jun 1899-b; Jul-Dec 1899-b; Jan-Jun 1900-b; Jul-Dec 1900--b; Jan-Jun 1901-b; Jul-Dec 1901-b; Jan-Jun 1902-b; Jul-Dec 1902-b; Jan-Jun 1903-b; Jul-Dec 1903-b; Jan-Jun 1904-b; Jan-Jun 1905-b; Mar 5 1915-u

HANOVER GAZETTE Hanover; 1810-u; Sep 16 1813-u; Apr 13 1815-u; Oct 23 1817-u; Apr 5 1837-u; Aug 24 1843-u; May 11 1846-u; Apr 29 1846-u; Apr 11 1850-u; Apr 18 1850-u; Jun 30 1858-u; Aug 4 1859-u

HANOVER GUARDIAN Hanover - Weekly; Apr 21 1819-u; Apr 28 1819-u; May 5 1819-u; May 12 1819-u; May 19 1891-u; May 26 1819-u; Jun 16 1819-u; Jun 30 1819-u 2 cop.; Aug 8 1819-u; Aug 25 1819-u; Sep 1 1819-u; Sep 15 1819-u; Sep 22 1819-u; Sep 29 1819-u; Nov 3 1819-u; Nov 10 1819-u; Nov 17 1819-u; Nov 24 1819-u; Dec 15 1819-u; Dec 22 1819-u; Jan 19 1820-u; Jan 26 1820-u; Feb 2 1820-u; Feb 9 1820-u; Feb 16 19820-u; Feb 23 1820-u; Mar 1 1820-u; Mar 8 1820-u; Mar 29 1820-u; Apr 12 1820-u; Apr 19 1820-u; May 3 1820-u; May 10 1820-u; May 17 1820-u; May 24 1820-u; May 31 1820-u; Jul 19 1820-u; Jul 26 1820-u; Aug 2 1820-u; Aug 9 1820-u; Aug 16 1820-u; Aug 23 1820-u; Aug 30 1820-u; Sep 6 1820-u; Sep 13 1820-u; Sep 27 1820-u; Oct 4 1820-u; Feb 19 1823-u; Jun 4 1823-u; Jul 2 1823-u; Jul 9 1823-u; Jul 16 1823-u; Aug 6 1823-u; Aug 13 1823-u; Oct 22 1823-u; Mar 10 1824-u; Mar 16 1824-u; Mar 14 1826-u; Jan 23 1827-u

HANOVER HERALD Hanover - Weekly; Jun 19 1841-u; Jun 29 1872-Jun 20 1984-b; Jun 20 1874-Jun 17 1876-b; Jul 1 1876-u; May 29 1880-u; Sep 24 1881-u; Jun 14 1884-Jun 6 1885-b; Nov 29 1901-u; Oct 23 1930-u

DAS HANOVER INTELLIGENZBLATT Hanover; Apr 7 1824-Apr 13 1826-b; Apr 7 1824-Apr 13 1826-m

HANOVER SPECTATOR Hanover - Weekly; Feb 18 1846 -u; Feb 16 1848-u; Nov 10 1848-u; Dec 1 1848-u; Oct 8 1852-u; Jan 4 1856-u; Jan 11 1856-u; Jan 18 1856-u; Apr 18 1856-u; May 2 1856-u; May 9 1856-u; May 16 1856-u; Jun 6 1856-u; Jun 13 1856-u; June 20 1856-u; Jun 27 1856-u; Jul 4 1856-u; Jul 11 1856-u; July 25 1856-u; Aug 1 1856-u; Aug 8 1856-u; Aug 15 1856-u; Aug 22 1856-u; Aug 129 1856-u; Sep 5 1856-u; Sep 12 1856-u; Sep 19 1856-u; Sep 26 1856-u; Oct 3 18565-u; Oct 10 1856-u; Oct 17 1856-u; Oct 24 1856-u; Oct 31 1856-u; Nov 7 1856-u; Nov 14 1856-u; Nov 28 1856-u; Dec 5 1856-u; Dec 12 1856-u; Dec 19 1856-u; May 12 1857-u; May 15 1865-u; Mar 21 1872-u; Apr 14 1875-u; Apr 28 1875-u; May 5 1875-u; May 19 1875-u; May 26 1875-u; Jun 2 1875-u; Jun 9 1875-u; Jun 16 1875-u; Jun 23 1875-u; Jun 30 1875-u; Jul 7 1875-u; July 14 1875-u; Jul 21 1875-u; Jul 28 1875-u; Aug 4 1875-u; Aug 18 1875-u; Aug 25 1875-u; Sep 1 1875-u; Sep 8 1875-u; Sep 15 1875-u; Sep 22 1875-u; Sep 29 1875-u; Oct 13 1875-u; Oct 20 1875-u; Oct 27 1875-u; Nov 3 1875-u; Nov 10 1875-u; Nov 17 1875-u; Nov 24 1875-u; Dec 1 1875-u; Dec 8 1875-u; Dec 15 1875-u; Dec 22 1875-u; Dec 29 1875-u; Jan 5 1876-u; Jan 12 1876-u; Jan 19 1876-u; Jan 26 1876-u; Feb 2 1876-u; Feb 9 1876-u; Feb 16 1876-u; Feb 23 1876-u; Mar 1 1876-u; Mar 8 1876-u; Mar 15 1876-u; Mar 22 1876-u; Mar 29 1876-u; Apr 5 1876-u; Jul 11 1877-u; Nov 5 1885-u; Feb 17 1887-u; Feb 24 1887-u; Mar 3 1887-u; Mar 10 1887-u; Mar 17 1887-u; Mar 24 1887-u; Mar 31 1887-u; Apr 7 1887-u; Apr 14 1887-u; Apr 21 1887-u; Apr 28 1887-u; May 5 1887-u; May 12 1887-u; May 19 1887-u; May 26 1887-u; Jun 2 1887-u; Jun 9 1887-u; Jun 16 1887-u; Jun 23 1887-u; Jun 30 1887-u; Jul 7 1887-u; Jul 14 1887-u; Jul 21 1887-u; Jul 28 1887-u; Aug 4 1887-u; Aug 11 1887-u; Aug 18 1887-u; Aug 25 1887-u; Sep 1 1887-u; Sep 15 1887-u; Sep 22 1887-u; Sep 29 1887-u; Oct 6 1887-u; Oct 13 1887-u; Oct 20 1887-u; Oct 27 1887-u; Nov 3 1887-u; Nov 10 1887-U; Nov 17 1887-u; Nov 24 1887-u; Dec 1 1887-u; Dec 8 1887-u; Dec 15 1887-u; Dec 22 1887-u

HANOVER WEEKLY RECORD Hanover - Weekly; Jan 2 - Dec 1920-b; 1900-b; 1901-b

HANOVERION AND YORK AND ADAMS COUNTIES ADVERTISER Hanover; Apr 17 1828-u (incomplete); May 1 1828-u; May 8 1828-u; May 15 1828-u; May 22 1828-u; May 29 1828-u; Jun 10 1828-u; June 10 1828-u; June 17 1828-u; June 24 1828-u; Jul 1 1828-u; Jul 8 1828-u; Jul 15 1828-u; Aug 12 1828-u; Aug 26 1828-u; Sep 2 1828-u; Sep 16 1828-u; Sep 23 1828-u; Sep 30 1828-u; Oct 7 1828-u; Oct 11 1828-u; Oct 14 1828-u; Oct 28 1828-u; Nov 4 1828-u; Nov 11 1828-u; Nov 18 1828-u; Nov 25 1828-u; Dec 17 1828-u; Jan 6 1829-u; Jan 13 1829-u; Jan 20 1829-u; Feb 3 1829-u; Feb 10 1829-u; Feb 24 1829-u; Mar 3 1829-u; Mar 10 1829-u; Apr 14 1829-u; May 5 1829-u; May 12 1829-u; May 19 1829-u; May 26 1829-u; Feb 17 ? (date indiscernible)-u

HARPER'S WEEKLY New York New York - Weekly; Aug 31 1861-u; Oct 5 1861-u; Oct 12 1861-u; Oct 19 1861-u; Nov 9 1861-u; May 31 1862-u; Jun 7 1862-u; Jun 19 1862-u; Jun 21 1862-u; Jun 28 1862-u

HERITAGE NEWS Columbia, Lancaster; 1994

HOME TOWN NEWS - Monthly; Aug 1944-u; Oct 1944-u; Nov 1944-u; Dec 1944-u; Jan 1945-u; Feb 1945-u; Mar 1945-u; Apr 1945-u; May 1945-u; Jun 1945-u; Jul 1945-u; Aug 1945-u; Sep 1945-u; Oct 1945-u

DER INTELLIGENCER Adams Co. PA. Abbottstown; Nov 21 1837-u

INTERNATIONAL COMMENTS Sep 1877-u; Dec 1877-u; Mar 1879-u

JACK'S SHEPARD'S DAILY - Daily; Nov 4 1871-u; Nov 16 1871-u; Feb 27 1872-u; Mar 7 1872-u; Apr 13 1872-u; Jun 19 1872-u; Jun 26 1872-u; Aug 2 1872-u; Aug 16 1872-u; Christmas 1872-u; 1872-u; Jan 24 1873-u; Feb 28 1873-u; Jul 16 1873-u; Aug 1 1873-u; Jul 18 1873-u

THE JACK SHEPHERD'S GOSPEL TRUMPET;

JACK SHEPHERD'S OPINION; or

JACK SHEPHERD'S TRUMPET; see Jack Shepherd's Daily

JOHNSTOWN TRIBUNE-Cambria Co. Pa. Johnstown; June 14 1889-u

LANCASTER INTELLIGENCER-Lancaster Co. PA. Lancaster; May 11 1878-u

LEWISBERRY FARMER & YORK & CUMBERLAND COUNTY ADVERTISER Lewisberry; June 26 1835-u

LITERARY RECORD AND JOURNAL OF THE LINEAN ASSOCIATION OF PENNA. COLLEGE Adams Co. PA, Gettysburg; Nov 1844-u; Dec 1844-u; Jan-Dec 1845-u; Jan-Dec 1846-u; Jan-Dec 1847-u; Jan-Oct 1848-u

LUTHERAN MISSIONARY JOURNAL MONTHLY; Jan 1884-u; Feb 1884-u

MARYLAND RECORDER Taney Town (Maryland); July 30 1832-u

DIE MINERVA Hanover; Dec 1809-u

MONTHLY FRIEND Hanover - Monthly; Aug 1843-u; Sep 1843-u; Oct 1843-u; Nov 1843-u; Dec 1843-u; Jan 1844-u; Feb 1844-u; Mar 1844-u; Apr 1844-u; May 1844-u; Jun 1844-u; Jul 1844-u; Aug 1844-u; Sep 1844-u; Oct 1844-u; Nov 1844-u; Dec 1844-u; Jan 1845-u; Feb 1845-u; Mar 1845-u; Apr 1845-u; May 1845-u; Jun 1845-u; Jul 1845-u; Aug 1845-u; Sep 1845-u; Oct 1845-u; Nov 1845-u; Dec 1845-u; Jan 1846-u; Mar 1846-u; Apr 1846-u; Jun 1846-u; Jul 1846-u 2 cop.; Mar 1847-u; Jul 1848-u; Aug 1848-u; Sep 1848-u; Oct 1848-u; Feb 1849-u;

Mar 1849-u; Apr 1849-u; Jul 1849-u; Aug 1849-u; Aug 1849-u supplement; Sep 1849-u; Sep 1849-u supplement; Oct 1849-u; Jan 1850-u; Mar 1850-u; May 1859-u; Jul 1850-u; Aug 1850-u; Sep 1850-u; Dec 1850-u; 1851-Carriers new yr's address-2 cop.-u; May 1851-u; Jul 24 1851-u; Dec 1851-u; 1852-carrier's New yr's address-u; Mar 1852-u; Jun 16 1852-u; Aug 26 1852-u; Dec 1852-u; 1853 carrier's New yr's address-u; Aug 3 1853-u; Apr 26 1854-u; Aug 1854-u; Aug 3 1854-u; Sep 2 1854-u; Dec 16 1854-u; 1855-Carrier's New Yr's address-u; 1855-no month listed-u; Mar 1868-u; Aug 1874-u; Sep 1874-u; Jul 1875-u; Nov 1880-u; Dec 1880-u (2 cop.); 1880-No month listed-u; 1891- no month listed -u; 1891-no month listed-u

MONTHLY REVIEW Oct 1869-b; Sep 1870-b

MORNING JOURNAL Oct 21 1970 (2 cop.)-u

NATIONAL GAZETTE WEEKLY York Weekly; Aug 1 1948 (3 cop.)-u

NEW FREEDOM SHOPPER Jul 9 1947 -u

NEW OXFORD ITEM Adams Co. PA. New Oxford; The New-boy's Annual Address-u (no date)

NEW YORK ILLUSTRATED NEWS-New York New York; July 6 1861-u

NEWS LEADER Red Lion; Nov 23 1950-u

OUR MISSION York - Monthly; Nov 1873-u; Feb 1874-u

OWL Wrightsville Monthly; Sept 1868-u

PENNSYLVANIA CHRONICLE York; Nov 7 1787 (transcript)-u; Nov 7 1787 (photocopy) -u; Apr 2 1788 (photocopy) -u

PENNSYLVANIA GAZETTE Jan 4 1775-Nov 1776-m; Feb 5 1777-May 30 1781-m; Dec 20 1777-Jun 20 1778-b(scrap book of cop. of originals); Dec 20 1777 (not original)-u; May 2 1778 (not original)-u; May 2 1778-postscript(8 cop.)(not originals)-u; May 9 1778-postscript (not original)-u; Feb 9 1783-u

PENNSYLVANIA HERALD AND YORK

PENNSYLVANIA REPUBLICAN York - Weekly; Jan 6 1826-u; Mar 11 1827-u; Mar 16 1830-Mar 1 1831-b; Mar 16 1830-u; Sep 7 1830 York Republican & Anti Masonic Expositor; Oct 4 1830-u; Nov 30 1830-u; Dec 7 1830-u; Dec 14 1830-u; Jan 4 1831-Dec 27 1831-b; Jan 25 1831-u; Mar 15 1831-Mar 5 1832-b; Apr 19 1831-u; Mar 13 1832-Mar 13 1833-b; Jan 1 1834-Dec 23 1835-b; Nov 5 1834-Mar 16 1836-b; Nov 11 1835-u; Jan 13 1836-u; Mar 16 1836-u; Mar 23 1836-Mar 15 1837-b; Apr 27 1836-u;

Jun 29 1836-u; Aug 3 18367-u; Aug 10 1836-u; Dec 7 1836-u; Mar 22 1837-Mar 14 1838-b; May 10 1837 (2 cop.)-u; May 24 1837-u; Jun 7 1837-u; Jul 19 1837-u; Dec 28 1837-u; Mar 21 1838-Mar 13 1839-b; May 26 1838(2 cop.)-u; Jun 13 1838-u; Mar 20 1839-Mar 11 1840-b; Jul 31 1839-u; Dec 25 1839-u; Mar 18 1840-Mar 24 1841-b; Dec 9 1840-u; Feb 3 1841-u; Mar 31 1841-Mar 23 1841-b; May 25 1841-u; Mar 30 1842-Mar 22 1843-b; Mar 27 1844-Mar 19 1845-b; Mar 26 1845-Mar 18 1846-b; Mar 25 1846-Mar 24 1847-b; Mar 4 1846-u; Jul 9 1846-u; Dec 9 1846-u 2 cop.; Mar 31 1847-Mar 22 1848-b; Jun 23 1847-u; Aug 16 1848-u; Aug 23 1848-u; Oct 11 1848-u; Nov 8 1848-u; Jun 6 1849-u; Oct 10 1849-u; Mar 27-1850-u; May 20 1850-u; Jun 26 1850-u; Jan 1 1852-u carrier's address; Jan 21 1852-u; Feb 16 1853-u; Aug 31 1853-u; Oct 19 1853-u; Dec 12 1853-u; Dec 21 1853-u; Jan 4 1854-u; Aug 9 1854-u 2 cop.; Aug 16 1854-u; Aug 23 1854-u; Sep 20 1854-u; Sep 27 1854-u; Oct 4 1854-u; Oct 11 1854-u; Nov 29 1854-u; Nov 14 1855-u; Nov 21 1855-u; Oct 30 1856-u extra issue; Jan 1 1859-u carrier's address; Jan 5 1859-u; Dec 5 1860-u; Dec 19 1860-u; Jan 9 1861-u; Jan 16 1861-u; Feb 6 1861-u; Feb 27 1861-u; Mar 6 1861-u; Mar 13 1861-u; Mar 20 1861-u; May 15 1861-u; May 22 1861-u; May 29 1861-u; Jun 5 1861-u; Jun 12 1861-u; Jul 6 1861-u; Jul 13 1861-u; Aug 3 1861-u; Aug 24 1861-u; Sep 5 1861-u; Sep 19 1861-u; Oct 10 1861-u; Oct 17 1861-u; Oct 31 1861-u; Jan 1 1862-u; Feb 26 1862-u; Mar 5 1862-u; Mar 26 1862-u; Apr 9 1862-u; Apr 16 1862-u; Jun 4 1862-u; Jun 11 1862-u; Jul 22 1862-u; Jul 30 1862-u; Aug 27 1862-u; Sep 3 1862-u; Sep 9 1862-u; Oct 29 1862-u; Nov 5 1862-u; Nov 12 1862-u; Nov 19 1862-u; Dec 3 1862-u; Dec 10 1862-u; Dec 31 1862-u; Jan 7 1863-u; Jan 21 1863-u; Feb 4 1863-u; Feb 11 1863-u; Feb 18 1863-u; Feb 25 1863-u; Mar 4 1863-u; Mar 13 1863-u; Mar 25 1863-u; Apr 1 1863-u; Apr 22 1863-u; Apr 29 1863-u; May 6 1863-u; May 3 1863-u; Jul 1 1863-u; Jul 1 1863-m; Jul 20 1863-u; Dec 6 1863-u; President's Message; Mar 2 1964-u; Mar 16 1864-u; Mar 30 1864-u; Apr 6 1864-u; Apr 20 1864-u; Oct 19 1864-u; Apr 19 1865-u; Apr 26 1865-u; Jun 5 1867-u; Feb 26 1878-u; Jan 5 1870-u; Jan 19 1870-u; Aug 3 1870-u; Aug 24 1870-u; Apr 1 1871-u; Feb 8 1873-u; Aug 6 1873-u; Jan 24 1874-u; Aug 8 1874-u; Mar 3 1876-u; Mar 12 1880-u 2 cop.; Apr 2 1880-u; Apr 8 1881-u; Jul 8 1881-u; Jan 1 1882-u Carrier's address to patrons; 1 undated issue

PENNSYLVANIFCHER GRAAFSBOFE 1775-u

PEOPLE'S ADVOCATE Nov 30 1847-u; Nov 17 1847-u; Sep 11 1849-Jul 22 1851-b; Aug 5 1851-Jul 19 1853-b; Jul 26 1853-Jul 3 1855-b;

Aug 2 1853-u; Sep 13 1853-u; Nov 8 1853-u; Dec 20 1853-u; Dec 27 1853-u; May 9 1854-u; Jul 4 1854-u; Jul 18 1854-u; Jul 25 1854-u; Aug 8 1854-u; Aug 15 1854-u; Aug 22 1854-u; Aug 29 1854-u; Sep 12 1854-u; Sep 19 1854-u; Sep 26 1854-u; Oct 3 1854-u; Oct 17 1854-u; Nov 28 1854-u; Mar 27 1855-u; May 8 1855-u; Aug 14 1855-u; Sep 18 1855-u; Oct 2 1855-u; Nov 20 1855-u; Nov 27 1855-u; Dec 4 1855-u; Jan 22 1855-u; Jan 26 1855-y; Aug 25 1857-u; May 18 1858-u

RECORD HERALD Hanover - Daily; Sep 9 1905-u; Jan-Apr 1906-b; May-Aug 1906-b; Sep-Dec 1906-b; Jan-Apr 1907-b; May-Aug 1907-b; Sep-Dec 1907-b; Jan-Apr 1908-b; May-Aug 1908-b; Sep-Dec 1908-b; Jan-Apr 1909-b; May-Aug 1909-b; Jan-Apr 1910-b; May-Aug 1910-b; Sep-Dec 1910-b; Jan-Apr 1911-b; May-Aug 1911-b; Sep-Dec 1912-b; Jan-Apr 1913-b; May-Aug 1913-b; Nov-Dec 1913-b; Jan-Apr 1914-b; May-Aug 1914-b; Nov-Dec 1914-b; Jan-Apr 1915-b; Mar 4 1915-u; May-Aug 1915-b; Sep-Dec 1915-b; Jan-Apr 1916-b; May-Aug 1916-b; Sep-Dec 1916-b; Jan 16-1917-u; Apr 18 1917-u; Sep-Dec 1917-b; Sep 13 1918-u; Jun 28 1919-u; Mar 2 1919-u; Jan-Apr 1920-b; May-Aug 1920-b; Sep-Dec 1920-b; Jan-Apr 1921-b; May-Aug 1921-b; Sep-Dec 1921-b; Jan-Apr 1922-b; Sep-Dec 1922-b; Jan-Apr 1923-b; May-Aug 1923-b; Sep-Dec 1923-b

RED LION ECHOES Red Lion; Jun 1944-u; Jul 1944-u 2 cop.; Sep 1944-u 2 cop.; Nov 1944-u; Dec 1944-u; Jan 1945-u; Feb 1945-u; Mar 1945-u; Apr 1945-u; May 1945-u; Jun 1945-u; Jul 1945-u; Aug 1945-u; Sep 1945-u; Oct 1945-u; Nov 1945-u; Dec 1945-u; Jan 1946-u; Feb 1946-u; Mar 1946-u; May 1946-u

DER REPUBLIKENISCHE Jan 10 1829-u; Jan 24 1829-u; Aug 28 1829-u; Dec 30 1836(photocopy) -u; Jul 19 1839 (2 cop.) -u; Aug 23 1839 (?) (2 cop.)-u

SELF HELP York - Monthly; Jan 1901-u; Feb 1901-u; Mar 1901-u; Apr 1901-u; Jun 1901-u; Aug 1901-u; Sep 1901-u; Oct 1901-u; Nov 1901-u; Dec 1901-u; Jan 1902-u; Feb 1902-u; Mar 1902-u; Apr 1902-u; May 1902-u; Jun 1902-u; Jul 1902-u; Aug 1902-u

SEMI-WEEKLY GAZETTE; Jan 3 1894-Dec 29 1894-b; Jan 2 1895-Dec 29 1894-b; Jan 1 1896-Dec 30 1896-b; Jan 2 1897-Dec 29 1897-b; Jan 1 1898-Dec 31 1898-b; Jan 4 1899-Dec 30 1899-b; Jun 3 1900-Dec 29 1900-b; Jan 2 1901-Jun 29 1901-b; Jul 3 1901-Dec 28 1901-b; Jan 1 1902-Dec 31 1902 (2 cop.)-b; Jan 2 1904-Dec 31 1904-2 cop.-b

SHIPPENSBURG MESSENGER Cumberland Co. Pa. Shippensburg; June 28 1797-m

SHOPPER Red Lion and Dallastown; Jun 5 1947-u; Jul 17 1947-u; Jul 31 1947-u; Sep 29 1966-u; Sep 25 1969-u; Oct 9 1969-u; Oct 23 1969-u; Nov 20 1969-u; Dec 18 1969-u; Jan 15 1970-u; Jan 29 1970-u; Feb 12 1970-u; Feb 26 1970-u; Mar 12 1970-u; Mar 26 1970-u; Apr 9 1970-u; Apr 23 1970-u; Jun 11 1970-u; Jul 16 1970-u; Jul 15 1971-u; Jul 29 1971-u; Aug 26 1971-u; Sep 9 1971-u; Sep 23 1971-u; Oct 7 1971-u; Oct 21 1971-u

SHOPPER West Manchester and West York; Mar 18 1971-u; Apr 15 1971-u; Jun 17 1971-u; Jul 22 1971-u; Sep 16 1971-u; Oct 14 1971-u

SOUTHERN YORK COUNTY FREE PRESS Dec 12 1974-u; Jul 17 1975-u 2 cop.; Aug 21 1975-u; Sep 4 1975-u; Sep 11 1975-u; Aug 21 1975-u; Dec 12 1975-u

SOUTHERN YORK COUNTY REPORTER Feb 13 1964-u; Mar 12 1964-u; May 14 1964-u; Jul 16 1964-u; Aug 13 1964-u; Oct 8 1964-u; Dec 10 1964-u; Jan 14 1965-u; Feb 11 1965; Mar 11 1965

SPHERE York - Weekly/Monthly; Apr 1911-u; May 1911-u; Jun 1911-u; Jul 1911-u; Aug 1911-u; Sep 1922-u; Oct 1911-u; Nov 1911-u; Dec 1911-u; Jan 1912-u 2 cop.; Feb 1912-u; Mar 1912-u; May 1912-u; Jun 1912-u; Jul; Aug 1912-u; Sep 1912-u; Oct 1912-u; Nov 1912-u; Dec 1912-u; Jan; Feb 1913-u; Mar 1913-u; Apr 1913-u; May 1913-u; Jun; Jul 1913-u; Sep 1913-u; Oct 1913-u; Dec 1913-u; Apr 1914-u; May 1914-u; Oct 1914-u; Dec 1914-u; Jan 1915-u; Jan 1916-u; Aug 5 1916-u; Aug 19 1916 undated special Edition 2 cop.

SPRING GROVE RIPPLET Spring Grove; Apr 4 1913-u; Jan 19 1917-u; Apr 27 1917-u

STANDARD March 23 1912-u

STAR Delta and Cardiff, Maryland Weekly; Apr 1953-Dec 1956-u; Oct 23 1953-u; Dec 25 1953-u; Jan 2 1954-u 2 cop.; Jan 8 1954-u 2 cop.; Jan 15 1954-u 3 cop.; Jan 22 1954-u 2 cop.; Jan 29 1954-u; Feb 15 1954-u 2 cop.; Feb 12 1954-u 3 cop.; Feb 18 1954-u 3 cop.; Feb 26 1954-u ; Mar 5 1954-u 3 cop.; Mar 12 1954-u 2 cop.; Mar 19 1954-u; Mar 26 1954-u 2 cop.; Apr 2 1954-u 2 cop.; Apr 9 1954-u; Apr 16 1954-u; Apr 23 1954-u 2 cop.; Apr 30 1954-u; May 14 1954-u; May 21 1954-u; May 28 1954-u; Jun 4 1954-u 2 cop.; Jun 18 1954-u; Jun 25 1954-u; Jul 2 1955-u 2 cop.; July 16 1954-u; Jul 9 1954-u 2 cop.; Jul 30 1954-u; Aug 2 1954-u; Aug 13 1954-u 2 cop.; Aug 27 1954-u; Sep 3 1954-u; Sep 10 1954-u; Sep 17 1954-u; Sep 24 1954-u;

Oct 1 1954-u; Oct 8 1954-u; Oct 15 1954-u; Oct 22 1954-u; Oct 29 1954-u; Nov 5 1954-u; Nov 12 1954-u; Nov 19 1954-u; Nov 26 1954-u; Dec 3 1954-u; Dec 10 1954-u; 1955-u; 1957-u; Jan 2 1958-; Dec 25 1958-u; Jan 1 1959-; Dec 31 1959-u; 1960-u, 1961-u, 1962-u, 1963-u, 1964-u, 1965-u,1966-u, 1967-u; 1968-u, 1969-u, 1970-u, 1971-u, 1972-u, Jan 20 missing, Jan 20 1972-u, 1973-u (Dec 6 missing); Jan 3 1974-u; Jan 10 1974-u; Jan 31 1974-u; Feb 7 1974-u; Feb 21 1974-u; Feb 28 1974-u; Mar 14 1974-u; Mar 28 1974-u; Apr 4 1974-u; Apr 11 1974-u; Apr 25 1974-u; May 2 1974-u; May 9 1974-u; May 16 1974-u; May 16 1974-u; May 23 1974-u; may 30 1974-u; Jun 6 1974-u; Jun 13 1974-u; Jun 20 1974-u; Jun 27 19074-u; Jul 4 1974-u; Jul 11 1974-u; Jul 18 1974-u; Jul 25 1974-u; Aug 1 1974-u; Aug 8 1974-u; Aug 15 1974-u; Aug 22 1974-u; Aug 29 1974-u; Sep 5 1974-u; Sep 12 1974-u; Sep 19 1974-u; Sep 26 1974-u; Oct 3 1974-u; Oct 10 1974-u; Oct 17 1974-u; Oct 24 1974-u; Oct 31 1974-u; Nov 7 1974-u; Nov 14 1974-u; Nov 21 1974-u; Nov 28 1974-u; Dec 5 1974-u; Dec 12 1974-u; Dec 19-1974-u; Dec 26 1974-u; Jan 2 1975-u; Jan 9 1975-u; Jan 16 1975-u; Jan 30 1975-u; Feb 6 1975-u; Feb 13 1975-u; Feb 20 1975-u; Feb 27 1975-u; Mar 6 1975-u; Mar 13 1975-u; Mar 20 1975-u; Mar 27 1975-u; Apr 3 1975-u; Apr 10 1975-u; Apr 17 1975-u; Apr 24 1975-u; May 1 1975-u; May 8 1975-u; May 15 1975-u; May 22 1975-u; May 29 1975-u; Jun 5 1975-u; Jun 12 1975-u; Jun 19 1975-u; Jun 26 1975-u; Jul 3 1975-u; Jul 10 1975-u; Jul 17 1975-u; Jul 24 1975-u; Jul 31 1975-u; Aug 7 1975-u; Aug 14 1975-u; Aug 21 1975-u; Aug 28 1975-u; Sep 4 1975-u; Sep 11 1975-u; Sep 18 1975-u Sep 25 1975-u; Oct 9 1975-u; Oct 12 1975-u; Oct 16 1975-u; Oct 23 1975-u; Nov 6 1975-u; Nov 13 1975-u; Nov 20 1975-u; Nov 27 1975-u; Dec 4 1975-u; Dec 11 1975-u; Dec 18 1975-u; Dec 25 1975-u; Jan 1 1976-u; Jan 8 1976-u; Feb 5 1976-u; Feb 12 1976-u; Feb 19 1976-u; Feb 26 1976-u; Mar 4 1976-u; Mar 11 1976-u; Mar 18 1976-u; Mar 25 1976-u; Apr 1 1976-u; Apr 8 1976-u; Apr 15 1976-u; Apr 22 1976-u; Apr 29 1976-u; May 6 1976-u; May 13 1976-u; May 20 1976-u; May 27 1976-u; Jun 13 1976-u; Jun 10 1976-u; Jun 24 1976-u; Jul 1 1976-u; Jul 8 1976-u; Jul 15 1976-u; Jul 22 1976-u; Jul 29 1976-u; Aug 5 1976-u; Aug 12 1976-u; Aug 19 1976-u; Aug 26 1976-u; Sep 2 1976-u; Sep 9 1976-u; Sep 16 1976-u; Sep 30 1976-u; Oct 7 1976-u; Oct 14 1976-u; Oct 21 1976-u; Oct 28 1976-u; Nov 4 1976-u; Nov 11 1976-u; Nov 18 1976-u; Nov 25 1976-u; Dec 4 1976-u; Dec 9 1976-u; Dec 16 1976-u; Dec 23 1976-u; Dec 30 1976-u; Jan 6 1977-u; Jan 13 1977-u; Jan 20 1977-u; Jan 27 1977-u; Feb 3 1977-u; Feb 10 1977-u; Feb 17 1977-u; Feb 24 1977-u; Mar 3 1977-u 2 cop.; Mar 17 1977-u; Mar 24

1977-u; Mar 26 1977-u; Mar 31 1977-u; Apr 7 1977-u; Apr 14 1977-u; Apr 21 1977-u; Apr 28 1977-u; May 5 1977-u; May 12 1977-u 2 cop.; May 18 1977-u; Jun 2 1977-u; Jun 9 1977-u; Jun 16 1977-u; Jun 23 1977-u; Jun 30 1977-u; Jul 7 1977-u; Jul 14 1977-u; Jul 21 1977-u; Jul 28 1977-u; Aug 11 1977-u; Aug 4 1977-u; Aug 18 1977-u; Aug 25 1977-u; Sep 1 1977-u; Sep 8 1977-u; Sep 15 1977-u; Sep 29 1977-u; Oct 6 1977-u; Oct 13 1977-u; Oct 20 1977-u; Oct 27 1977-u; Nov 4 1977-u; Nov 10-1977-u; Nov 17 1977-u; Nov 24 1977-u; Dec 1 1977-u; Dec 15 1977-u; Dec 22 1977-u; Dec 8 1977-u; Jan 5 1978-u; Jan 12 1978-u; Jan 19 1978-u; Jan 26 1978-u; Feb 2 1978-u; Feb 9 1978-u; Feb 16 1978-u; Feb 23 1978-u; Mar 2 1978-u; Mar 9 1978-u; Mar 16 1978-u; Mar 23 1978-u; Mar 30 1978-u; Apr 6 1978-u; Apr 13 1978-u; Apr 20 1978-u

STAR AND SENTINEL- Adams Co. PA. Gettysburg; July 1 1961-u

STARS & STRIPES NATIONAL TRIBUNE - Weekly; 1919 Special issue-u; Feb 7 1919-u; Mar 7 1919-u; Mar 14 1919-u; Mar 21 1919-u; Jul 21 1960-u; Mar 16 1961-u; Sep 18 1961-u; Oct 5 1961-u; Oct 12 1961-u; Oct 19 1961-u; Oct 26 1961-u; Nov 2 1961-u; Nov 9 1961-u; Nov 16 1961-u; Nov 23 1961-u; Nov 30 1961-u; Dec 7 1961-u; Dec 14 1961-u; Dec 21 1961-u; Jan 4 1962-u; Jan 11 1962-u; Jan 18 1962-u; Apr 26 1962-u; May 3 1962-u; May 10 1962-u; May 17 1962-u; Jul 19 1962-u; Jul 2 1962-u; Aug 9 1962-u; Aug 16 1962-u; Aug 23 1962-u; Jan 24 1963-u; Jan 31 1963-u; Feb 7 1963-u; Feb 14 1963-u; Feb 21 1963-u; Feb 28 1963-u; Mar 7 1963-u; Mar 141963-u; Mar 28 1963-u; Apr 4 1963-u; Apr 11 1963-u; Apr 118 1963-u; Apr 25 1963-u; May 2 1963-u; May 9 1963-u; May 16 1963-u 1 undated special supplement

STATE JOURNAL Philadelphia, Pa.; Jul 23 1859-u 2 cop.; Jul 30 1859-u; Aug 6 1959-u; Aug 13 1859-u; Aug 20 1859-u; Aug 27 1859-u; Sep 3 1859-u; Sep 10 1859-u; Sep 17 1859-u; Oct 1 1859-u; Oct 8 1859-u; Oct 15 1859-u; Oct 22 1859-u; Nov 12 1859-u; Nov 19 1859-u

STEWARTSTOWN NEWS/ STEWARTSTOWN WEEKLY; Jan 6 1905-Dec 29 1905-b; Jan 5 1906-Dec 28 1906-b; Jan 4 1907-Dec 27 1907-b; Jan 3 1908-Dec 25 1908-b; Jan 1 1909-Dec 31 1909-b; Jan 7 1910-Dec 30 1910-b; Jan 6 1911-Dec 29 1911-b; Jan 5 1912-Dec 31 1912-b; Oct 15 1914-u; Jan 7 1915-Dec 27 1917-b; Jul 22 1892-u; Dec 28 1894-u; Jan 11 1895-u; Apr 15 1915-u; Jul 8 1915-u; Nov 11 1915-u; Dec 23 1915-u; Dec 30 1915-u; May 17 1917-u; Jan 3 1918-Dec 30 1920-b; Feb 13 1919-u; Jan 6 1921-Dec 27 1923-b; Jan 3 1924-Dec 30 1926-b; Jan 6 1927-Feb 9 1928-b; Feb 16-

1928-u; Feb 23 1928-u; Mar 1 1928-u; Mar 8 1928-u; Mar 15 1928-u; Mar 22 1928-u; Mar 29 1928-u

STEWARTSTOWN STAR Stewartstown; July 4 1890-u

STINGER 1 undated issue -u

SUN Red Lion; Dec 1936-Feb 1938-u; Feb 1938-Dec 1938-u; 1939, 1940, 1941 Nov 1942

SUNDAY NEWS - Weekly; Oct 5 1969-u supplement; Jul 1974-u; Aug 1974-u; Oct 1974-u missing Oct 13; Sep 1974-u; Nov 1974-u 2 cop. of Nov 14; Dec 1974-u; Jan 1975-u missing Jan 5; Feb 1975-u; Mar 1975-u; Apr 1975-u; May 1975-u; Jun 1975-u; Jul 1975-u missing Jul 6; Aug 1975-u; Sep 1975-u; Oct 1975-u; Nov 1975-u 2 cop. of Nov 30; Dec 1975-u 2 cop. of Dec 26; Jan 1976-u; Feb 1976-u 2 cop. of Feb 1; Mar 1976-u; Apr 1976-u (missing Apr 25); May 1976-u; Jun 1976-u; Jul 1976-u (missing Jul 4); Aug 1976-u; Sep 1976-u; Oct 1976-u; Nov 1976-u missing Nov 14; Dec 1976-u missing Dec 26; Jan 1977-u; Feb 1977-u; Mar 1977-u; Apr 1977-u; May 1977-u; Jun 1977-u; July 1977-u; Aug 1977-u; Sep 1977-u

SUNDAY PATRIOT NEWS Dauphin Co. Pa. Harrisburg - Weekly; Sep 18 1949-u; Aug 25 1974-u; Apr 27 1975-u

SUSQUEHANNA SHOPPER; June 20 1947-u

TEACHER'S JOURNAL - Monthly; Jan 1874-u; Feb 1874-u; Mar 1874-u; Feb 1976-u; Jan-Dec 1977-u; Jan-Dec 1878-u; Jan-Dec 1879-u; Jan-Dec 1880-u; Apr 1884-u; Jun 1901-u

TELEPHONE - Monthly; Dec 1882-u; Jan 25 1883-u; Feb 1883-u (2 cop.); Mar 1883-u 2 cop.; Jun 1883-u; Jul 1883-u; Aug 1883-u

TIME TABLE RECORD - Monthly; Apr 1890-u; Oct 1907-u; Oct 1918-u

TOWN AND COUNTRY REPORTER Red Lion; Sep 27 1955-u; Oct 20 1955-u; Nov 3 1955-u; Nov 17 1955-u; Dec 1 1955-u; Dec 15 1955-u; Dec 22 1955-u; Dec 29 1955-u; Jan 5 1956-u 2 cop.; Jan 19 1956-u; Jan 26 1956-u; Jan 31 1956-u; Feb 9 1956-u; Feb 16 1956-u 2 cop.; Mar 1 1956-u; Mar 8 1956-u; Mar 15 1956-u; Mar 22 1956-u; Mar 29 1956-u; Apr 12 1956-u; Apr 19 1956-u; Apr 25 1956-u; May 2 1956-u; May 16 1956-u; May 30 1956-u; Jun 6 1956-u

TRUE DEMOCRAT - Weekly; Jun 7 1864-Apr 25 1865-b*; Aug 30 1864; Jan 1 1865-u-Carrier's address to the patrons; Mar 28 18665-u; May 23 1865-u; Jan 2 1866-Dec 29 1868-b; Mar 6 1866-u; May 8 1866-u; Jan 3 1871-Dec

31 1872-b*; Aug 13 1872-u; Jun 10 1873-May 11 1875-b; Aug 30 1881-u; Sep 27 1881-u; Oct 25 1881-u; Nov 1 1881-u; Jan 3 1864-u; Nov 22 1870-u; Dec 20 1870-u

ULSTER COUNTY GAZETTE Ulster Co. NY-Kingston; Jan 4 1800 (4 cop.)-u

UNIONS FREUND; Nov 1817-u

VOLKSBERICHTER EIN YORKER WOCHEMBLATT Jul 25 1799-Jul 23 1801-m; Dec 1799-u; Jan 1801-u; Feb 1802-u

WEAVER'S MUSICAL MONTHLY York - Monthly; Sep 1879-u

WEEKLY BULLETIN Dillsburg - Weekly; Jul 2 1908-u; Sep 28 1934-u; Nov 9 1934-u; May 31 1935-u; Nov 15 1935-u; Sep 18 1936-u; Apr 21 1939-u; Aug 25 1939-u; Aug 8 1940-u; Nov 14 1940-u; Jan 16 1941-u; Jan 20 1941'-u; Jan 23 1941-u; Jan 30 1941-u; Feb 6 1941-u; Feb 13 1941-u; Feb 20 1941-u; Feb 27 1941-u; Mar 6 1941-u; Mar 13 1941-u; Mar 20 1941-u; Mar 27 1941-u; Apr 3 1941-u; Apr 10 1941-u; Apr 17 1941-u 2 cop.; Apr 24 1941-u; May 1 1941-u; May 8 1941-u; May 15 1941-u; May 22 1941-u; May 29 1941-u; Jun 5 1941-u; Jun 12 1941-u; Jun 19 1941-u; Jun 26 1941-u; Jul 7 1941-u; Jul 10 1941-u; Jul 24 1941-u; Aug 21 1941-u; Aug 29 1941-u; Sep 4 1941-u; Sep 11 1941-u; Sep 18 1941-u 2 cop.; Sep 25 1941-u; Oct 9 1941-u; Oct 16 1941-u; Oct 23 1941-u; Oct 30 1941-u; Nov 6 1941-u; Nov 13 1941-u; Nov 20 1941-u; Nov 27 1941-u; Dec 4 1941-u; Dec 11 1941-u; Dec 18 1941-u; Dec 23 1941-u; Jan 8 1942-u; Jan 15 1942-u; Jan 22 1942-u; Jan 29 1942-u; Feb 5 1942-u; Feb 12 1942-u; Feb 19 1942-u; Feb 26 1942-u; Mar 5 1942-u; Mar 12 1942-u; Mar 19 1942-u; Mar 26 1942-u; Apr 2 1942-u; Apr 9 1942-u; Apr 16 1942-u; Apr 23 1942-u; Apr 30 1942-u; May 7 1942-u; May 14 1942-u; May 21 1942-u; May 28 1942-u; Oct 8 1942-u; Oct 22 1942-u; Oct 29 1942-u; Nov 5 1942-u; Nov 12 1942-u; Nov 19 1942-u; Nov 26 1942-u; Dec 3 1942-u; Jan 7 1943-u; Jan 14 1943-u; Jan 21 1943-u; Jan 28 1943-u; Feb 4 1943-u; Feb 11 1943-u; Feb 18 1943-u; Feb 25 1943-u; Mar 4 1943-u; Mar 11 1943-u; Mar 18 1943-u; Mar 25 1943-u; Apr 1 1943-u; Apr 8 1943-u; Apr 15 1943-u; Apr 22 1943-u; Apr 29 1943-u 2 cop.; May 6 1943-u; May 13 1943-u; May 20 1943-u; May 27 1943-u; Jun 10 1943-u; Jun 17 1943-u; Jun 24 1943-u; Jul 1 1943-u; Jul 22 1943-u; Jul 29 1943-u 2 cop.; Aug 5 1943-u; Aug 12 1943-u; Aug 19 1943-u 2 cop.; Aug 26 1943-u; Sep 2 1943-u; Sep 9 1943-u; Sep 23 1943-u 2 cop.; Sep 30 1943-u 2 cop.; Oct 7 1943-u; Oct 28 1943-u 2 cop.; Dec 2 1943-u; Dec 16 1943-u; Dec 23 1943-u; Dec 30 1943-u; Jan 8 1948-u; Jan 15 1948-u; Jan 22 1948-u; Jan 29 1948-u; Feb 12 1948-u; Feb 19 1948-u; Feb 26 1948-u; Mar 4 1948-u; Mar 11 1948-u; Mar 18 1948-u; Mar 25 1948-u; Apr 1 1948-u; Apr 8 1948-u; Apr 15 1948-u; Apr 22 1948-u; Apr 29 1948-u; May 6 1948-u; May 13 1948-u; May 20 1948-u; May 27 1948-u; Jun 13 1948-u; Jun 10 1948-u; Jun 17 1948-u; Jun 24 1948-u; Jul 1 1948-u; Jul 15 1948-u; Jul 22 1948-u; Jul 29 1948-u; Aug 5 1948-u; Aug 12 1948-u; Aug 19 1948-u; Aug 26 1948-u; Sep 2 1948-u; Sep 16 1948-u; Sep 23 1948-u 2 cop.; Sep 30 1948-u; Oct 7 1948-u; Oct 14 1948-u; Oct 21 1948-u; Oct 28 1948-u; Nov 4 1948-u; Nov 11 1948-u; Nov 18 1948-u; Nov 25 1948-u; Dec 2 1948-u; Dec 9 1948-u; Dec 16 1948-u; Dec 23 1948-u; Jan 13 1949-u; Jan 20 1949-u; Jan 27 1949-u; Feb 3 1949-u; Feb 10 1949-u; Feb 17 1949-u; Feb 24 1949-u; Mar 3 1949-u; Mar 10 1949-u; Mar 17 1949-u; Mar 24 1949-u; Mar 31 1949-u; Apr 7 1949-u; Apr 14 1949-u; Apr 21 1949-u; Apr 28 1949-u; May 5 1949-u; May 12 1949-u; May 19 1949-u; May 26 1949-u; Jun 2 1949-u; Jun 9 1949-u; Jun 16 1949-u; Jun 30 1949-u; Jul 14 1949-u; Jul 21 1949-u; Jul 28 1949-u; Aug 4 1949-u; Aug 11 1949-u; Aug 18 1949-u; Aug 25 1949-u; Sep 1 1949-u; Sep 6 1949-u; Sep 15 1949-u; Sep 22 1949-u; Sep 29 1949-u; Oct 6 1949-u; Oct 13 1949-u; Oct 20 1949-u; Oct 27 1949-u; Nov 3 1949-u; Nov 10 1949-u; Nov 17 1949-u; Nov 24 1949-u; Dec 1 1949-u; Dec 8 1949-u; Dec 15 1949-u; Dec 22 1949-u; Jan 5 1950-u; Jan 12 1950-u; Jan 19 1950-u; Jan 26 1950-u; Feb 2 1950-u; Feb 9 1950-u; Feb 16 1950-u; Feb 23 1950-u; Mar 2 1950-u; Mar 9 1950-u; Mar 16 1950-u; Mar 23 1950-u; Mar 30 1950-u; Apr 6 1950-u; Apr 13 1950-u; Apr 20 1950-u; Apr 27 1950-u; May 4 1950-u; May 11 1950-u; May 18 1950-u; May 25 1950-u; Jun 1 1959-u; Jun 8 1950-u; Jun 15 1950-u; Jun 22 1950-u; Jun 29 1950-u; Jul 20 1950-u; Aug 10 1950-u; Aug 17 1950-u; Aug 24 1950-u; Aug 31 1950-u; Sep 7 1950-u; Sep 13 1950-u; Sep 28 1950-u; Oct 5 1950-u; Oct 12 1950-u; Oct 19 1950-u; Oct 26 1950-u; Nov 2 1950-u; Nov 9 1950-u; Nov 16 1950-u; Nov 23 1950-u; Nov 30 1950-u; Dec 7 1950-u; Dec 14 1950-u; Dec 21 1950-u; Jan 4 1951-u; Jan 11 1951-u; Jan 18 1951-u; Jan 25 1951-u; Feb 1 1951-u; Feb 8 1951-u; Feb 15 1951-u; Feb 22 1951-u; Mar 1 1951-u; Mar 8 1951-u; Mar 15 1951-u; Mar 22 1951-u; Mar 29 1951-u; Apr 5 1951-u; Apr 12 1951-u; Apr 19 1951-u; Apr 26 1951-u; May 3 1951-u; May 10 1951-u; May 17 1951-u; May 24 1951-u; May 31 1951-u; Jun 7 1951-u; Jun 14 1951-u; Jun 21 1951-u; Jun 28 1951-u; Jul 12 1951-u; Jul 19 1951-u; Jul 26 1951-u; Aug 2 1951-u; Aug 9 1951-u; Aug 16 1951-u; Aug 23 1951-u; Aug 30 1951-u; Sep 6 1951-u; Sep 13 1951-u; Sep 20 1951-u; Sep 27 1951-u; Oct 4 1951-u; Oct 11 1951-u; Oct 18 1951-u; Oct 25 1951-u; Nov 1

1951-u; Nov 8 1951-u; Nov 15-1951-u; Nov 22 1951-u; Nov 29 1951-u; Dec 6 1951-u; Dec 13 1951-u; Jan 3 1952-u; Jan 10 1952-u; Jan 17 1952-u; Jan 24 1952-u; Jan 31 1952-u; Feb 7 1952-u; Feb 14 1952-u; Feb 21 1952-u; Feb 28 1952-u; Mar 6 1952-u; Mar 13 1952-u; Mar 20 1952-u; Mar 27 1952-u; Apr 3 1952-u; Apr 10 1952-u; Apr 17 1952-u; Apr 24 1952-u; May 1 1952-u; May 8 1952-u; May 15 1952-u; May 22 1952-u; May 29 1952-u; Jun 5 1952-u; Jun 12 1952-u; Jun 19 1952-u; Jun 26 1952-u; Jul 10 1952-u; Jul 17 1952-u; Jan 30 1958-u

WEEKLY DISPATCH - Weekly; Jul 1 1884-u; Apr 7 1885-u; Jul 28 1885-u; Jan 3 1894-Dec 29 1894-b; Jan 1 1897-Dec 31 1897-b; Jan 7 1898-Dec 3 1898-b; Jan 6 1899-Dec 15 1899-b; Jan 5 1900-Dec 28 1900-b

WEEKLY YORK REPUBLICAN; see The Pennsylvania Republican

WEST YORK AREA NEWS -ETTE- -West York; Aug 23 1962-u 3 cop.; Sep 20 1962-u; Oct 18 1962-u; Nov 15 1962-u; Dec 20 1962-u; Jan 17 1963-u; Feb 21 1963-u; Sep 19 1963-u; Oct 31 1963-u; Oct 17 1963-u; Nov 21 1963-u; Dec 19 1963-u; Jan 16 1964-u; Feb 20 1964-u; Mar 19 1964-u; pr 16 1964-u; May 21 1964-u; Jun 18 1964-u; Jul 16 1964-u; Aug 20 1964-u; Sep 17 1964-u; Oct 15 1964-u; Nov 19 1964-u; Dec 17 1964-u; Jan 21 1965-u; Feb 18 1965-u; Mar 18 1965-u

WRIGHTSVILLE HERALD .-Wrightsville; Dec 26 1946-; Jan 2 1948-u; May 2 1947-u; May 9 1947-u; May 16 1947-u 2 cop.; May 30 1947-u 2 cop.; Jun 6 1947-u; Jun 13 1947-u; Jun 20 1947-u; Jun 27 1947-u; Jul 4 1947-u; Jul 11 1947-u; Aug 1 1947-u; Aug 8 1947-Aug 22 1947-u; Aug 29 1947-u; Sep 5 1947-u; Sep 19 1947-u; Sep 26 1947-u; Oct 3 1947-u; Oct 10 1947-u; Oct 24 1947-u; Oct 31 1947-u; Nov 7 1947-u; Nov 14 1947-u; Nov 21 1947-u; Nov 28 1947-u; Dec 5 1947-u; Dec 12 1947-u; Dec 19 1947-u; Feb 13 1948-u; Feb 27 1948-u; Jul 23 1948-u; 1949-u. 1950-u, 1951-u, 1952-u, 1953-u

WRIGHTSVILLE STAR Wrightsville - Weekly; May 20 1870-; May 16 1873-b; Apr 24 1874-u; May 7 1875-u; Jul 7 1876-u; May 20 1881; May 11 1883-b; May 18 1883-; May 15 1885-b; May 22 1885; May 13 1887-b; May 20 1887; May 10 1889-b; Jan 10 1901-u; Jan 28 1901-u; Jul 12 1901-u; Jul 19 1901-u; Jul 26 1901-u; Aug 2 1901-u; Aug 9 1901-u; Aug 16 1901-u; Aug 23 1901-u; Aug 30 1901-u; Sep 20 1901-u; Sep 27 1901-u; Oct 13 1901-u; Oct 25 1901-u; Nov 8 1901-u; Nov 15 1901-i; Nov 22 1901-u; Nov 29 1901-u; Dec 20 1901-u; Jan 3 1902-u; Jan 31 1902-u; Feb 7 1902-u; May 23 1902-u; Sep 5 1902-u; Sep 12 1902-u; Sep 19 1902-u; Oct 3 1902-u; Dec 5 1902-u; Dec 12 1902-u; Dec 26 1902-u; Aug 14 1903-u; Cot 2 1903-u; May 13 1904-u; Jun 24 1904-u; Feb 10 1905-u; Jul 14 1905-u; Jul 28 1905-u; Aug 4 1905-u; Aug 19 1905-u; Sep 1 1905-u; Oct 13 1905-u; Feb 15 1907-u; Sep 3 1909-u; Apr 21 1912-u; Nov 8 1912-u

WRIGHTSVILLE SUN Wrightsville; September 9 1880-u

Y.C.I. CHRONICLE (Literary Section); Jan 31 1931-u; Mar 22 1935-u; May 3 1935-u; Nov 25 1936-u 2 cop.; May 21 1937-u; Mar 4 1938-u; Jun 1 1938-u

YORK COUNTIAN Dec 19 1902-u

YORK COUNTY FARMER Dec 23 1831-Jan 2 1834-b; Apr 5 1832-u; Apr 18 1833-u; May 23 1833-u; Jun 13 1833-u; Sep 19 1833-u

YORK COUNTY PLANNER York; Sept 1963-u; Dec 1963-u; Mar 1964-u 2 cop.; Jul 1966-u

YORK COUNTY STAR AND WRIGHTSVILLE ADVERTISER Wrightsville - Weekly; Apr 6 1854-Apr 19 1855-b; Jul 19 1855-u; May 7 1857-May 24 1860-b; Mar 18 1858-u; Apr 15 1858-u; Jul 8 1858-u; May 31 1860-Jan 2 1862-b; Jul 11 1861-u; Oct 24 1861-u; May 18 1866-Jul 12 1867-b; May 18 1866-; May 14 1869-b; May 21 1869-; May 13 1870-b

YORK DAILY - Daily; Mar 22 1871-Jun 2 1918-m; Jan 5 1874-u; May 11 1876-u; Jan 1 1876-Jun 30 1876-b; Jul 1 1876-Dec 4 1876-b; Jul 4 1876-u; Sep 14 1877-u Morning Edition; Jan 1 1877-u; Jan 1 1878-u-Carrier's address to the patrons; Sep 12 1878-u; Feb 14 1881-u; Sep 21 1882-u; Sep 23 1887-u; Sep 28 1887-u; Apr 1 1981-u Illustrated Trade Edition; Jul 16 1895-u; Jul 30 1895-u; (incomplete); Mar 31 1898-u; Sep 4 1899-u; Supplement; Jan 24 1903-u undated to the patrons-u

YORK DAILY RECORD York - Daily; Oct 23 1970 (first issue)-u; Jan 1971-u, Feb 1971-u, Mar 1971-u, Apr 1971-u, May 1971-u, ; Jun 1972-u, Jul 1971-u, 2 cop., Aug 1971-u, Sep 1971,u; Oct 1971-u, Nov 1971-u, Jan 1972-u, Feb 1972-u, Mar 1972-u; Apr 1972-u, Jun 1972-u, Sep 1972-u, w/o 4,6,12, Oct 1972-u,; Nov 1972-u, Dec 1972-u, Jan 1973-u, Jan 1973-b, Feb 1973-b; Feb 1973-u, Mar 1973-b, Apr 1973-b, Apr 1973-u, May 1973-b; May 1973-u, Jun 1973-u, Jun 1973-b, Jul 1973-u, Aug 1973-u,; Sep 1973-u, Oct 1973-u, Nov 1973-u, Dec 1973-u, Jan 1974-u,; Feb 1974-u, Mar 1974-u, Apr 1974-u (w/o 8,9-11,12,26,27)-u; May 1974-u, (w/o 9,13,27), Jun 1974-u (w/o 24), Jul 1974-u; (w/o 5,9,10),Aug 1974-u, Oct 1974-u, Nov 1974-u, Dec 23 1974-; Jun 3 1975-m (4 rolls), Jul 3

1975-u, Oct 12 1976-u, Nov 1 1976-u; Nov 2 1976-u, Nov 4 1976-u, Nov 5 1976-u, Nov 6 1976-u, Nov 8 1976-u, ; Nov 9 1976-u; Nov 12 1976-u; Nov 13 1976-u; Nov 16 1976-u 2 cop.; Nov 17 1976-u; Nov 18 1976-u; Nov 19 1976-u; Nov 22 1976-u; Nov 23 1976-u; Nov 24 1976-u; Nov 26 1976-u; Nov 27 1976-u; Nov 29 1976-u; Nov 30 1976-u; Dec 1 1976-u; Dec 2 1976-u; Dec 3 1976-u; Dec 4 1976-u; Dec 7 1976-u; Dec 8 1976-u; Dec 9 1976-u; Dec 10 1976-u 2 cop.; Dec 11 1976-u 2 cop.; Dec 13 1976-u; Dec 14 1976-u; Dec 15 1976-u; Dec 16 1976-u; Dec 17 1976-u; Dec 18 1976-u ; Dec 20 1976-u 2 cop.; Dec 21 1976-u; Dec 22 1976-u; Dec 23 1976-u; Dec 27 1976-u; Dec 28 1976-u; Dec 29 1976-u; Dec 30 1976-u; Jan 3 1977-u; Jan 4 1977-u; Jan 5 1977-u; Jan 6 1977-u; Jan 10 1977-u; Jan 11 1977-u; Jan 12 1977-u; Jan 14 1977-u; Jan 15 1977-u; Jan 17 1977-u; Jan 18 1977-u; Jan 19 1977-u; Jan 20 1977-u; Jan 21 1977-u; Jan 24 1977-u; Jan 25 1977-u; Jan 26 1977-u; Jan 27 1977-u; Jan 28 1977-u; Jan 28 1977-; Jan 30 1977-m; Jan 29 1977-u; Feb 11 1977-u; Feb 12 1977-u; Feb 14 1977-u; Feb 15 1977-u; Feb 16 1977-u; Feb 171977-u; Feb 18 1977-u; Feb 19 1977-u; Feb 21 1977-u; Feb 22 1977-u; Feb 23 1977-u; Feb 24 1977-u; Feb 25 1977-u; Feb 26 1977-u; Feb 28 1977-u; Mar 1 1977-u; Mar 2 1977-u; Mar 3 1977-u; Mar 4 1977-u; Mar 5 1977-u; Mar 7 1977-u; Mar 8 1977-u; Mar 9 1977-u; Mar 10 1977-u; Mar 11 1977-u; Mar 12 1977-u; Mar 14 1977-u; Mar 15 1977-u; Mar 17 1977-u; Mar 18 1977-u; Mar 19 1977-u; Mar 21 1977-u; Mar 23 1977-u; Mar 24 1977-u; Mar 26 1977-u; Mar 28 1977-u; Mar 29 1977-u; Mar 31 1977-u; Apr 1 1977-u; Apr 2 1977-u; Apr 5 1977-u; Apr 6 1977-u; Apr 7 1977-u; Apr 8 1977-u; Apr 11 1977-u; Apr 12 1977-u; Apr 13 1977-u; Apr 14 1977-u; Apr 15 1977-u; Apr 16 1977-u; Apr 19 1977-u; Apr 20 1977-u; Apr 22 1977-u; Apr 25 1977-u; Apr 26 1977-u; Apr 27 1977-u; Apr 28 1977-u; Apr 30 1977-u; May 3 1977-u; May 4 1977-u; May 5 1977-u; May 6 1977-u; May 9 1977-u; May 9 1977-u; May 10 1977-u; May 11 1977-u; may 12 1977-u; May 13 1977-u; May 14 1977-u; May 16 1977-u; May 17 1977-u; May 18 1977-u; May 19 1977-u; may 20 1977-u; May 21 1977-u; May 23 1977-u; May 24 1977-u; May 25 1977-u; May 26 1977-u; May 27 1977-u; May 31 1977-u; Jun 1 1977-u; Jun 2 1977-u; Jun 3 1977-u; Jun 4 1977-u; Jun 6 1977-u; Jun 7 1977-u; Jun 8 1977-u; Jun 9 1977-u; Jun 11 1977-u; Jun 13 1977-u; Jun 14 1977-u; Jun 15 1977-u; Jun 16 1977-u; Jun 17 1977-u; Jun 18 1977-u; Jun 20 1977-u; Jun 21 1977-u; Jun 22 1977-u; Jun 23 1977-u; Jun 25 1977-u; Jun 27 1977-u; Jun 29 1977-u; July 1977-u, Aug 1977-u m. Sept 1977-u m, Oct 1977-u m, ; Oct 7 missing, Nov 1977-u m, Dec 1977-u m, Jan 1978 u m, ; Jan 2 1971-Nov 30 1983-m

DER YORK DEMOCRAT- Feb 28 1834-u

YORK DEMOCRAT- Oct 1906-u; Oct 1908-u

YORK DISPATCH- Daily; Sep 27 1881-u; Jan 1 1882-u Carrier's address to the patrons-3 cop.; Oct 5 1883-u; Jan 1 1884-u; Carriers address to the patrons; June 26 1884-u; Jun 28 1884-u; Jun 1 1886-Dec 29 1886-b; Jul 1 1887-Dec 30 1887-b; Jan 2 1888-Dec 29-1888-b; Jul 2 1888-Dec 30 1889-b; Jan 2 1889-Jun 29 1889-b; Jul 2 1889-Dec 30 1889-b; Jan 3 1890-Jun 30 18990-b; Jul 1 1890-Dec 31 1890-b; Jan 1 1891-Jun 30 1891-b; Jul 2 1891-Dec 31 1891-b; Jan 1 1892-Jun 30 1892-b; Jul 1 1892-Dec 30 1982-b; Jan 3 1893-Jun 30 1893-b; Jul 1 1893-Nov 29 1893-b; Jan-Apr 1894-u; Feb 8 1894-u; May-Aug 1894-u; May 24 1894-u; Nov 30 1893-May 28 1895-b; May 29 1895-Nov 27 1895-b; Nov 29 1895-May 28 1895-b; may 29 1896-Nov 30 1896-b; Aug 25 1896-u; Dec 1 1896-May 28 1897-b; May 29 1897-Nov 27 1897-b; Nov 29 1897-May 28 1898-b; May 30 1898-Nov 28 1898-b; Nov 29 1898-May 27 1899-b; May 29 1899-Nov 28 1899-b; Sep 4 1899-u 2 cop.; Sep 5 1899-u; May 29 1900-Nov 26 1900-b; Nov 28 1900-May 27 1901-b; May 29 1901-Nov 27 1901-b; Jul-Aug 1902-u; Sep-Oct 1902-u; Nov-Dec 1902-u; Jan-Feb 1903-u; mar-Apr 1903-u; May-Jun 1903-u; Jul-Aug 1903-u; Sep-Nov 1903-u; Aug 1 1904-u; Jun 19 1905; Jun 30 1975-m; (Mar, Apr, May 1905 missing); Jul 21 1908-u; Apr 24 1908-u; Aug 4 1911-u; Aug 7 1911-u; Aug 24 1911-u; Mar 28 1925-u; Aug 25 1933-u; Oct 4 1934-u; Oct 5 1934-u; May 18 1938-u; Sep 1 1953-u; Nov 22 1963-u; Nov 23 1963-u; Nov 25 1963-u; Dec 4 1963-u; Feb 1 1977-; Jul 30 1977-m; Feb 4 1977-u; Feb 5 1977-u; Feb 7 1977-u; Feb 8 1977-u; Feb 9 1977-u; Feb 10 1977-u; Feb 11 1977-u; Feb 12 1977-u; Feb 16 1977-u; Feb 25 1977-u; Feb 26 1977-u; Feb 28 1977-u; May 2 1977-u; May 3 1977-u; May 5 1977-u ; May 7 1977-u; May 9 1977-u; May 10 1977-u; May 11 1977-u; May 12 1977-u; May 13 1977-u; May 14 1977-u; May 16 1977-u; May 17 1977-u; May 19 1977-u; May 20 1977-u; May 21 1977-u 2 cop.; May 23 1977-u; May 24 1977-u; May 25 1977-u; May 26 1977-u; May 31 1977-u; Jun 1 1977-u; Jun 2 1977-u; Jun 3 1977-u; Jun 6 1977-u; Jun 7 1977-u; Jun 9 1977-u; Jun 10 1977-u; Jun 13 1977-u; Jun 14 1077-u; Jun 15 1977-u; Jun 16 1977-u; Jun 17 1977-u; Jun 18 1977-u; Jun 20 1977-u; Jun 22 1977-u; Jun 23 1977-u; Jun 25 1977-u; Jun 27 1977-u; July 1977-u, Aug 1977-u, Sept 1977-u, Oct 1977-u; Jun 19 1905-Dec 31 1983-m

YORK DRUGGIST Spring 1882-u

YORK EVENING PRESS - Daily; May 1901-Oct 1901-b; Nov 1901-Apr 1902-b; May 1 1902-Oct 31 1902-b; Nov 1902-Apr 1903-b; May 1

1903-Oct 31 1903-b; Nov 1903-Apr 1904-b; May 1904-Oct 1904-b; Nov 1904-Apr 1905-b; May 1905-Jan 1906-b; Nov 7 1905-u

YORK EVENING - Daily; July 5 1876-u

YORK EVENING RECORD - Daily; Oct 17 1877-u; Oct 18 1877-u; Oct 19 1877-u; Nov 1 1877-u; Jan 19 1878-u; Feb 26 1878-u; Feb 29 1878-u; Mar 2 1878-u; Mar 5 1878-u; Mar 7 1878-u; Mar 8 1878-u; Mar 9 1878-u; Mar 11 1878-u; Mar 14 1878-u; Mar 15 1878-u; May 3 1878-u; Nov 1 1878-u

YORK EVENING TELEGRAM - Daily; Sep 24 1874-u 2 cop.; Sep 25 1874-u; Oct 12 1874-u; Oct 13 1874-u; Oct 14 1874-u; Oct 17 1874-u; Oct 26 1874-u; Nov 5 1874-u; Nov 27 1874-u; Dec 1 1874-u; Dec 16 1874-u; Jan 7 1875-u; Jan 18 1875-u; Jan 19 1875-u; Jan 20 1875-u; Jan 21 1875-u; Jan 22 1875-u 2 cop.; Jan 25 1875-u; Jan 27 1875-u; Jan 30 1875-u 2 cop.; Feb 1 1875-u; Feb 2 1875-u 2 cop.; Feb 5 1875-u; Feb 6 1875-u; Feb 13 1875-u; Jun 25 1875-u; Jun 28 1875-u; Jun 29 1875-u; Jun 30 1875-u; Jul 1 1875-u; Jul 2 1875-u; Jul 3 1875-u; Jul 6 1875-u; Jul 7 1875-u; Jul 8 1874-u; Jul 12 1875-u; Jul 14 1875-u; Jul 15 1875-u; Jul 16 1875-u; Jul 19 1875-u; Jul 22 1875-u; Jul 23 1875-u; Jul 26 1875-u; Jul 27 1875-u; Jul 28 1875-u; Aug 26 1875-u

YORK GAZETTE (GERMAN) May 20 1796-Jul 18 1797-m scattered; Sep 7 1798-u; Jan 24 1800-u; Sep 26 1804-u; Mar 23 1821-Mar 1 1882-b; May 1882-Feb 1823-b; Mar 14 1823-Mar 12 1824-b; Mar 19 1824-Mar 10 1826-b; Dec 31 1824-u; Mar 31 1826-; Feb 29 1828-b; Jun 8 1827-u; May 9 1828-u; Mar 1821, Feb 3 1829-m; Feb 20 1834-m; Jan 1 1830-u; Dec 25 1835-u; Apr 9 1852-u; May 19 1854-u; Aug 15 1854-u; Jan 13 1860-u; May 16 1862-u; Oct 21 1870-u

YORK GAZETTE ENGLISH - Weekly/Daily; Nov 30 1815-Apr 11 1816-b; Dec 28 1815-u; Apr 18 1816-Mar 28 1818-b; Mar 27 1817-May 21 1818-b; Aug 1817- 2 cop.-u; Oct 16 1817-u; Feb 26 1818-u; Dec 10 1818-u; Dec 17 1818-u; May 1819-Feb 1820-b; Jan 11 1820-u; Feb 1820-Apr 1821-b; May 15 1821-Apr 30 1822-b; May 7 1822-Apr 27 1824-b; May 1823-May 1824-b; May 1824-May 1825-b; May 18 1824-May 16 1826-b; Nov 29 1825-u; May 1826-May 1828-b; May 1829-May 1830-b; may 1830-May 1831-b; May 1831-May 1832-b; May 22 1833-May 28 1833-b; Jun 1833-May 1834-b; Nov 6 1833-u; Nov 12 1833-u; Jan 1835-May 1836-b; Mar 1836-Dec 1837-b; May 1836-Feb 1838-b; 1838-1840-b; Jan 1840-Dec 1841-b; Jan 1842-Dec 1843-b; Jan 1844-May 1845-b; May 1845-Apr 1847-b; Jan 1847-Dec 1849-b; May 1847-Apr

1849-b; Jan 1850-Dec 1851-b; Jan 1851-Dec 1853-b; Jul 20 1852-u; Jan 1854-Dec 1855-b; Apr 4 1854-u; Sep 4 1855-u; Jan 1856-Dec 1857-b; 1860-1861-b; Jan 7 1862-Jan 6 1863-b; Jan 13 1863-Dec 15 1863-b; Jan 1864-Dec 1865-b; Jan 17 1865-u; Jan 2 1866-Dec 28 1869-b; Mar 6 1866-u; Oct 4 1866-extra edit-u; Mar 10 1868-u; Jan 1870-Dec 1871-b; Jan 1872-Dec 1873-b; Jan 1874-Dec 1875-b; Jan 1876-Dec 1877-b; Jan 1878-Dec 1879-b; Jan 1880-Dec 1881-b; Jan 1882-Dec 1883-b; Jan 1 1882-carrier's address to the patrons; Jan 1884-Dec 1885-b; Jan 1886-Dec 1886-b; Jan 1887-Dec 1887-b; Jan 1888-Dec 1888-b; Feb 9 1888-u; Jan 1889-Dec 1889-b; Jan 1891-Dec 1891-b; Jan 1892-Dec 1892-b; Jan 1893-Dec 1893-b; Jan 1 1894-Carrier's address to the patrons-u; Jan 1895-Dec 1895-b; Jan 1898-Dec 1898-b; Jan 1901-Jan 1901-b; Jul 1901-Dec 1901-b; Apr 1902-Jun 1902-b; Jul 1902-Nov 19 1902-b; Nov 20 1902-Mar 31 1903-b; Jan 1903-Dec 1903-b; Jan 1904-Jun 1904-b; Apr 1905-Jun 1905-b; Oct 1905-Dec 1905-b; Apr 1906-Jun 1906-b; Jul 1906-Sep 1906-b; Jan 1907-Mar 1907-b; Jul 1907-Sep 1907-b; Jan 1908-Mar 1908-b; Apr 1908-Jun 1908-b; Jan 1909-Mar 1909-b; Apr 1909-Jun 1909-b; Jan 1910-Apr 1910-b; May 1910-Aug 1910-b; Sep 1910-Dec 1910-b; Jan 1911-Mar 1911-b; Apr 1911-Jun 1911-b; Jul 1911-Sep 1911-b; Oct 1911-Dec 1911-b; Jan 1912-Mar 1912-b; Feb 1912-Apr 1912-b; May 1912-Aug 1912-b; Sep 1912-Dec 1912-b; Jan 1913-Apr 1913-b; May 1913-Aug 1913-b; Sep 1913-Dec 1913-b; Jan 1914-Apr 1914-b; May 1914-Aug 1914-b; Sep 1914-Dec 1914-b; Jan 1915-Apr 1915-b; May 1915-Aug 1915-b; jul 1915-Aug 1915-b; Sep 1915-Dec 1915-b; Nov 30 1815-Jan 31 1917 m; Jan 1916-Apr 1916-b; May 1916-Aug 1916-b; Sep 1916-Dec 1916-b; Jan 1917-Mar 1917-b; Mar 1917-Apr 1917-b; Apr 30 1917-u; May 1917-Jun 1917-b; Sep 1917-Oct 1917-b; Nov 1917-Dec 1917-b; Jan 1918-Mar 1918-b; Apr 1918-Jun 1918-b; Jul 1918-Aug 1918-b

YORK GAZETTE AND PUBLIC ADVERTISER Jul 11 1816-u; Nov 7 1816-u

YORK HIGH WEEKLY Apr 11 1924-u; Sep 5 1924-u; Sep 12 1924-u; Sep 19 1924-u; Sep 26 1924-u; Oct 3 1924-u; Oct 24 1924-u; Oct 17 1924-u; Oct 31 1924-u; Nov 7 1924-u; Nov 14 1924-u; Nov 21 1924-u; Dec 5 1924-u; Dec 12 1924-u; Dec 19 1924-u; Jan 9 1925-u; Jan 16 1925-u; Jan 23 1925-u; Jan 30 1925-u; Feb 6 1925-u; Feb 20 1925-u; Feb 27 1925-u; Mar 13 1925-u; Mar 20 1925-u; Mar 27 1925-u; Apr 3 1925-u; Apr 9 1925-u; Apr 17 1925-u; May 1 1925-u 2 cop.; May 27 1925-u; May 14 1926-u; May 24 1926-u; Sep 1926-Jun 1927-b; Dec 23 1926-u; Mar 27 1927-u; May 12 1927-u 3 cop.;

May 23 1927-u 2 cop.; Sep 1927-Jun 1928-b; Oct 12 1927-u; Oct 28 1927-u; Nov 4 1927-u; Nov 11 1927-u 2 cop.; Dec 2 1927-u; Dec 9 1927-u; Dec 2 ? 1927-u; Jan 6 1928-u; Jan 20 1928-u; Feb 3 1928-u; Feb 10 1928-u; Feb 17 1928-u; Feb 24 1928-u; Feb 28 1928-u; Mar 2 1928-u; Mar 9 1928-u; Mar 16 1928-u; Mar 23 1928-u; Mar 30 1928-u; Apr 13 1928-u; Apr 20 1928-u; May 4 1928-u; May 10 1928-u; May 23 1928-u; Sep 1928-June 1929-b; Sep 7 1928-u; Sep 14 1928-u; Sep 21 1928-u; Sep 28 1928-u; Oct 12 1928-u; Oct 19 1928-u; Oct 26 1928-u; Nov 2 1928-u 2 cop.; Nov 9 1928-u; Nov 16 1928-u; Nov 23 1928-u; Dec 7 1928-u; Dec 14 1928-u; Dec 21 1928-u 2 cop.; May 29 1929-u; Sep 1929-Jun 1930-b; Sep 1930-Jun 1931-b; Jan 16 1931-u; Feb 6 1931-u 2 cop.; Feb 20 1931-u; Feb 27 1931-u; Mar 20 1931-u; Apr 17 1931-u; Apr 24 1931-u; May 8 1931-u; May 22 1931-u; Sep 1931-Jun 1932-b; Sep 4 1931-u; Sep 11 1931-u; Sep 18 1931-u; Sep 25 1931-u; Oct 2 1931-u; Oct 16 1931-u; Oct 30 1931-u 2 cop.; Nov 6 1931-u 2 cop.; Nov 13 1931-u; Nov 20 1931-u; Dec 1 1931-u; Dec 4 1931-u; Dec 18 1931-u; Jan 8 1932-u; Jan 13 1932-u; Feb 5 1932-u; Feb 12 1932-u; Feb 19 1932-u; Feb 26 1932-u; Mar 4 1932-u; Mar 11 1932-u; Mar 18 1932-u; Mar 24 1932-u; Apr 8 1932-u; Apr 15 1932-u; Apr 22 1932-u; Apr 29 1932-u; May 13 1932-u; May 20 1932-u; May 25 1932-u; Sep 9 1932-u 2 cop.; Sep 16 1932-u; Nov 4 1932-u; Nov 11 1932-u 2 cop.; Nov 18 1932-u; Dec 2 1932-u; Dec 16 1932-u; Dec 23 1932-u; Sep 1935-Jun 1935-b; Sep 1935-Jun 1936-b; Dec 6 1935-u; Jan 10 1936-u; Jan 17 1936-u; Feb 28 1936-u; Mar 20 1936-u; Sep 1936-Jun 1937-b; Sep 1937-Jun 1938-b; Sep 1938-Jun 1939-b 2 cop.; Sep 1929-Jun 1940-b 2 cop.; Sep 1940-Jun 1941-b; Sep 1941-Jun 1942-b; Sep 1942-Jun 1943-b; Sep 1943-Jun 1944-b; Sep 1944-Jun 1945-b; Sep 1945-Jun 1946-b; Sep 1946-Jun 1947-b; Sep 1947-Jun 1948-b; Sep 1948-Jun 1949-b; Sep 1949-Jun 1950-b; Sep 1950-Jun 1951-b

YORK J C (JUNIOR COLLEGE) NEWSLET-TER Nov 1965-u; Nov 1965-u

YORK LABOR NEWS - Weekly; Jan 6 1917-u; Dec 23 1916-u; Jan 13 1917-u; Feb 17 1917-u; Mar 10 1917-u; Mar 17 1917-u; 1 undated issue

YORK NEWSLETTER AND ADVERTISER York; Mar 1921-u

YORK PENNSYLVANIAN - Weekly; Dec 16 1854-u; Oct 14 1858-u Extra Edition; Sep 3 1859-u; Aug 31 1862-u Extra Edition; Jul 9 1864-u; Oct 14 1865-u; Jun 13 1866-u; Mar 9 1867-u; May 4 1867-u; Jan 22 1870-u; Nov 16 1872-u; Feb 8 1873-u; Feb 22 1873-u; Sep 6 1873-u; Aug 15 1874-u; Dec 26 1874-u; Apr 28

1877-u; Aug 9 1879-u; Apr 3 1880-u; Feb 19 1881-u; Apr 7 1894-u; Jul 21 1894-u; 1 undated extra edition -u

YORK PRESS Oct 1897-Mar 1898-b; Apr 1 1898-Oct 1899-m; May 13 1898-u; Jul 2 1898-u; Oct 1898-Apr 1899-b; Jan 19 1899-u; Apr 20 1899-Oct 12 1899-b; Sep 5 1899-u 2 cop.; Sep 6 1899-u; Sep 7 1899-u; Oct 13 1899-Apr 7 1900-b; Apr 9 1900-Sep 29 1900-b; Oct 1 1900-Apr 30 1901-b; Jan 3 1903-Dec 30 1903-m

YORK RECORDER - Weekly; Jan 29 1800-; Feb 21 1805-m; Mar 5 1800-u; Mar 14 1804-u; Aug 1 1804-u; Aug 23 1806-u; Apr 14 1810-; Apr 3 1813-m; Aug 15 1812-u; Aug 30 1814-u; Nov 22 1814-u; Jan 1 1821-; Dec 31 1825-m; Jan 17 1821-u; Oct 21 1823-u; Jan 1 1826-; Mar 31 1830-m; Jan 3 1826-u; Mar 21 1826-u; Apr 4 1826-u; Apr 25 1826-u; May 2 1828-u; May 16 1826-u; May 23 1826-u; Nov 13 1827-u; Jan 5 1830-; Mar 9 1830-b; Feb 2 1830-u

YORK REPUBLICAN see The Pennsylvania Republican

YORK REPUBLICAN AND ANTI-MASONIC EXPOSITOR Weekly; see The Pennsylvania Republican

YORK SEMI-WEEKLY PRESS Jun 20 1899-Jun 19 1900-b; Jun 22 1900-May 7 1901-b

YORK UNION York - Monthly; Jun 1894-u

YORK WEEKLY - Weekly; Oct 10 1874-u; Feb 17 1882-u; Mar 17 1882-u; Mar 31 1885-u; Feb 18 1887-u; Apr 17 1891-u incomplete; Dec 25 1891-u; Jan 1 1892-u; May 23 1899-u; Jul 28 1899-u; Aug 8 1899-u; Aug 11 1899-u; Sep 8 1899-u; May 18 1903-u; Feb 29 1904-u

YORK WEEKLY ADVERTISER see The Pennsylvania Chronicle

YORK WEEKLY GAZETTE Jan 4 1890-Dec 27 1890-b

YORK WEEKLY PRESS Aug 19, 1898-Jun 16 1899-b

Y'S - J'S JOURNAL Feb 24 1919-special edition-u; Dec 19 1832-(3 cop.)-u

YOUTH'S HERALD Jan 1886-u; Mar 1886-u

Chapter 12
ORIGINS OF SETTLERS

The purpose of this section is to point researchers to publications where they can obtain information on the overseas origins of their York County ancestors. The names in the following list were included because they had at some time a connection with York County. [See also Calvin Schildknecht, *Monocacy and Catoctin*, Vol. 1 (pub. by Beidel Printing House, Shippensburg, PA) and Vol. 2 (pub. by Family Line Publications, Westminster, MD).]

References

A-001: *Adams County Church Records of the 18th Century*. Westminster: Family Line Publications, n.d.

B-001; Burgert, Annette K. *York County Pioneers from Friedelsheim and Gonnheim in the Palatinate*. Worthington: AKB Publications, c.r.1984.

B-002: Burgert, Annette K. *Eighteenth Century Emigrants from German Speaking Lands to North America: Volume II: The Western Palatinate*.

B-003: Burgert, Annette K. *Eighteenth and Nineteenth Century Emigrants from Lachen-Speyerdorf in the Palatinate*. AKB Publications, 1989.

B-004: Burgert, Annette K. *Eighteenth Century Emigrants from Pfungstadt, Hessen-Darmstadt to Pennsylvania*. Myerstown: AKB Publications, 1995.

B-005: Burgert, Annette K. *Brethren from Gimbsheim in the Palatinate to Ephrata and Bermudian in Pennsylvania*. Myerstown: AKB Publications, 1994.

B-006: Burgoyne, Bruce E. *Waldeck Soldiers of the American Revolutionary War*. Bowie: Heritage Books, 1991. [Checked through p. 69]

B-007: Burgert, Annette K. *Eighteenth Century Emigrants from the Northern Alsace to America*. Camden, ME: Picton Press, 1992.

B-008. Bates, Marlene S., and F. Edward Wright. *York County, Pennsylvania Church Records of the 18th Century. Volume 1*. Westminster: Family Line Publications, 1991.

B-009. Bates, Marlene S., and F. Edward Wright. *York County, Pennsylvania Church Records of the 18th Century. Volume 2*. Westminster: Family Line Publications, 1991.

B-010. Bates, Marlene S., and F. Edward Wright. *York County, Pennsylvania Church Records of the 18th Century. Volume 3*. Westminster: Family Line Publications, 1991.

B-011. Burgert, Annette K. *Eighteenth Century Emigrants from German Speaking Land to North America. Vol. I: The Northern Kraichgau*. Breinigsville: The Pennsylvania German Society, 1983.

B-012. Burgert, Annette K., and Henry Z. Jones, Jr. *Westerwald to America*. Calden, ME: Picton Press, 1989.

B-013. Burgert, Annette K. *Pennsylvania Pioneers from Wolfersweiler Parish, Saarland, Germany*. Worthington, OH: AKB Publications, 1983.

B-014. Burgert, Annette K. *The Hochstadt Origins of Some of the Early Settlers of Host Church, Berks County, Pennsylvania*. Worthington, OH: AKB Publications, 1983.

B-015. Burgert, Annette K. *Early Pennsylvania Pioneers from Mutterstadt in the Palatinate*. Worthington, OH: AKB Publications, 1983.

B-016. Burgert, Annette K. *Eighteenth Century Pennsylvania Emigrants from Hassloch and Bohl in the Palatinate*. Worthington, OH: AKB Publications, 1983.

B-017. Burgert, Annette K. *A Century of Emigration from Affoltern am Albis, Canton Zurich, Switzerland.* Worthington, OH: AKB Publications, 1984.

B-018. Burgert, Annette K. *Emigrants from Eppingen to America in the 18th and 19th Centuries.* Myerstown, PA: AKB Publications, 1987.

B-019. Burgert, Annette K. *Colonial Pennsylvania Immigrants from Frensheim in the Palatinate.* Myerstown, PA: AKB Publications, 1989.

0-001. Oertel, Prof. Dr. Burkhardt. *German Genealogical Queries and Research Reports... A 1990-1991 Project of the Pennsylvania Chapter of Palatines to America.* Elverson, PA: Old Springfield Shoppe, 1992.

P-001: "Surname Index," *The Palatine Immigrant,* 1 (2) 14.

S-001: South Central Penna. Gen. Soc.: *Special Publication Number 41: Abstracts and Identifications of Entries Giving European Origins in Church Records of South Central Pennsylvania...Book I.* York: The Society, 1990.

S-002: "Some Continental European Origins in Local Church Records," Typescript, HSYC.

Y-001: Yoder, Don, Ed. *Rhineland Emigrants.* Baltimore: Genealogical Publishing Co., 1985.

Name of Settler	Age if Shown	Date of Arrival	Reference
Adlum, Elizabeth Berwick	b. 1705	1732	S-001:3
Albert, Anna Margaretha		1739	0-001:50
Alberth, Lorentz	b. 1719	1754	A-001:18
Allenbach, Friederich	bap. 1714	1750	B-002:29
Alt, Valentine		1738	0-001:78
Baron, Anna Elisabetha	b. c.1751	1770	B-007:40
Battenfeld, Johann		1750	P-001:15
Battenfeld, Philip		1750	P-001:15
Battenfeld, Hans Adam		1750	P-001:15
Bauer, John Martin	b. 1707	1732	B-011:42
Baum, Jerg Simon		1751	B-011:43
Baumann, Daniel		1751	0-001:648
Beckel, Georg Valentin		1732	B-001:5
Becker, George		by 1759	S-001:1
Beitzel, John	b. 1712	1737	B-09:16
Beizel, Anna Elizabeth. See Eberhard, Anna Elizabeth			
Bender, Catherina. See Williart, Catherina.			
Benner, John		by 1761	S-001:1
Bentz, Joh. Weyrich		1728	B-011:54
Berlin, Georg Friedrich	b. 1722	1738	B-007:53
Berot(h), Franz Ludwig	b. 1699		S-002:58
Berthold, Peter	b. 1724	1748	0-001:14
Berwick, Elizabeth	b. 1735	1732	B-009:284
Beyerfalck, Michel		1738	B-007:57

Bietenger, Peter	b. c.1703	1737	B-007:71
Billet, Kraft		1751	0-001:80
Billmeyer, Rosina		1732	B-009:289
Binckele, Peter	b. 1704		S-002:56
Bischof, Heinrich	b.1713	1736	0-001:406
Bischoff, Anna Margaretha	b. 1709	1738	B-011:63
Bischoff, Heinrich	b. c.1713	1733	B-007:77
Bleymeier, Martin		1749	B-011:67
Bohl, Anna Maria	b. 1726		S-002:51
Bohler, hans Martin		1738	B-001:5
Bracher, Catherina	b. 1705	1738	S-001:2
Brincker, Elisabetha Barbara		by 1759	S-001:1
Brinkmann, Catharina. See Heilmann, Catharina.			
Brotzman, Ludwig		1750	S-002:54
Brotzman, Ludwig	b. 1718	1750	B-009:16
Brungart, Martin		1752	B-007:94
Bucking, Caspar		1749	B-005:11
Buckle, Susanna Elizabeth		1750	P-001:17
Burckert, Paul	b. 1716	1736	S-001:2
Buschi, Joh. Nicolaus	b. 1723		A-001:17
Buser, Henry	b. 1725	1749	S-002:75
Clar, Jacob	bap. 1698	1740	B-002:76
Coblentz, Niclaus	b.1697	1743	B-001:6
Correll, Magdalena. See Schnazler, Magdalena.			
Cuntz/Kuntz, Jacob		1727	Y-001:5
Deeh, Joh. Nicolaus		1754	B:004:7
Depfer, George B.	b.1775		0-001:88
Derr, Maria Eva	b. 1737	1746	B-009:284
Detter, Nicolaus	b. 1712	1749	A-001:17
Diefenbach, Christoph	n.g.	n.g.	B-007:117
Diehl, (Joh.) Adam	b. c.1787	1739	B-002:88
Dietz, Conrad	b. 1711	1738	S-001:2
Doerkes, Henry	b. 1725	1753	S-002:32
Durr, Hans Georg		1747	B-011:95
Durr, Maria Eva	bap. 1738	1747	B-011:95
Eberhard, Anna Elizabeth	b. 1727		S-002:27
Eberhard, Anna Elizabeth	b. 1729		B-009:16
Eberle, Elizabeth	b. 1723		B-009:25
Ebert, Martin	b. 1724	1732	S-002:61

Ebert/Eberle, Elizabeth	b. 1723	1753	S-002:42
Eckert, Gertrude	b. 1709		S-002:63
Eichelberger, Frederick	bap.1693	1728	B-011:97
Einers, Elizabeth	b. 1728		B-009:12
Emig, Johannes	b. 1722	1732	B-007:142
Enders, Johann Peter	bap.1716	1740	B-012:61
Eners, Elizabeth	b. 1728		S-002:37
Etter, Elizabeth	b. 1726		S-002:47
Feiser, Elizabeth. See Eners, Elizabeth.			
Feiser, John	b. 1716	1740	S-002:67
Feiser, Peter	b. 1732	1744	S-002:45
Feisser, Elizabeth. See Schlatter, Elizabeth.			
Felger, Johann Heinrich	b. 1734	1753	B-012:65
Ferbert, Nikolaus		1727	P-001:19
Feuerstein, Johann Nicholas	b. 1735	1753	B-007:158
Feuser, Johannes Thiess	b. 1716	1740	B-012:68
Fickes, Hannah Regina	b. 1717		A-001:18
Fischel, John	b. 1703	1742	S-002:62
Fischel, John Adam	b. 1730	1742	S-002:70
Fischel, John Michael	b. 1736	1742	S-002-43
Fischel, Michael	b. 1736		S-002:76
Fischer, Joh. Nicklas	b. c.1714	1738	B-002:119
Fischer, Nicolaus		c.1747	S-002:86
Fischer, Michael		by 1761	S-001:1
Floetzer, Jacob	b. 1704		S-001:1
Foscher, Susanna Maria Klee		c.1747	S-002:86
Frank, Henrietta	b. 1831		S-002:50
Freisinger, Ludwig Fridrich		1754	0-001:112
Frey, Gottfried	bap.1721	1727	B-011:114
Frey, Jacob		1750	P-001:19
Frey, Tobias		1727	Y-001:8
Freytag, Nicholas		1738	B-001:7
Fritz, Maria Elizabeth	b. 1733	1742	B-009:284
Froschauer, John George		c.1747	S-002:80
Fuchs, Henrich	b. 1728		A-001:17
Funfrock, Johann Michael	b. 1735	1770	B-007:183
Funfrock, Johann Stephan	b. 1742	1770	B-007:183
Funfrock, Michael		1770	B-007:183
Galatin, Widow Eleanora	b. 1724		S-002:53

Gansshorn, Johann Georg	b. 1725	1750	Y-001:22
Gantzhorn, Hans Georg		1750	B-011:119
Gartner, Hans Peter		1731	B-007:187
Geiger, Anna Margaret	b. 1722		S-002:56
Geisi, John Conrad	b. 1718	1741	B-016:11
Geiss, Margaret	b. 1715	1738	B-009:290
Gentes, Daniel	b. 1738	1773	B-002:133
Gerber, Jacob		1733	S-001:3
Gerber, John	b. 1726	1733	B-009:283
Gerber, Philip	b. 1730	1733	B-009:282
Gernion, Elizabeth	b. 1709		P-001:20
Gerret, Peter		1749	B-007:202
Geyer, Johann Adam	b.1726	1744	B-012:80
Gobel, Antoni	b.1718	1733	B-011:134
Grau, Johann Conrad	b.1711	1753	B-012:84
Greb, Johann Theiss	b.1731	1753	B-012:86
Greb, Johann Gerhard	b. 1743	1753	B-012:87
Griesinger, John	b.c1708	1733	0-001:422
Groll, Christian	b. 1707		S-001:2
Grossman, Simon		1749	0-001:236
Gump, George	b. 1709	1732	S-002:72
Gump, John George	b. 1709	1732	S-002:29
Gump, Salome. See Schwing, Salome.			
Haentschi, Barbara. See Spittler, Barbara.			
Hahn, Anna Maria	b. 1706	1743	B-009:289
Haller, Christopher	b. 1710		S-002:69
Haller, Jorg Christopher	b.1710	1752	B-011:146
Hauck, Hans Martin	b. 1716	1752	B-007:231
Hauck, Hans Michel	b. 1719	1749	B-007:229
Hauck, Joh. Bernhard	b. 1728	1749	B-007:229
Hausman, Conrad	b. 1715	1754	S-001:3
Heckendorn, Barbara. See Spittler, Barbara.			
Heckendorn, John	b. 1716	1736	S-002:52
Heckler, Hans Georg	b. 1708	1754	B-007:238
Heckler, Hans Martin	bapt. 1735	1754	B-007:238
Heilmann, Catharina	b. 1730	1750	S-002:35
Heintz, Philip	b. 1692	1738	B-002:158
Hekedorn, John	b. 1716	1736	B-009:14
Hekele, Johann Georg	b. 1735	1749	A-001:18

Henneman, Johann Philipp	b. 1714	1749	B-005:15
Herbach, George	b. 1726	1738	B-009:18
Hermsdorff, John Carl	b. 1710	1754	S-001:3
Heyer, Johan Friderich	b. 1720	1743	B-001:7
Heyer, Vallandien	b. 1725	1743	B-001:7
Heylmann, Anna Maria	b. 1723	1750	S-002:54
Hockstatter, Nicklaus		1749	B-007:255
Hoehneisen, Bernhard	b. 1713	1752	S-002:64
Hoeneise, Elizabeth	b. 1719		B-009:26
Hoeneisen, Elizabeth	b. 1719	1752	B-009:11
Hoeneisen, John			B-009:29
Hoens, Marcus	b. 1719	1738	S-002:59
Hoens, Philip	b. 1720	1738	S-002:68
Hoff, Adam			S-002:55
Hoff, Johan Adam	b. 1704	1730	B-001:9
Hoffeins, George	b. 1726	1751	S-001:1
Hofin, Anna Maria	b.1735		0-001:428
Holzapfel, Errasmus	b.1711	1731	B-011:173
Honig, Nicklas		1739	B-007:259
Horch, Elias	b. 1718	1751	B-011:175
Horn, Georg Friedrich	b. 1731	1750	B-007:260
Hornig, Catherine (m. Bauer)	b. 1715	1751	S-001:3
Hoss, Hans Philip	b. c.1712	1738	B-003:6
Huber, Anna Barbara	b. 1711		S-002:64
Hutig, Johann Andreas	b.c.1736	1751	0-001:596
Hutig, Philip		1748	0-001:522
Ilgenfritz, George	b. 1728		S-002:71
Isler, Johann Georg		1749	S-001:4
Johns, Carl	b. 1692	1704	B-009:283
Joho, Johannes	b. 1701	1738	B-007:280
Jung, Frederick	b.1730/5	1766	0-001:428
Kaufeldt, Nicklas	n.g.	1746	B-002:193
Kerber, Eva	b. 1717	1733	S-002:66
Kerber, Anna Elizabeth	b. 1727		S-002:59
Kern, Jacob		1749	B-007:289
Kieffer, Joh. Caspar	b. 1704	1748	B-002:198
Kiesel, Barbara	b. 1707	1729	S-002:73
Kirsch, Johann Jacob		1744	Y-001:18
Kirscheman, Hans Martin		1752	0-001:436

Klauer, Joh. Phillip	bapt.1711	1723	B-019:11
Klauer, Johannes	bapt.1720	1723	B-019:11
Klee, Joh. Nickel	bapt. 1706	1738	B-002:201
Klee, Hans Nickel	bapt. 1708	1739	B-002:200
Klein, Joh. Heinrich	b.1731	1737	0-001:646
Klein, Joh. Ludwig	b. c.1696	1742	B-002:204
Klein, Philip	b. 1740	1760	A-001:48
Klein, Casper		c.1747	S-002:79
Kleindienst, Catherine	b. 1729	1752	S-001:4
Kleindienst, Christina		by 1759	S-001:1
Kleindienst, David	b.c1734	1749	0-001:614
Klemer, Ludwig		c.1747	S-002:88
Klemmer, Joh. Hennrich	b. 1688	1730	B-001:11
Kling, Georg Anthon	b. 1723	1754	A-001:18
Klund, Jacob		c.1747	S-002:87
Klund, Maria Barbara Holl		c.1747	S-002:87
Knauff, John Henry		c.1747	S-002:81
Knortzer, Maria Catherine	b.1725	1738	B-011:210
Knortzer, Joh. Balthes	1738		B-011:210
Koch, Georg Adam		c.1747	S-002:85
Konig, Abraham	1751		B-007:309
Koppenhoefer, Anna Catharine	b. 1717	1732	B-009:290
Krafft, Hans Georg	b. 1726	1751	B-011:219
Krafft, (Joh.) Valentine	n.g.	1742	B-002:213
Kramer, Juliana	b. 1712		S-002:57
Kramer, Hans Adam		1721	B-001:12
Kreutz, John Henry		c.1747	S-002:78
Kummel, Jacob	b. 1705	1751	B-005:18
Kuntz, Catherine	b. 1720	1726	S-002:53
Kuntz, Georg		1732	B-007:318
Kunz, Adam		c.1747	S-002:89
Kutzmuller, Martin		c.1747	S-002:90
Landis, Christian	b. c1710	1736	0-001:351
Lang, Johann Georg	b. 1718	1749	B-011:229
Lanius, Jacob	b. 1708		S-002:57
Lanius, Jacob	b. 1708	1731	B-001:13
Lau, David	b. 1727	by 1749	B-007:328
Lau, Joh. Peter		by 1749	B-007:328
Lauer, Johann Christ.	b. 1728	1753	B-012:135

Lauer, Matthias	b. 1740	1753	B-012:135
Lauer, Johann heinrich	b. 1735	1753	B-012:135
Laumann, Georg Bernhard	b. 1710	1738	B-011:232
Lehman, Johannes	b. 1700	1727	B-003:10
Lehmer, Hannes		1749	A-001:18
Leib, Johannes	b. 1696	1727	B-011:236
Leichti, John Peter		1738	S-001:3
Leiss, Johann Peter		1749	B-012:137
Lohrey, John Michael	b. 1733	1749	B-009:290
Lorsch, J. Jacob		1752	0-001:516
Low, Conrad		1732	B-007:349
Low, Joh. Christman		1732	B-007:347
Luckebach, Johann Gerhard		1749	B-012:146
Macholdt, Joh. Nicolaus	n.g.	1749	B-002:230
Macholdt, Joh. Nicolaus	n.g.	1749	B-007:351
Mack, Rosina	n.g.		P-001:26
Mack, Rosina	b. 1705		S-002:72
Mang, (Joh.) Gotfried	bapt. 1716	1739	B-002:232
Mattheis, Catharine		1739	B-009:287
May, Johannes	1765		0-001:116
Mayer, Anna	1727		P-001:25
Meyer, Jacob	b. 1710	1753	S-002:30
Meyer, Nicholas	b. 1715	1737	0-001:50
Meyerhoffer, Vincenz Philip		by 1820	S-002:25
Miller, Rev. John Constantine	b. 1762		S-002:48
Mitzel, Michael	b.1736	1771	0-001:450
Moor, Cathertine Mattheis		1739	S-001:4
Moosbrugger, Jacob		by 1856	S-002:26
Mueller, Anna Dorothea	b. 1725		B-009:21
Muller, Anna Dorothea	b.1725		0-001:432
Muller, Franz Jacob	b. 1719		S-002:51
Muller, Hans Adam	b. 1700	1727	B-011:264
Nass, Mathias, Sr.	b. 1673	1731	B-007:375
Nass, Mathias, Jr.	b. c.1704	1731	B-007:375
Nebinger, Andreas	b.1720		0-001:454
Nunnemacher, Abraham	b. 1716	1749	B-007:382
Ohler, Johann Wilheklm		1737	B-001:14
Ottinger, Jacob	b. 1716	1738	B-011:276
Peitzel, John	b. 1712	c.1737	S-002:34

Name	Birth	Year	Reference
Peter, Anna Maria		1727	P-001:27
Pfaff, Peter	b. 1727	1749	S-002:65
Pfarr, Johan Jkacob		1738	B-001:14
Pfefferman, Anthony	b.1721	1730s	0-001:396
Pfluger, Hans Georg	b.c1706	1731	0-001:56
Raus, Lucas	b. 1723		A-001:17
Rebmann, Anna Maria	b. 1715	by 1740	B-007:399
Reichman, Jacob		by 1760	S-001:1
Reiff, Hans Jacob		1739	B-007:402
Reissinger, Hans Martin	b. 1722	1737	B-011:286
Reiter, Susanna	b. 1704		S-002:58
Resser, Anna Maria	b. 1683		B-009:284
Reuel, William. See Riel, William.			
Rhein, John Martin	b. 1718	1738	S-001:2
Riel, William	b. 1705	1742	S-002:63
Rodenburger, Regina Margaret	b. 1711	1743	S-001:4
Roemer, Frederick			S-002:60
Roemer, Johann Frederick	b.1715	1741	0-001:432
Rohrbach, Christian	n.g.	1739	B-002:274
Roser, Adam		1753	0-001:32
Roth, Rev. John	b. 1726		S-002:28
Rothrock, Philip	b. 1713	1733	S-002:53
Rudisile, Andreas	b. 1717	1749	B-011:302
Rudisile, Joh. Jacob	b. 1706	1729	B-011:303
Rudisile, Joh. Jacob		1752	B-011:303
Rudisille, Philip	b. 1697	1727	Y-001:9
Rummel, Jacob	b. 1726	1749	S-001:2
Rupp, Jacob	b. 1731	1749	B-011:307
Ruppert, John Adam		1731	B-011:308
Sarbach, Jacob	b. 1721	1742	B-011:310
Schaer, Anna Barbara		by 1759	S-001:1
Schaffer, Joh. David	bap. 1713	1739	B-007:425
Schank, Elizabeth. See Hoeneisen, Elizabeth.			
Schank, Joseph	b. 1718		S-002:74
Schenck, Andrew	b. 1709	1732	B-009:289
Scherrer, Joh. Augustus	b. 1711	1730	B-003:30
Scheubele, Catherine	b. 1717	1736	S-002:52
Schiehl, Joh. Nicholas	n.g.	1739	B-002:281
Schiele, Jerg Leonhard		1747	B-011:318

Schindeldecker, Joh. Jacob	b. 1679	1737	B-002:283
Schlatter, Andreas		1732	B-011:318
Schlatter, Elizabeth	b. 1723		S-002:40
Schlepi, Adam	b. 1695	1741	B-007:432
Schmidt, Anna Catherine	b. 1722		S-001:2
Schmidt, Maria Elizabeth	b. 1707	1742	S-002:62
Schmidt, Mary Elizabeth	b. 1728	1754	B-009:284
Schnazler, Magdalena	b. 1723		S-002:39
Schneidmann, Sebastian		1749	B-005:25
Schnep, Lorentz	bap. 1711	1733	B-007:451
Schotter, Hend'k	b. 1721	1743	B-001:21
Schotter, Valentine	b. 1698	1743	B-001:21
Schreiber, Ulrich Kaser		c.1747	S-002:84
Schreiber, Andreas		c.1747	S-002:84
Schreyer, Christian		by 1727	B-001:15
Schreyer, Nicolaus		c.1747	S-002:83
Schreyer, John		c.1747	S-002:82
Schuler, Maria Catharina	b. 1724		S-002-46
Schultz, Catherine Kraemer		1731	B-001:4
Schultz, Johannes	b. 1707	1742	B-001:19
Schultz, John Martin	b. 1694	1731	S-001:4
Schultz, Martin	b. 1695	1731	B-001:20
Schultz, Valentin	n.g.	1738	B-002:298
Schumacher, Johannes	b.1731	1754	0-001:244
Schumacher, John	b. 1731		S-002-36
Schumacher, John	b. 1731		B-009:12
Schutz, Frederick	b.c1710	1732	B-011:332
Schwab, Johann George		1727	Y-001:10
Schwab, Johann Georg		1727	P-001:31
Schwartzbach, Johann Adam	b. 1706	1749	B-005:26
Schwinck, Salome		1749	S-001:2
Schwing, Salome	b.1722	1749	S-002:31
Seib, Juliana	b. 1720		S-002:55
Seib, Juliana	b.1720	1732	B-011:339
Seiffert, Joh. Adam	b. 1723	1749	B-011:340
Seiler, Ulrich, Sr.		1738	0-001:414
Seitz, Johann Joseph	1749		0-001:528
Shederon, Abraham	b. 1730	1751	S-001:2
Sohn, John George	b. 1694		S-001:3

Sommer, Michael	b. 1729	1754	S-001:4
Spahr, Johannes	b. 1703	1742	0-001:83
Spengler, Balthasar	b. 1706	1732	B-011:349
Spengler, Baltzer	b. 1708	1732	Y-001:12
Spengler, Bernhard	bapt.1719	1727	B-011:351
Spengler, Caspar		1727	Y-001:7
Spiess, Johann Ludwig	b. 1713	1749	B-012:204
Spittler, Barbara	b. 1726	1736	S-002:33
Stambach, Jacob	b. 1719	1739	B-007:477
Stauffer, Widow Barbara	b. 1707	1729	B-009:23
Stein, Johann Friedrich		by 1783	S-002:24
Stentz, Henry	b. 1694		S-001:2
Stettler, Christian		1738	B-007:588
Strubig, John Jacob	b. 1726		S-002:38
Struebig, John Jacob. See Strubig, John Jacob			
Tanneberg, David	b. 1728	1749	S-002:41
Thomas, Catharine	b. 1738	1739	S-002:70
Traub, Paul	b. 1725	1749	B-005:27
Triddel, Dorothy			B-009:281
Tritt(e), Hans Peter	b. 1715	1739	B-007:502
Tritten, Anna (m. Wampler)	b. 1686	1747	S-001:1
Tschop, Jacob	b. 1725		S-002:44
Tschudi, Magdalena	b. 1730		S-002:75
Vogler, Nicklas		1741	B-007:511
Votrin, John Daniel	b. 1711	1739	B-009:21
Votring, Johannes Daniel		1739	B-007:514
Wacker, Bernhart	bapt. 1731	1749	B-002:324
Wampffler, Joh. Christian	bapt. 1718	1748	B-007:522
Wampler, Christian		1747	S-001:1
Weigel, John Martin	b. 1703	1730	S-001:2
Weigel, Martin		1732	B-011:387
Weismuller, Anna Maria	b. 1719		B-009:3
Weller, George	b. 1709		S-002:66
Weller, Maria Magdalena		1737	B-009:16
Welsch, Joh. Jacob	bapt. 1716	1737	B-002:331
Welsch, Joh. Wilhelm	bapt. 1712	1737	B-002:332
Welschans, Abraham	bapt. 1713	1739	B-007:533
Welschans, Jacob	bapt. 1719	1741	B-007:534
Welschans, Joseph	bapt. 1714	1739	B-007:535

Weltzhoffer, Jacob		1731	B-001:22
Wenner, Margaret	b. 1732	1746	B-009:281
Wenner, Michael		1746	S-001:2
Werle, Maria	b. 1704		S-002:56
Weygand, Frederick	b. 1712		S-001:3
Wilcke, Rudolf		1727	P-001:35
Wilcke, Rudolf	b. c.1690	1727	Y-001:8
Will, George	bapt. 1747		S-002:77
Williart, Catharina		1746	B-009:18
Winemiller, Johann H.		1754	0-001:332
Winterbauer, Sebastian		1737	B-011:399
Wolf, Jacob	bapt. 1694	1737	B-002:338
Wollet, Frederick	b. 1770		S-002:49
Wodering, Johannes. See Votring, Johannes.			
Wurts, Hans Martin		1750	0-001:366
Zauck, Joh. Heinrich	1732		B-011:408
Ziegler, Johann George		1727	P-001:35
Ziegler, John George	b. 1697	1727	Y-001:8
Ziegler, Philip	b. 1677	1727	Y-001:7
Ziegler, Philip	b. 1677	1727	B-011:421
Ziegler, Philip George	1727		P-001:35
Zimmer, Mary Eliz. Schmidt	b. 1728	1754	S-001:3
Zimmerman, Johann Christ	b. 1727	1751	B-012:220
Zumwald, Andreas	b. c.1698	1737	B-002:3459

Chapter 13
OTHER COURT RECORDS

Abstracts from Common Pleas Docket, York county, Pennsylvania, April Term 1757 Through July Term 1761. Abstracted and Compiled by David P. Hively. (1991). SCPGS Spec. Pub. # 46.

Commissioners Accounts, 1846, CC 3 (3) 24, (4) 19; 4 (1) 16, (2) 20, (3) 40, (4) 43; 5 (2) 44, (3) 43

Proprietary Rights. PA (3) III.

Record Book of Overseers of the Poor, Borough of York, Pennsylvania, 1799-1804. (April 1984). SCPGS Spec. Pub. # 27.

Surviving Early Records of York County, PA - An Alphabetical Listing of All Names Found in York County Court of Quarter Sessions Docket Books, 1749-1754, and True Copies of 5 Known "Quarter Sessions" Documents, 1749-1754, Not Recorded (Abstracted in the Docket Books (1980). SCPGS Spec. Pub. # 12.

Surviving Early Records of York County, PA - Abstracts of All Known Existing Documents Submitted to York County Court of Quarter Sessions, 1749-1765 (1981). SCPGS Spec. Pub. # 14.

Chapter 14
PASSENGER LISTS AND IMMIGRATION RECORDS

The Alsace Emigration Book, Volume I. By Cornelia Schrader. Apollo, PA: Closson Press.

Auswanderungen aus Rheinpfalz und Saarland im 18. Jahrhundert. By Warner Hacker. HSYC.

A Century of Emigration from Affoltern am Albis, Canton Zurich, Switzerland. By Annette K. Burgert. Worthington, OH: AKB Publications, 1984.

Colonial Pennsylvania Immigrants from Frensheim in the Palatinate. Myerstown, PA: AKB Publications, 1989.

Early Pennsylvania Pioneers from Mutterstadt in the Palatinate. By Annette K. Burgert. Worthington, OH: AKB Publications, 1983.

Eighteenth and Nineteenth Century Emigrants from Lachen-Speyerdorf in the Palatinate. By Annette K. Burgert. AKB Publications, 1989.

Eighteenth Century Emigrants from German Speaking Land to North America. Vol. I: The Northern Kraichgau. By Annette K. Burgert. Breinigsville: The Pennsylvania German Society, 1983.

Eighteenth Century Emigrants. Volume II. The Western Palatinate. By Annette K. Burgert. Birdsboro: Pennsylvania German Society, 1985 Annual Volume.

Eighteenth Century Pennsylvania Emigrants from Hassloch and Bohl in the Palatinate. By Annette K. Burgert. Worthington, OH: AKB Publications, 1983.

Eighteenth Century Emigrants from the Northern Alsace to America. By Annette K. Burgert. Camden, ME: Picton Press, 1992.

Eighteenth Century Emigrants from Pfungstadt, Hessen-Darmstadt to Pennsylvania. By Annette K. Burgert. Myerstown: AKB Publications, 1995.

Emigrants from Baden and the Briesgau. By Werner Hacker. Reviewed in ONTG 11 (3) 2-3.

Emigrants from Eppingen to America in the 18th and 19th Centuries. By Annette K. Burgert. Myerstown, PA: AKB Publications, 1987.

The Emigration from Nassau-Dillenberg to America in the Eighteenth Century; The Conduct of the Government Towards It and the Ensuing Fates of the Emigrants. By Adolf Gerber. Trans. by Lissy L. Weirich. 1984.

Germans to America, 1850-. This series contains passenger arrivals from German ports, and when it is finished, will include German arrivals up to 1900.

The Hochstadt Origins of Some of the Early Settlers of Host Church, Berks County, Pennsylvania. By Annette K. Burgert. Worthington, OH: AKB Publications, 1983.

Kurpfaelzische Auswanderer vom Unteren Neckar: Rechtrheinische Gebiete der Kurpfals. By Warner Hacker. Donated to HSYC.

Pennsylvania German Pioneers: A Publication of the Original Lists of Arrivals in the Port of Philadelphia from 1727 to 1808. By Ralph Beaver Strassburger. Edited by William John Hinke. 3 vols. Norristown: The Pennsylvania German Society, 1934.

Pennsylvania Pioneers from Wolfersweiler Parish, Saarland, Germany. By Annette K. Burgert. Worthington, OH: AKB Publications, 1983

Rhineland Emigrants. Ed. by Don Yoder. Baltimore: Genealogical Publishing Co., 1985

Westerwald to America. By Annette K. Burgert, and Henry Jones. Camden, ME: Picton Press. Reviewed in ONTG 15 (4) 2.

York County Pioneers from Friedelsheim and Gonnheim in the Palatinate. By Annette K. Burgert. 1984.

Chapter 15
PERIODICALS AND OTHER PUBLICATIONS

SPECIAL PUBLICATIONS OF THE
SOUTH CENTRAL PENNSYLVANIA GENEALOGICAL SOCIETY

(The following is a list of titles.

\# 1 - Notarial Docket of George Caruthers, 1810-1812 (1977).

\# 2 - Private Records of Rev. George Jacob Martz, 1869-1878.

\# 3 - Alphabetical Listing...of Information on ... Tombstones of Zion United Methodist Church, Freeland, MD.

\# 4 - Gravemarkers and Tombstones in Bermudian Church of the Brethren, Washington Township. (1976).

\# 5 - Assessed Inhabitants of York County..., For Townships now in York County, 1762, Book 1 (1978).

\# 6 - Assessed Inhabitants of York County..., For Townships now in Adams County, 1762, Book 2 (1978).

\# 7 - Sundry Genealogical Materials..., Book I. 1. Introduction. 2. Notes on Andrew Armstrong, 1782. 3. Admin. Bond of John Miller, with a List of Soldiers Killed on the Sullivan Expedition. 4 and 5 - From the Parish Telephone (Pub. by Rev. Adam Stump); obituaries of Elmer Ellsworth Brooks (1901) and Sarah Anne Eyster (1907). 6. Plot map and ... Gravestones of Chestnut Grove Presbyterian Church, Codorus Twp.

\# 8 - Surviving Early Records of York County, PA - Collector's Warrants: County Tax of 1762 (for '63), Hellam Twp.; County Tax of 1767 (for '68): Cumberland and Newberry (Fragment) Twp.; Provincial Tax of 1767 (for '68): Germany, Hamiltonban and Newberry Twp. (1979).

\# 9 - Surviving Early Records of York County, PA - Constable's Returns: Newberry Twp., 1765; Paradise Twp., 1769; York Twp., 1769 (1979).

\# 10 - Gravemarkers and Tombstones in Altland's Meeting House, Paradise Township, (1980).

\# 11 - Alphabetical list of Taxables on Collector's Warrants, for 1771 (1980).

\# 12 - - Surviving Early Records of York County, PA - An Alphabetical Listing of All Names Found in York County Court of Quarter Sessions Docket Books, 1749-1754, and True Copies of 5 Known "Quarter Sessions" Documents, 1749-01754, Not Recorded (Abstracted in the Docket Books (1980).

\# 13 - Some Records of Associate Reformed Church at Airville, Lower Chanceford Township (1981).

\# 14 - Surviving Early Records of York County, PA - Abstracts of All Known Existing Documents Submitted to York County Court of Quarter Sessions, 1749-1765 (1981).

\# 15 - An Alphabetical Listing of Heads of Households (with age and sex of all members of households) Included in the 1800 Census of York County, PA (Book I (of Two) - Surnames A-L (1981).

\# 16 - Same. Book II (of Two) - Surnames M-Z (1981).

\# 17 - Records of the Reformed Church in Shippensburg, PA, Cumberland County, 1770-1842; Includes Tombstone Inscriptions.

\# 18 - An Alphabetical Listing of Heads of Households (with age and sex of all members of households) Included in the 1800 Census of Adams County, PA (1982).

\# 19 - Record of Apprentices, 1860-1911 (1982).

20 - Genealogical Excerpts from Will Book A, 1749-1762 (1982).

21 - Death Registration Book, 1852-1855 (1983).

22 - Birth Registration Book, 1852-1855 (1983).

23 - They Went West Or More Precisely, Information Found in Newspapers of Astoria, Fulton County, IL, 1886-1917, and Crawford County, OH, 1891-1938, Pertaining to Descendants of Families from South Central Pennsylvania and Adjacent Areas (July 1983).

24 - Abstract of Pennsylvania Records of Naturalizations, 1695-1773, Found in *Colonial Records (Minutes of the Provincial Council)*, Volumes 1, 2, 3, 4, 9, & 10; *The Statutes at Large of Pennsylvania,* Volumes II, III, IV, V, VI, VII & VIII; *Pennsylvania Archives,* Series 1, Volumes 1, 2, 3, & 4. (Oct. 1983).

25 - Sundry Genealogical Materials. Book II. 1. Abstracts of Six Unprobated Wills. 2. Marriages Performed by Rev. John Jacob Strine. 3. Abstracts from Case of Charles Cecil's [Calvert?] Claims to Lands in York County, 1681-1764. 4. Early Interments in Ziegler's Church Cemetery, 1772-1810, and in Friedensaal's Church Cemetery, 1759-1810.

26 - Sundry Genealogical Materials ... , Book III. 1. York County, PA, "Delinquent" Taxables, 1758-1768. 2. Jacob Michael's Unprobated Will (1769, York Twp., York County, PA). Abstract of the Journals of Jacob C. Schultz (Time Keeper for the Northern Central Railway Co., of MD and PA, 1856-1876). 4. The 1863 Letter of George W. Finlaw (pertains to Civil War Incident in York County, PA. (Feb. 1984).

27 - Record Book of Overseers of the Poor, Borough of York, Pennsylvania, 1799-1804. (April 1984).

28 - Marriage Registration Book, 1852-1855 (1984).

29 - An Alphabetical Listing of Heads of Households ... Included in the 1800 Federal Census of Cumberland Co, PA (1984-1985).

30 - Notarial Docket of John Morris, Esq., of the Borough of York, York County, 1792-1809 (1985).

31 - Sundry Genealogical Materials..., Book IV. 1. Abstracts of Marriages and Apprenticeships in the Docket Books of Charles Brandon, JP, Middletown, Dauphin County 2. Unpublished Baptisms Performed by John Casper Stoever. 3. Docket book of John Reeser of Conewago Twp., 1839-1852. 4. Index of Recorded Wills 1749-1875, for Fairview Twp., Newberry Twp., and Lewisberry Boro, York County.

32 - Genealogical Abstracts of Adams County, Pennsylvania, Birth, Marriage, and Death Registrations, 1852-1855 (1986).

33 - An Abstract of the 1865 York County, Pennsylvania, Assessors Military Roll (1986-1987).

34 - Sundry Genealogical Materials..., Book V. 1. Comparative Monetary Values of Early Pennsylvania. 2. Rev. Thomas Barton, Itinerant Missionary of the Church of England, 1755-1759, in York and Cumberland County, PA (Part 1 - Biographical Introduction. Part 2 - Marriages Performed, 1755-1759. Part 3 - Letter from Thomas Barton, York in Pennsylvania, To The Lord Bishop of Oxford, 12 March 1757). 3. Warrington (Friends) Meeting House Cemetery, Warrington Township...: Entries in the Grave Diggers Account Book, 1822-1847, Compared with Inscriptions on Tombstones, 1822-1847, Existing in 1934. 4. Pipe Creek (Friends) Meeting House Cemetery, Carroll County, MD: Graves Identified in the 1882 *History of Western Maryland,* by Scharf, compared with Inscriptions on Tombstones Existing in 1934. 5. Surname Index. (1987)

35 - "Poor" Children Named on the Tax Lists, 1811-1844, York County, Pennsylvania. (1987-1988).

36 - Family Records From Bibles, Volume 1 (1988).

37 - Sundry Genealogical Materials..., Book VI. 1. 1814 Petition for Public Clock in York Borough. 2. List of Subscribers for German Bible, Published in 1819, Lancaster, Pennsylvania. 3. Genealogical Abstracts of Eighteenth Century Original and Mostly Unpublished Deeds Pertaining to Adams County, Pennsylvania. Surname Index (1988).

38 - York County, Pennsylvania, Land Appraisement Certificates Issued by the County Commissioners, 1835-1850 (1988).

39 - The GAR: Its Organization and the Men of Post # 37 (1988-1989).

40 - Abstracts of Unrecorded Wills of York County, Pennsylvania (1989).

41 - Abstracts and Identifications of Entries Giving European Origins in Church Records of South Central Pennsylvania and Adjacent Areas. Book I (1990).

42 - The Journal of James L. Purdy: Hopewell Township, York County, Pennsylvania and Mansfield, Richland County, Ohio... (1990).

43 - Gone to Ohio... Ashland,. Brown, Columbiana, Harrison, Jefferson and Richland Counties, From Pennsylvania Counties: Adams, Cumberland, Dauphin, Franklin, Lancaster and York. Compiled by Gloria L. Aughenbaugh (1990).

44 - Alphabetized, Cross References and Coded Indexes to the 1876 Atlas of York County, Pennsylvania, in Two Volumes. Volume 1: Individual Name Index. Compiled and Edited by Patricia R. Gross, Leonard A. Heilman and Samuel J. Saylor (1991).

45 - Alphabetized, Cross References and Coded Indexes to the 1876 Atlas of York County, Pennsylvania, in Two Volumes. Volume 2: Subject Index. Compiled and Edited by Patricia R. Gross, Leonard A. Heilman and Samuel J. Saylor (1991).

46 - Abstracts from Common Pleas Docket, York County, Pennsylvania, April Term 1757 Through July Term 1761. Abstracted and Compiled by David P. Hively. (1991).

47 - Notes and Documents Concerning the Manorial History of the Town of York, York County, Pennsylvania. Compiled by Henry James Young (1992).

48 - Index of Tavern Licenses Allowed by York County, Pennsylvania: 1749-1806. Comp. by John R. McGrew (1992).

49 - An Everyname Index to Orphans' Court book A (1749-1762) Plus Introductory text. Comp. by Patricia A. Gross and Leonard A. Heilman. (1992).

50 - Tombstone Inscriptions from St. Mary's Cemetery (Old Section) Silver Run, Maryland. Compiled by Wendy Bish and Larry Bolin. (1992).

51 - Index to the Taxables of Hanover and Heidelberg Township, York County, Pennsylvania, 1750-1817. By John R. McGrew. 1993).

52 - Sundry Genealogical Materials..., Book VII. 1. Welsh Immigrant Information from the *Delta Herald and Times*. 2. Slate Ridge Cemetery, Peach Bottom Twp., Tombstone Inscriptions. 3. Slateville Presbyterian Cemetery, Peach Bottom Twp., Tombstone Inscriptions. 4. Examples of Genealogical Information found in Religious Publications. 5. Almshouse Births, 1864-1874. 6. Shiloh Cemetery, West Manchester Twp., Record of Burials, 1930-1975. 7. Petition to Divide Chanceford Twp., 1805. 8. List of Constables, York County, 1785. 9. Notes on the Confusing of Given Names Among the Pennsylvania Germans.

53 - Gone to Ohio ... Champaign, Crawford and Wood Counties From Pennsylvania Counties: Adams, Cumberland, Dauphin, Franklin, Lancaster and York. Comp. by Gloria L. Aughenbaugh. (1993).

Ancestral Charts of Members of the SCPGS

There are two volumes, with a third volume containing an every name index to both volumes.

Codorus Chronicles

This quarterly is published by Southwest Pennsylvania Genealogical Services. It contains abstracts of York County source materials (will abstracts, quarter session records, naturalizations, tax lists, etc.) queries, Each issue contains a surname index.

Our Name's the Game

This is the periodical of the South Central Pennsylvania Genealogical Society. It contains news of the society, book reviews and queries; began publication with Vol. 1 - , 1975.

Chapter 16
PROBATE RECORDS

Abstracts of Adams County Pennsylvania Wills, 1800-1826. By Kevin L. Greenholt. Westminster: Family Line, 1988.

Abstracts of Unrecorded Wills of York County, Pennsylvania (1989). SCPGS Spec. Pub. # 40.

Abstract of Wills Probated in Lancaster and York Counties Between 1745 and 1800. By Randy J. Miller. Gettysburg: Adams County Historical Society. Reviewed in ONTG 20 (6) 2.

Abstracts of York County, Pennsylvania, Wills, 1749-1819. Westminster: Family Line Publications, 1995. (Based on the works of volunteers of the Historical Society of Pennsylvania in the early 1900s; should be used with caution as the original abstracts were not entirely error-free).

Admin. Abstracts Book AA, 1794, CC 1 (1) 9, (2) 9, (3) 9, (4) 9; 1796-1797, CC 2 (2) 9; 1796, 2 (3) 9; 1796-98, 2 (4) 9; 1798, 3 (1) 5, (3) 5; 1798-1799, 3 (4) 5; 1799, 4 (1) 5, (2) 5, (3) 5; 1799-1800, (4) 5; 1800, 5 (2) 5, (3) 5, (4) 5; 1800-1801, (5) 5; 1801, 6 (1) 5; 1796-1803, 6 (2) 5; 1794-1813, 6 (3) 5.

Admin. Abstracts Book BB. 1801-1802, CC 6 (3) 5.

Admin. Abstracts Book TT, 1860, CC 1 (1) 18, (2) 11, (3) 11, (4) 11; 1861, CC 2 (2) 11, 2 (3) 11; 1861-1862, 2 (4) 11; 1862, 3 (1) 6, (3) 6, (4) 6; 4 (1) 6, (2) 6, (3) 6, (4) 6; 1862-1863, 5 (2) 6; 1863, 5 (3) 6, (4) 6, (5) 6; 6 (1) 6, (2) 6, (3) 6.

An Everyname Index to Orphans' Court Book A (1749-1762) Plus Introductory text. Comp. by Patricia A. Gross and Leonard A. Heilman. (1992). SCPGS Spec. Pub. # 49.

Genealogical Excerpts from Will Book A, 1749-1762. South Central Pennsylvania Genealogical Society: Special Publications # 20 1982.

Index to the Probate Inventories of York County, Pennsylvania, 1749-1850. David A. and Brenda L. Paup. Westminster: Family Line Publications, n.d.

"Original Wills, Bonds, Inventories and Accounts in the York County Court House," ONTG 1 (10) Supp.

Orphans Court Abstracts Volume A, 1749-1750, CC 1 (1) 11; 1750, CC 1 (2) 13, (3) 13, (4) 13; 1752, CC 2 (2) 13; 1752-3, 2 (3) 13; 1753, 2 (4) 13; 3 (1) 7; 1753-1754, 3 (3)) 17; 1754, 3 (4) 7; 4 (1) 7, (2) 7; 1754-1755, 4 (3) 7; 1755, 4 (4) 7; 5 (2) 7, (3) 7; 1755-1756, 5 (4) 7; 1756, 5 (5) 7; 6 (1) 7, (2) 7, (3) 7.

Orphans Court Dockets, 1749-1887 (transcripts): GSP.

Orphans Court Records, 1749-1754 (transcripts): GSP.

Will Abstracts, 1749-1820 (transcripts): GSP.

Will Abstracts, Book A, 1758, CC 3 (4) 2.

Will Abstracts Book F, 1782, CC 1 (1) 5, (2) 5, (3) 5, (4) 5; 1783-1784, 2 (2) 5; 1784, CC 2 (3) 5, (4) 5; 3 (1) 3; 1784-1785, 3 (3) 3, (4) 3; 1785, 4 (1) 3, (2) 3,; 1783-1785, 4 (3) 3.

Will Abstracts Book G, 1785, CC 4 (3) 3, (4) 3; 5 (2) 3, (3) 3, (4) 3, (5) 3; 1786, 6 (1) 3, (2) 3, (3) 3.

Will Abstracts Book Q, 1828, CC 1 (1) 7, (2) 7, (3) 7, (4) 7; 1829, CC 2 (2) 7, 2 (3) 7; 1829-1830, 2 (4) 7; 1830, 3 (1) 4, (3) 4, (4) 4; 5 (1) 4; 1830-1831, 4 (2) 4; 1831, 4 (3) 4, (4) 4; 5 (2) 4, (3) 4, (4) 4, (5) 4; 1831-1832, 6 (1) 4; 1832, 6 (2) 4, (3) 4.

Will and Admin. Abstracts, Book A, 1749-1750, CC 1 (1) 3; 1749-1751, CC 1 (2) 3, (3) 3, (4) 3; 1754-1755, CC 2 (2) 3; 1755 2 (3) 3; 1755-156, 2 (4) 3; 1756-1757, 3 (1) 2, (3) 2, (40) 2; 4 (1) 2; 1758, 4 (2) 2, (3) 2; 1759, 4 (4) 2; 5 (2) 2, (3) 2; 1760, 5 (4) 2, (5) 2; 1760-1761, 6 (1) 2; 1761, 6 (2) 2; 1761-1762, 6 (3) 2.

Wills and Administrations, 1749-1858 (transcripts) : GSP.

Chapter 17
TOWNSHIPS

Name	Date formed	Parent Township
Carroll, Twp.	1831	Monaghan and Franklin
Chanceford, Twp.	1745	

While part of Lancaster County it may have been part of Lower Hellam Twp.

Name	Date formed	Parent Township
Codorus, Twp.	1747	
Conewago, Twp.	1818	Dover and Newberry
Dover, Twp.	1747	
East Hopewell, Twp.	1885	Hopewell
East Manchester, Twp.	1887	Manchester
Fairview, Twp.	1803	Newberry
Fawn, Twp.	1745	Lower Hellam
Franklin, Twp.	1809	Monaghan
Heidelberg, Twp.	1750	Manheim
Hellam, Twp.	1739	Original Twp.
Hopewell, Twp.	1767	Shrewsbury
Jackson, Twp.	1857	Paradise
Lower Chanceford, Twp.	1805	Chanceford
Lower Windsor, Twp.	1838	Windsor
Manchester, Twp.	1742	
Manheim, Twp.	1747	
Monaghan, Twp.	1745	Lancaster
Newberry, Twp.*	1742	
North Codorus, Twp.	1838	Codorus
North Hopewell, Twp.	1885	Hopewell
Paradise, Twp.	1747	
Peach Bottom, Twp.	1815	Fawn
Penn, Twp.	1880	Heidelberg
Shrewsbury, Twp.	1742	
Spring Garden, Twp.	1821	Hellam and York
Springettsbury, Twp.	1819	Spring Garden
Springfield, Twp.	1835	Shrewsbury
Warrington, Twp.	1744	
Washington, Twp.	1803	Warrington
West Manchester, Twp.	1799	Manchester
West Manheim, Twp.	1858	Manheim
Windsor, Twp.	1758	Hellam

*Newberry [Township, York County, PA] The Beginning, 1700-1900, mentioned, ONTG 16 (4) 2.

A Genealogy of the Townships of York County

YORK COUNTY 1749

Original Township 1749	Timeline (1800 – 1850 – 1900)	Present Township	Date Erected
Chanceford 1745		Chanceford	1745
	Lower Chanceford 1805?	Lower Chanceford	1805?
Codorus 1747?		Codorus	1747?
	North Codorus 1838	North Codorus	1838
Dover 1745		Dover	1745
	Conewago 1818	Conewago	1818
Newberry 1742		Newberry	1742
	Fairview 1803	Fairview	1803
Fawn 1745		Fawn	1745
	Peach Bottom 1815	Peach Bottom	1815
Hellam 1738?		Hellam	1738?
	Spring Garden 1821	Spring Garden	1821
	Springettsbury 1891	Springettsbury	1891
York 1745	Windsor 1758	Windsor	1758
	Lower Windsor 1838	Lower Windsor	1838
		York	1745
Manchester 1740		Manchester	1740
	West Manchester 1799	West Manchester	1799
	East Manchester 1887	East Manchester	1887
Manheim 1747?		Manheim	1747?
	West Manheim 1858	West Manheim	1858
Heidelberg 1749		Heidelberg	1749
	Penn 1880	Penn	1880
Monaghan 1745		Monaghan	1745
	Carroll 1831	Carroll	1831
	Franklin 1809	Franklin	1809
Paradise 1747		Paradise	1747
Shrewsbury 1742? (Strasburg)	Jackson 1853	Jackson	1853
		Shrewsbury	1742?
	Springfield 1835	Springfield	1835
	Hopewell 1767	Hopewell	1767
	North Hopewell 1885	North Hopewell	1885
	East Hopewell 1885	East Hopewell	1885
Warrington 1744		Warrington	1744
	Washington 1802	Washington	1802
	ADAMS COUNTY 1800	ADAMS COUNTY	1800

By permission of Jonathan R. Stayer

A Genealogy of the Townships of York County

York County was erected from Lancaster by Act of August 19, 1749.

Hellam Township was the Lancaster County township from which most York townsips were formed.

The Susquehanna River has never been a part of York County. It lies in Lancaster County.

Adams County was erected from York on January 22, 1800.

The town of York was laid out for John, Thomas and Richard Penn by Thomas Cookson in 1741.

KEY

————	Original township boundary
– – – –	Present township boundary
··········	Temporary township boundary
————	Approximate boundary of Springettsbury Manor
——→	Direction of township division
<u>Hellam</u>	Original township
←•—•—	Originally extended into Adams County

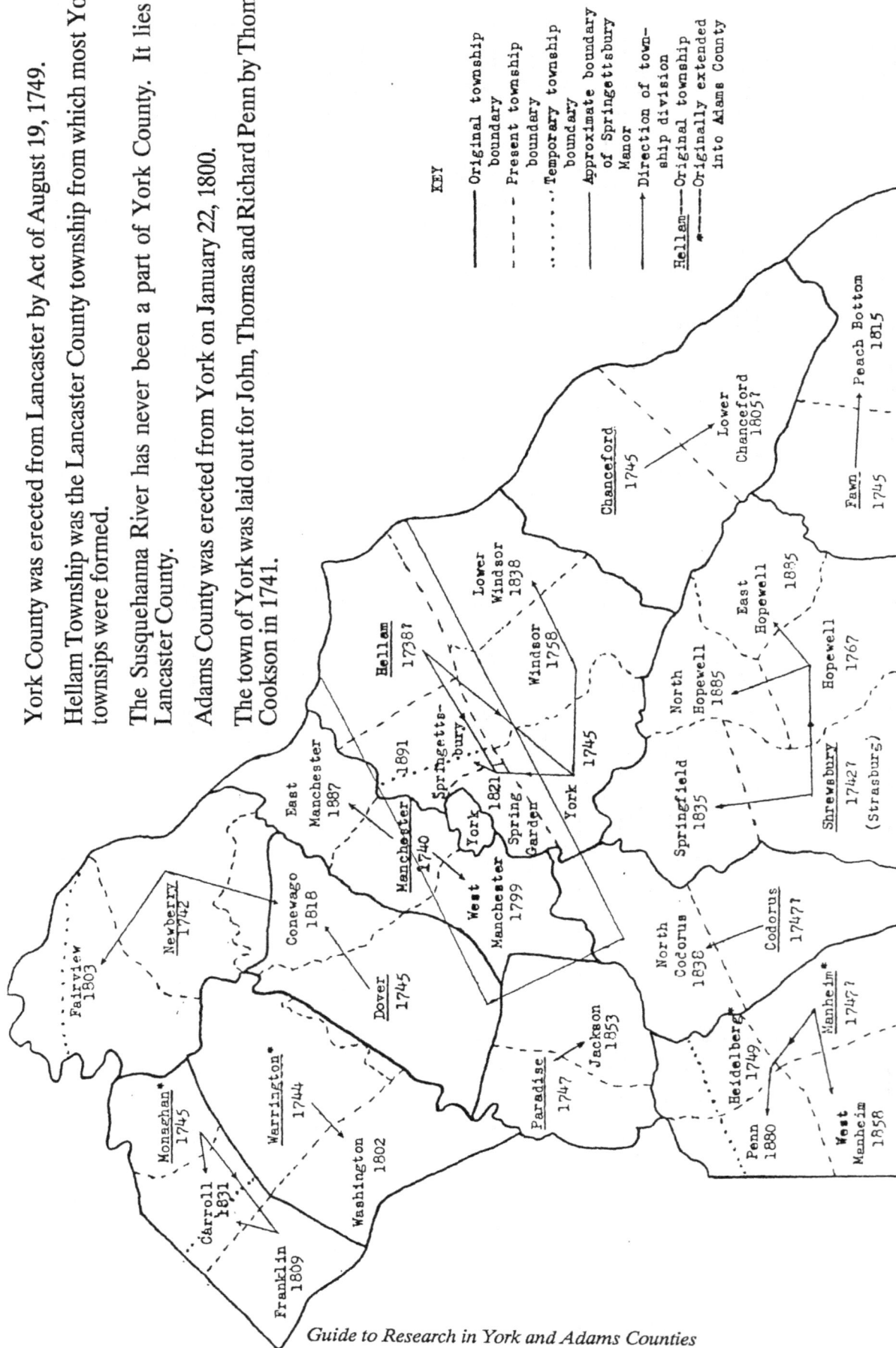

Fairview
1803

Newberry
1742

Conewago
1818

East Manchester
1887

Dover
1745

Manchester
1740

Springetts-
bury 1891

Springetts-
bury

York

Spring
Garden

West
Manchester
1799

Lower
Windsor
1838

Windsor
1758

<u>Hellam</u>
1738?

York
1745

Chanceford
1745

Lower
Chanceford
1805?

North
Hopewell
1885

East
Hopewell
1885

Hopewell
1767

Fawn
1745

Peach Bottom
1815

Monaghan*
1745

Warrington*
1744

Washington
1802

Franklin
1809

Carroll
1831

Paradise
1747

Jackson
1853

North
Codorus
1838

<u>Codorus</u>
1747?

Springfield
1835

<u>Shrewsbury</u>
1742?
(Strasburg)

Heidelberg*
1749

Penn
1880

<u>Manheim</u>
1747?

West
Manheim
1858

Guide to Research in York and Adams Counties

A Genealogy of the Townships of Adams County

Original Township 1749	Date Erected	Genealogy (1800 – 1825 – 1850 – 1875)	Present Township	Date Erected
Berwick	1747		Berwick	1747
		Hamilton 1810	Hamilton	1810
		Oxford 1847	Oxford	1847
Cumberland	1749		Cumberland	1749
		Franklin 1785	Franklin	1785
		Butler 1859	Butler	1859
Menallen	1745		Menallen	1745
Heidelberg*	1749	Conewago 1801	Conewago	1801
Manheim*	1747?	Union 1841	Union	1841
Germany	1749?		Germany	1749?
Mount Pleasant	1749		Mount Pleasant	1749
Hamiltonban	1749		Hamiltonban	1749
		Liberty 1801	Liberty	1801
		Freedom 1838	Freedom	1838
		Highland 1863	Highland	1863
Huntington	1745		Huntington	1745
Monaghan*	1745	Latimore 1807	Latimore	1807
Warrington*	1744			
Mount Joy	1749		Mount Joy	1749
Reading	1746		Reading	1746
Straban	1746		Straban	1746
Tyrone	1745		Tyrone	1745
			YORK COUNTY	1749

*Township of York County

By permission of Jonathan R. Stayer

A Genealogy of the Townships of Adams County

Adams County was erected from York on January 22, 1800. The original townships of Adams County were townships of York until the division of the two counties. Mongahan, Warrington, Heidelberg and Manheim were townships of York County which contributed land to Adams County.

KEY:

——————— Original township boundary

- - - - - Present township boundary

——————— Approximate boundary of the Manor of Maske

——————→ Direction of township division

Tyrone——— Original township

*———— Originally extended into York County

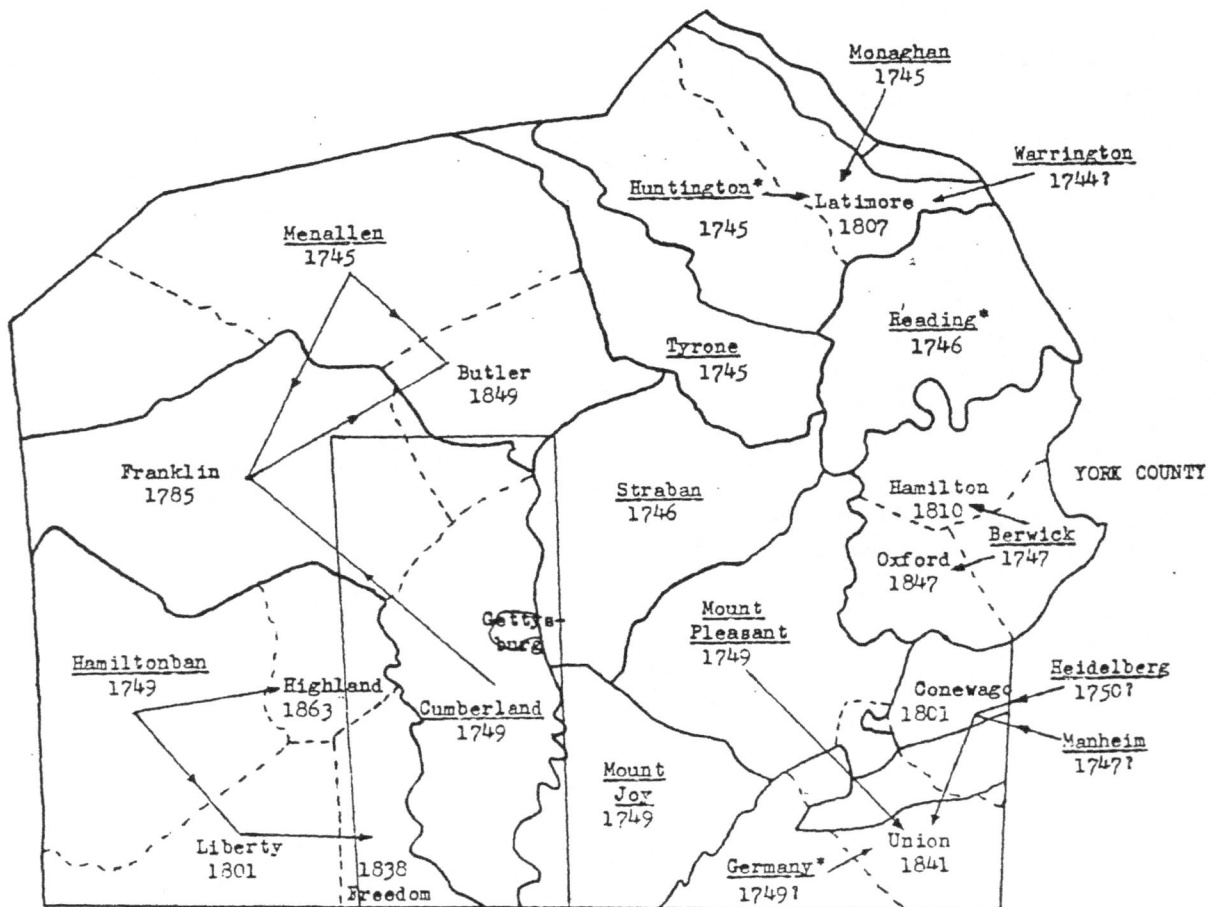

By permission of Jonathan R. Stayer

Chapter 18
VITAL RECORDS

Birth and death certificates after 1906 can be obtained from the Pennsylvania Department of Health, Division of Vital Records, New Castle, PA. Death certificates cost $3.00. Birth certificates cost $4.00.

Almshouse Births, 1864-1874. (SCPGS Spec. Pub. # 52).

Birth Register, Book 1, 1893, CC 5 (4) 23, (5) 23; 6 (1) 27, (2) 27, (3) 31.

Birth Registration Book, 1852-1855, SCPGS Spec. Pub. # 22 (1983).

Death Register, Book 1, 1893, CC 5 (4) 24, (5) 24; 6 (1) 28, (2) 28, (3) 32.

Death Registration Book, 1852-1855 (SCPGS Spec. Pub. # 21, 1983). Family Records From Bibles, Volume 1 (SCPGS Spec. Pub. # 36, 1988).

Genealogical Abstracts of Adams County, Pennsylvania, Birth, Marriage, and Death Registrations, 1852-1855 (SCPGS Spec. Pub. # 32, 1986).

Genealogical Abstracts of York County Death Registration Book, 1852-1855 (transcripts): GSP.

Marriage Licenses, Book A, 1885, CC 4 (1) 12, (2) 17, (3) 39, (4) 15; 5 (2) 25; 1885-1886, 5 (3) 25, (4) 25, (5) 25; 6 (1) 29, (2) 29, (3) 32.

Marriage Registration Book, 1852-1855 (SCPGS Spec. Pub. # 28, 1984).

York County (PA) Residents Married in Maryland: Volume I -- Harford County, Books 1-4, 1865-1930. By Samuel J. Saylor. Reviewed in ONTG 15 (5) 2-3.

York County (PA) Residents Married in Maryland: Volume II -Baltimore County, 1898-1931. By Samuel J. Saylor. Reviewed in ONTG 15 (?) 1.

Chapter 19
VISITING YORK AND ADAMS COUNTIES

Included here are suggestions of places to stay, places to eat, and places to visit (in case the researcher is accompanied by friends and family who do not want to spend their time doing research). The author cannot recommend one place over another: names and addresses are supplied for the researcher to make a decision. Much of the information in this section has been culled from brochures distributed by the businesses listed below.

Places to Stay in York

The Christopher Kolter House Bed and Breakfast, 403 North Main Street, Shrewsbury, PA, 17361, is in a restored house dating from 1876. Phone (717)-235-5528.

The Yorktowne Hotel, 48 East Market St., York, PA 17401. Phone (717)-848-1111, or 1-800-233-9324. Fax: (717)-854-7678. The hotel, a restored National Historic Landmark, is in the heart of town, and is within walking distance of the Historical Society, the Court House, and the Martin Library.

There are also numerous motels along US Rt. 30 in the York area.

Places to Stay in Gettysburg

Heritage Motor Lodge is located in the heart of the historical area, close to shops, museums, the Bus Tour Center, and also close to four restaurants. Phone (717)-334-9281. AM-VISA and MASTER CHG. accepted. AAA Recommended.

Holiday Inn is located on Baltimore Avenue, next to the Jennie Wade House.

Places to Eat in York

"Autographs," is a coffee shop at the Yorktowne Hotel.

The Central Market, about 3 blocks west of the Historical Society, between Philadelphia St., Beavor St. and Cherry Lane.

"Uncle's," is on Duke St., north of Market. It is open Monday through Friday for breakfast and lunch, located about 2 blocks west of the Historical Society.

Places to Eat in Gettysburg

The Tavern in the Village, located on Baltimore St., Gettysburg; offers a variety of meals and beverages. Phone (717)-334-5648

General Pickett's Buffet on Steinwehr Avenue is in the same building as the Gettysburg Battle Theatre.

Places to Visit (or Shop) in York County

For additional information write the York County Convention & Visitors' Bureau, 1 Market Way East, P. O. Box 1229, York, PA 17405, or Phone (717)-848-4000, or 1-800-673-2429.

Farmer's Daughter, a large craft and garden center, is at 351 West Railroad Avenue, Route 851, west of Shrewsbury. it is open all year, but hours are seasonal. Phone (717)-235-3309.

The Fire Museum of York County, Inc., at 757 West Market St., York, PA 17404, contains equipment and displays York County's Fire Companies, some dating back to colonial times. Open on Saturdays and some Sundays, April through November. Phone (717)-843-0464 for further details.

Shrewsbury Antique Center, from I-83 follow Route 851 West about 1/2 mile; turn right onto Highland Drive (before you reach the traffic light). Phone (717)-235-6637 or (717)-235-5797. Open every day, 10 A.M. to 5 P.M.

Shrewsbury, PA, has six antique stores located at 9 S. Main, 2 N. Main, 10 &12 N. Main, 13 N. Main, 16 n. Main and 21 n. Main Streets

Stewartstown Railroad, at W. Pennsylvania Avenue and Hill St. (Route 851), Stewartstown. Write P. O. Box 155, Stewartstown, PA, 17363, or phone (717)-993-2936 for information and schedule.

The York County Colonial Court House, West Market at Pershing Avenue, is the site where our first Constitution was adopted, the place where the first national Thanksgiving Day Proclamation was issued, and the scene of many other historic events. Phone: (717)-846-1977.

Places to Visit (or Shop) in Adams County

For more information, write the Gettysburg Tour Center, 778 Baltimore St., Gettysburg, PA 17325, or: Phone (717)-334-6296.

The Electric Map is on Taneytown Road, and is a must-see for Civil War Buffs.

Gettysburg Battle Theatre on Steinwehr Avenue. See the film "America at Gettysburg."

The Hall of Presidents and First Ladies, on Baltimore Avenue next to the Soldier's Museum, uses a multi-media approach to tell the story of America in the sound of the Presidents and first Ladies "own voices." The Smithsonian Collection of First Ladies' Gowns is reproduced. The Hall also contains the "Eisenhower at Gettysburg" Exhibit.

The Jennie Wade House, on Baltimore Avenue, is a carefully restored home that tells the story of Jennie Wade, "Gettysburg's Heroine."

The Lincoln Train Museum is on Steinwehr Avenue between the Wax Kusumn and the Battle Theatre. One can "ride" with Lincoln on his historic train trip to Gettysburg, and see model railroads. Open March-November. Phone (717)-334-5678.

Soldier's National Museum, "The Showcase of the Civil War," is located on Baltimore Avenue, across from the Battlefield Bus Tours. It has displays of 10 major battles and a large private collection of battlefield relics.

INDEX

-A-

A. R. Wentz Library, 11
    Resources, 11
Abbottstown, 16
    Community History, 16
Abbreviations, vi

Accounts, Lancaster County, 5, 12, 107

Adams County, 15, 16, 17, 18, 19, 105
    Burial Grounds, 38
    Cemeteries, 33
    Church Records, 42, 52
    County History, 16
    Court House, 11
    Directories and Lists, 41
    Migration from, 17
    Naturalization, 74
    Origins of Settlers, 89
    Special Publications, 104, 106
    Tax Lists, 40
    Tombstone Records, 39
    Vital Records, 113
Adams County Historical Society, 9
    Holdings, 9
    Land, 71, 72
    Publications, 9, 10
    Research, 9
Administrations, 107

Administration accounts, 5

Administration bonds, 5, 107

Administration inventories, 5

Albright, Clayton M., 57

Almshouse births, 113

Allen, Ruth Bailey, 64

Ancestral Charts of Members of the SCPGS, 106

Ancestral File (LDS), 8

Archives, Court Houses and Institutions, 1

Archives of Evan. Lutheran Church, Adams County, 11

Ashland County, 17

Atlas, York County, 13

Aughenbaugh, Gloria L., 17, 106

-B-

Baltimore County, Census records (microfilm) at HSYC, 2

Bates, Marlene S., 42, 89

Bates, Samuel, 73

Battey, F. A., 15, 17

Becker, Gloria O., 17

Bedford County, 17

Bell, Raymond M., 66

Bell, Raymond Martin, 59

Bell, Rev. P. G., 60

Berks County, 55

Bibliography, 15
    Business Records, 15
    Ethnic Groups, 17
    General, 15
    Guides, 15
    Houses and Structures, 17
    Regional Histories, 15
Billet, Donald F., 59

Births
    Birth Certificates, Microfilm for York Co., 2
    Birth records, 1893-1906, 5
    Birth Registration Book, 113
    Births, Microfilm holdings of HSYC, 2
Bish, Wendy, 105

Bittinger, Dr. Emmert F., 62

Bittinger, Lucy Forney, 60

Black, Arthur Geiger, 65

Bloom, Robert L., 16

Boldsboro Historical Association, 16

Bolin, Larry, 105

Bowser, Addison Bartholomew, 58

Brackbill, Martin H., 71

Bradsby, H. C., 16

Bricker, Florence M., 42

Brossman, Schuyler, 15

Brown County, 17

Brua, Lynn Austin, 58

Bucks County, 55

Burgert, Annette K., 89, 90, 102

Burgoyne, Bruce E., 89

Burial Grounds, Adams County, 38

Business Records, Manheim Township, 15

-C-

Camenisch, Ruth Clotfelter, 60

Carroll County (MD), Census records (microfilm) at HSYC, 2

Carroll County, Maryland, Special Publications, 104

Carter, W. C., 15, 17

Catchings, Fermine Baird, 58

Catholic records, at John T.R. Historical Society, 7

Cemeteries, 19, 33
    Adams County, 33
    Cemetery Inscriptions, 1

Cemetery Inscriptions
  Card File, 1
Historical Society of York
  County, 19
Special Publicatons, 105
York County, 19
Census, 1, 2, 6, 8, 10

Center County, 55

Church Records, 42
  Christian Protestant, 42
  Church of the Brethren, 42
  General, 42
  Lutheran, 43
  Mennonite, 43
  Reformed, 43
  Roman Catholic, 43
  Society of Friends, 43
  United Brethren in Christ,
    43
  United Methodist, 43
Church Records of Adams
  County, 42, 43, 52
  Berwick Boro, 52
  Butler Township, 52
  Conewago Township, 53
  Cumberland Township
    (Gettysburg), 53
  Franklin Township, 53
  Germany Township, 53
  Hamilton Township, 54
  Huntington Township, 53
  Latimore Township, 54
  Menallen Township, 54
  Mount Joy Township, 54
  Mount Pleasant Township,
    54
  Other, 54
  Oxford Township, 54
  Traban, 54
Church Records of York Coun-
  ty, 43
  Carroll Township, 43
  Chanceford Township, 44
  Codorus Township, 44
  Conewago Township, 44
  Dover Township, 44
  East Hopewell Township,
    45

East Manchester
  Township, 45
Fairview Township, 45
Fawn Township, 45
Franklin Township, 45
Heidelberg Township, 45
Hellam Township, 45
Hopewell Township, 46
Jackson Township, 46
Lower Chanceford
  Township, 46
Lower Windsor Township,
  46
Manchester Township, 46
Manheim Township, 46
Monoghan Township, 47
Newberry Township, 47
North Codorus Township,
  47
North Hopewell Township,
  47
Paradise Township, 47
Peach Bottom Township,
  47
Penn Township, 47
Shrewsbury Township, 48
Spring Garden Township,
  48
Springettsbury Township,
  48
Springfield Township, 48
Warrington Township, 48
Washington Township, 49
West Manchester
  Township, 49
West Manheim Township,
  49
Windsor Township, 49
York City, 50
York Township, 49
Church Records Outside York
  and Adams, 55
  Berks County, 55
  Bucks County, 55
  Center County, 55
  Cumberland County, 55
  Dauphin County, 55
  Delaware Church Records
    at HSYC, 56

Franklin County, 55
Maryland Church Records
  at HSYC, 55
Civil Cases (Court of Common
  Pleas), 5
Clark, Raymond B., Jr., 15
Clint, Florene, 15
Clippinger, Joan S., 16
Codorus, Community History,
  16
Codorus Chronicles, 106
Codorus Township, 13
  Middle Region Draft
    Maps, 13
  Special Publications, 106
  West Region Draft Maps,
    13
  Steltz Region Draft Maps,
    13
  Upper Region Draft Maps,
    13
Columbiana County, 17
Community Histories, 16
  Abbottstown, 16
  Codorus, 16
  Dallastown, 16
  Dover, 16
  Goldsboro, 16
  Jacobus, 16
  New Freedom, 16
  North Codorus, 16
  Red Lion, 16
  Wellsville, 16
  York, 16
Conewago Township, Special
  Publications, 104
Congregational History File,
  Adams County, 11
Constables, List of, 18
County Histories, 16
  Adams County, 16
  Lancaster County, 16
  York County, 16
Court house records
  Adams County, 11
  Birth, 5

Clerk of Courts Office, 5
Death, 5
Divorces, 5
Land Office, 5
Marriage Applications and licenses, 5
Prothonotary's Office, 5
Recorder of Deeds Office, 5
Register of Wills Office, 5
Sheriff's Office, 5
Tax records, 5
Veterans' Office, 5
York County, 5
York Legan Record, 5
Court houses, 1

Court Records, 101
Commissioners Accounts, 101
Common Pleas Dockets, 101
Early Records, 101
Proprietary Rights, 101
Crawford, Hazel Sheffer, 64

Criminal cases, 5

Cronbaugh, Lois E. Wilson, 59

Cross References, 2

Cross, Harold E., 57

Cumberland County, 17, 55, 105
Census records (microfilm) at HSYC, 2
Special Publications, 104, 106

-D-

Dallastown, 16
Community History, 16
Dalton, Sharon A., 48

Dauphin County, 17, 55, 105
Census records (microfilm) at HSYC, 2
Special Publications, 104, 106
Davenport, John Scott, 63

Death Certificates,
Adams County, 10

Microfilm for York Co., 2
Death Notices, Adams County, Gettysburg Newspapers, 10

Death records, 1893-1906, 5

Deaths,
Death Registration Book, 113
Microfilm holdings of HSYC, 2
Newspaper notices, 2, 75
Deckard, Percy Edward, 59

Deeds, 5
Adams County, 10
Delaware Church Records at HSYC, 56

Diedrich, Marjorie H., 61

Diehl, Harry A., 59

Directories, 40

Directories and Lists, 41
Adams County, 41
Divorces, 5

Doolittle, Lewis L., 17

Dover, 16
Community History, 16
Dover Township, 19

Dover Township Board of Supervisors, 16

Drury, Rev. A. W., 63

Dull, Keith, 57, 58, 60, 61, 62, 63, 64, 65, 66

-E-

Earhart, Ronald E., 59

East Hopewell Township, 19

Egeland, Janice A., 60

Eisenhart, Ruth M., 59

Eisenhart, Wilkes S., 16

Eisenhart, Willis W., 57

Emenheiser, Doris L., 43

Emery, William F., 45

Ethnic groups, 17

Evangelical and Reformed Historical Soc., 42

-F-

Fairview Township, Special Publications, 104

Families, Genealogical Reports, 2

Family File Folders, 1

Family Histories, 57

Family histories, At Martin Memorial Library, 6

Family Histories,
Collections of Family Histories, 57
Family Reports, 67
Individual Family Histories, 57
Family histories at Martin Memorial Lib., 6

Family Reports, 67

Farm Journal Illustrated Farmer's Dir., York County, 13

Fetters, William B., 67

Fetters, William Brooke, 66

Fields, Helen S., 51

Folker, Howard O., 60

Forney, John K., 60

Franklin County, 17, 55, 105
Census records (microfilm) at HSYC, 2
Special Publications, 106
Freeland, Barney F., 60

Frey, Samuel Clarence, 60

-G-

Gamble, Anna Dill, 43

Garber, William Berry and Judity B., 58

Garrett, Walter E., 45

Geiselman, John, 16

Genealogical Reports, 2

Genealogical Society of Pennsylvania, Land, 71

General, York County, 15

Gerber, Adolf, 102

Gerberich, Albert H., 60

Gibson, John, 15, 17, 57

Gingerich, Hugh G., 57

Gipe, Florence M., 44

Giuseppi, M. S., 74

Glatfelter, Charles H., 18, 42, 44, 48

Glatfelter, Dr. Charles, 9

Glatfelter, Dr. Charles H., 43, 72

Glenn, Elmer Q., 47

Glossbrenner, A. J., 15, 17

Goff, Philip G., 60

Goldsboro, 16
    Community History, 16
    Houses and Structures, 17
Gould, William L., 42

Granquist, Mabel G., 66

Gras, E. Maurice, 67

Greater Dover Bicentennial Committee, 16

Greenholt, Kevin, 64

Greenholt, Kevin L., 107

Griffin, Benjamin T., 50

Gross, Patricia R., 13, 105

Guardian accounts, 5

-H-

Hacker, Warner, 102

Hacker, Werner, 102

Hamilton, James Alexander, 61

Hanover Area Historical Society, 6

Hanover Public Library, Holdings, 6

Hanover Township, Special Publicatiosn, 105

Harford County, Census records (microfilm) at HSYC, 2

Harrison County, 17

Heidelbaugh, James E., 61

Heidelberg Township, 19
    Special Publicatiosn, 105
Heidleberg Township, 13
    North Region Draft Maps, 13
    South Region Draft Maps, 13
Heilman, Leonard A., 13, 105

Heisey, John W., 15

Heiss, Willard, 43

Hellam Township, 19

Himes, J. A., 63

Historical Society of Pennsylvania, 42

Historical Society of York County, 1, 15, 16, 42
    Cemeteries, 19
Hitchins, Mary Beale, 58

Hively, David P., 101

Hively, Dr. Neal Otto, 13, 71

Hively, Neal Otto, 72

Hopewell Township, 14
    East Hopewell Draft Maps, 14
    North Hopewell Draft Maps, 14
    South Hopewell Draft Maps, 14
    Special Publications, 105
Horan, Col. John P., 63

Houses and Structures, Goldsboro, 17

-I-

IGI (International Genealogical Index), 8

Illing, Rev. Traugott Frederick, 51

Illinois, 18
    Astoria, Fulton County, Newspapers, 18

Immigration Records and Passenger Lists, 102

Individual Family Histories, 57

Institutions, 1

Inventories, Lancaster County, 12

Irish, Donna R., 42

-J-

Jacobus, 16
    Community History, 16
Jefferson County, 17

Jewett, Julia A., 63

John Timon Reily Historical Society, 7, 57

Jones, Henry, 102

Jones, Henry Z., Jr., 89

-K-

Kaltreider Library, 7

Kauffman, Charles Fahs, 62

Kilbourne, John Dwight, 61

Kittle, Mrs. Flora H., 61

Knipe, James Lloyd, 63

Knisely, George W., 62

Konkel, Richard, 40, 75

Koontz, Mrs. Azariah H., 62

-L-

Lancaster County, 15, 16, 17, 105
    Census records (microfilm) at HSYC, 2
    County History, 16
    Land, 71
    Special Publications, 106
Lancaster County Archives, 12

Lancaster County Historical Society, 12

Lancaster Theological Seminary, Philip Schaff Library, 12

Lancaster-Mennonite Historical Society, 11
    Holdings, 11

Land, 5, 71
  Appraisement Certificates (York), 72
  Calendar of Transactions, 71
  Deed Abstracts, 71
  Deeds, 71
  Land Drafts, 71
  Land Record Card File, 1
  Land records, Microfilm holdings of HSYC, 2
  Land surveys, Adams County, 10
  Real estate sales, 1
  Warrant Registers, 71
  Warrant Registers (Lancaster County), 71, 72
  Warrant Registers (York County), 72
  York County Draft Warrant Maps, 72
Lau, Michael W., 62, 65
Laucks-Xanders, Amanda Lydia, 65
LDS Family History Center, 7
Leamer, Laurence E., 62
Lewisberry Boro, Special Publications, 104
Lichtenwalter, Gladys E. G., 59
List of Township Officers,
  Adams County, 10
  York County, 10
Longaker, A B., 62
Lower Chanceford Township, 19
Lybarger, Donald F., 60

-M-

McAllister, Mary Catherine, 63
McGaughey, Polly Rachel, 63
McGrew, John R., 18, 105
McJohn, James F., 63
McTeer, Frances Davis, 59
Manchester Township, 19
Manheim Township, 13, 15

Business Records, 15
North Region Draft Maps, 13
South Region Draft Maps, 13
Maps, 13
Marriages,
  Adams County newspapers (marriage indices), 10
  Applications, 5
  Certificates, Microfilm holdings of HSYC, 2
  Cross References from wills, Orphans Court, 2
  Licenses, 5, 113
  Marriage Registration Book, 113
  Marriage returns for Adams County, 10
  Newspaper notices, 2, 75
  York County newspapers (indices to marriage notices), 2
Martin Memorial Library, 6
Martin, Levi E., 59
Maryland,
  Church records, 56
  Silver Run tombstone inscriptions, 105
  York residents married in Baltimore Co., 113
  York residents married in Harford Co., 113
Meals, Kathryn M., 18
Mennonite, family histories, 17
Microfilm, Holdings of HSYC, 2
Middletown, Special Publications, 104
Middletown Ferry, 17
  Houses and Structures, 17
Migration, 17
Military, 73
  Civil War, 73, 104
  Korea (index), 8
  Revolutionary War, 2, 73
  Viet Nam (index), 8
  War of 1812, 73

World War I, 73
Miller, Randy J., 107
Mogan, Donna Morton, 63
Monaghan Township, 19
Munger, Donna Bingham, 71

-N-

Naturalization, 5, 74
  Adams County, 74
  Card File, 1
New Freedom, 16
  Community History, 16
Newberry Township, 19
  Special Publications, 104
Newspapers,
  Abstracts and Indices, 75
  At Martin Memorial Library, 6
  Death Index, 75
  Deaths, 75
  Items, 75
  Marriage Index, 75
  Marriages, 75
  Martin Memorial Library, 6
  Newspaper records, 2
  Obituary Indexes, 6, 10, 75
  York County, 75
North Codorus, 16
  Community History, 16
  East Region Draft Maps, 13
  North Region Draft Maps, 13
  South Region Draft Maps, 13
North Codorus Township, 19

-O-

Oaths of allegiance, 5
Obituary Indices (newspaper),
  Adams County, Gettysburg Newspapers, 10
  Adams County, Hanover Newspapers, 10
  York County (death notices), 2
Occupations, 18
Oertel, Prof. Dr. Burkhardt, 90
Ohio,

Ashland County, 17, 105
Brown County, 17, 105
Carroll County, 18
Champaign County, 17, 106
Columbiana County, 17, 105
Crawford County, 17, 18, 106
Harrison County, 17, 18, 105
Jefferson County, 17, 105
Richland County, 17, 105
Richland County, Mansfield, 17
Sommerset County, 18
Tuscarawas County, 18
Wood County, 17, 106
O'Keefe, Barbara Brady, 57

Old Line Historic Society, 7

Olson, Helen Stambaugh, 64

Origins of Settlers, 89, 90

Orphans Court Dockets, 1, 5

Orphans court proceedings, Microfilm holdings of HSYC, 2

Orwig, Elmer W., 46, 63

Otstot, Charles, 13

Our Name's the Game, 106

-P-

Paradise Township, 19

Parish Registers, Adams County, 11

Passenger and Immigration Index (Filby), 9

Passenger Lists and Immigration Records, 102

Passports, 5

Pastoral Registers, 51

Patton, Alfreda, 62

Paup, David A. and Brenda L., 107

Penn Township, 13, 19

Pennabacker, Samuel Floyd, 43

Pennsylvania German Society, 15, 42, 102

Petersen, Florence Hepp, 60

Philip Schaff Library, Lancaster Theological Seminary, 12

Photograph collection, At Hanover Public Library, 6

Probate Records, 107. See also Accounts, Administrations,

Administration bonds, Administration inventories, Orphans

Court ..., Wills.

Prowell, George R., 15, 16

Purdy, James L., 17

-R-

Rahn, B. Elizabeth Shearer, 58

Rahn, Claude J., 57, 58, 61, 67

Reagan, Donald B., 65

Real estate sales, 1

Reamy, Martha, 75

Red Lion, 16
Community History, 16
Red Lion Area Historical Society, 7

Reed, John Elmer, 64

Regional Histories, York County, 15

Reiber, John R., 64

Replogle, Paul H., 64

Research, by mail, 4

Retailers, List of, 18

Rhyne, Dr. Howard S., 64

Richland County, 17

Romer, Mary Catherine, 64

Rowland, Ralph and Star, 62

Ruby, Edward O., 64

Ruby, Jay W., 64

Ruby, Rev. Edward C., 62

Ruby, Ruth, 64

Rudisill, Jim, 16

Rupp, Israel, 15, 16

Russell, George Ely, 60

-S-

Saylor, Samuel J., 13, 65, 105, 113

Schaff, Philip, Library, Lancaster Theological Seminary, 12

Schmitz, Maurine C., 57

Scholl, John William, 64

Schrader, Cornelia, 102

Seaman, Vashti, 61

Sechrist, Raymond Jacob, 16

Seitz, May Albright, 57

Seminary Archives, Adams County, 11

Septennial Censuses, Adams County, 10

Settlers, Index of Continental European Orgins, 3

Sheaffer, Carol M., M.D., 64

Sheaffer, Margaret E., 64

Sheely, Aaron, 16

Sheets, George R., 16, 49

Sherk, Thomas A., 65

Sherrick, James W., 65

Shrewsbury Township,
Middle Region Draft Maps, 13
North Region Draft Maps, 13
Southwest Region Draft Maps, 13
Springfield Region Draft Maps, 13
Shumaker, Edward Seitz, 62

Shuman, William C., 65

Smee, James, 64

Smith, Kenneth L., 42

Social Security Death Index, 8

Somerset County, 17

South Central PA Genealogical Society, 42, 103
   Special Publications, 103
South Central Pennsylvania, 17, 18

South Central Pennsylvania Gen. Society, 3
   Meetings, 3
   Newsletters, 3
   Our Name's The Game, 3
   Purpose, 3
   Queries, 3
   Research Committee, 4
   Resource persons, 4
   Special Publications, 3
   Surname Index File, 4
Southwest PA Genealogical Services, 106

Spahr, Max Curt, 65

Spangler, Edward W., 65

Special Publications of SCPGS:
   "Poor" Children, 1811-1844, 104
   Abstracts of Court Records, 103
   Adams County, 104
   Apprentices, 103
   Assessed Inhabitants, 103
   Birth Registrations, 104
   Cemeteries, 105
   Claims to Land (York County), 104
   Common Pleas Docket, 105
   Death Registrations, 104
   Early Records of York County, PA, 103
   Heads of Household, 103
   Land Appraisement Certificates, 104
   Manorial History of Town of York, 105
   Military Roll of 1865 (York County), 104
   Naturalization Abstracts (PA), 104

Newspapers - Crawford County, OH, 104
Newspapers - Fulton County, IL, 104
Notarial Docket, 104
Ohio, 106
Orphans' Court, 105
Silver Run, MD
   Tombstone Inscriptions, 105
South Central PA
   Genealogical Society, 103
Sundry Genealogical
   Materials, 103
Tavern Licenses, 105
Taxables on Collector's
   Warrants, 103
Tombstones and
   Gravemarkers, 103
Will Book, 104
Wills, 105
York County Atlas (1876), 105

Spring Garden Township, 19

Springettsbury Manor, 13, 14

Springettsbury Township, Land, 72

Springfield Township, North Region Draft Maps, 14

Stephens, Gertrude J., 57

Stevenson, George Urie, 66

Stewartstown Historical Society, 7

Stony Brook, 17
   Houses and Structures, 17
Strassburger, Ralph Beaver, 102

Strayer, Glenda S., 66

Strickler, Harry M., 66

Surname Index File, of SCPGS, 4

Sutton, Mrs. Charles W., 63

Swarr, Philip Cassell, 63

Swope, C. W., 66

Swope, H. E., 66

-T-

Tavern Licenses,
   Adams County, 10
   Special Publications, 105
Tax Lists,
   Adams County, 10
   By County, 41
   By Township, 40
   Microfilm at HSYC, 40
   Tax List Card, 2
   York County, 40
Tax Records,
   Microfilm holdings of HSYC, 2
   Microfilm holdings of HSYC, Fed. Direct, 2
Toews, John A., 43

Tombstone Records, 38
   Adams County, 10, 39
   Veterans, 5
   York County, 38
Torrence, Robert M., 65

Townships, 13, 108. See also Cemeteries, Newspapers.
   A Genealogy of the Townships of Adams County, 111-112
   A Genealogy of the Townships of York County, 109-110
   Butler, 52
   Carroll, 43
   Chanceford, 44
   Codorus, 13, 44m 106
   Conewago, 44, 53
   Cumberland (Gettysburg), 53
   Dover, 19, 44
   East Hopewell, 19, 45
   East Manchester, 45
   Fairview, 45
   Fawn, 45
   Franklin, 45, 53
   Germany, 53
   Hamilton, 53
   Hanover, 105
   Heidelberg, 13, 19, 45, 105
   Hellam, 19, 45

Hopewell, 14, 17, 46
Huntington, 53
Jackson, 46
Latimore, 54
Lower Chanceford, 19, 46
Lower Windsor, 46
Manchester, 19, 46
Manheim, 13, 46
Menallen, 54
Monaghan, 19
Monoghan, 47
Mount Joy, 54
Mount Pleasant, 54
Newberry, 19, 47
North Codorus, 13, 19, 47
North Hopewell, 47
Other, 54
Oxford, 54
Paradise, 19, 47
Peach Bottom, 47
Penn, 13, 19, 47
Shrewsbury, 13, 48
Spring Garden, 19, 48
Springettsbury, 48
Springfield, 13, 48
Straban, 54
Warrington, 19, 48
Washington, 19, 49
West Manchester, 19, 49
West Manheim, 13, 49
Windsor, 16, 49
York, 19, 49
Trout, George E., 66

-V-

Vendue (sales) lists,
  Lancaster County, 12
  York County, 5
Virdin, Donald, 57
Virdin, Donald Odell, 15
Visiting York County, 114
  Places to Eat in Gettys-
    burg, 114
  Places to Eat in York, 114
  Places to Stay in Gettys-
    burg, 114

Places to Stay in York, 114
Places to Visit (or Shop) in
  Adams Co., 115
Places to Visit (or Shop) in
  York County, 114
Vital Records, 113
  Adams County, 113
  Births, 2, 5, 113
  Deaths, 2, 113
  Marriage Licenses, 113
  Marriage Registration
    Book, 113
  York Residents Married in
    Maryland, 113
Vital Statistics Card File, 1, 2

-W-

Waggoner, Luella May, 58
Walmer, Margaret B., 49
Walsmith, Thelma Berkey, 59
Warrington Township, 19
  Special Publications, 104
Washington Township, 19
Weaner, Arthur, 72
Weidner, H. W., 61
Weiser, Frederick S., 47
Wellsville, 16
  Community History, 16
Wentz, A. R., Library, 11
  Resources, 11
West Manchester, 19
West Manheim Township, 13
  North Region Draft Maps,
    13
  South Region Draft Maps,
    13
Whiteford, A. W., 66
Wiley, Samuel T., 57
Wills, 5, 107
  Abstracts, 107
  Adams County, 2
  Baltimore County, 2
  Berks County, 2
  Bucks County, 2
  Chester County, 2
  Cumberland County, 2

Delaware, 2
Franklin County, 2
Indices, 2
Lancaster County, 2, 12
Maryland, 2
Microfilm holdings of
  HSYC, 2
Montgomery County, 2
Philadelphia County, 2
York County, abstracts, 1
Wilson, Charles Hellen, 67
Wilson, George Henry, 67
Windsor Township, 16
Woodroofe, Helen Hutchin-
  son, 15, 42
Wright, F. Edward, 42, 75, 89
Wright, Mary Ruth, 58
Wrightsville, 17
  Houses and Structures, 17
Wyand, Florence L., 74
Wyand, Jeffrey A., 74

-Y-

Yoder, Don, 44, 102
York, City of 17, 19
  Community History, 16
  Houses and Structures, 17
York County, 13, 15, 17, 18, 19,
  105
  Atlas, 13
  Archives, 5
  Cemeteries, 19
  Church Records, 43
  Codorus Chronicles, 106
  Compiled Church Records
    and Guides, 42, 43
  County History, 16
  Court house, 4
  Court Records, 101
  Directories and Lists, 41
  Draft Maps, 72
  Family Reports, 67
  Farm Journal Illustrated
    Farmer's Dir., 13
  History of, 17

Land Appraisement Certificates, 72

Land Records, 71

Manorial History of Town of York, 72, 105

Migration, 17

Military, 73

Naturalization, 74

Newspapers, 75

Officers, 18

Origins of Settlers, 89

Special Publications, 103-106

Springettsburg Manor, 14

Tax Lists, 40

Tax records, Microfilm holdings of HSYC, 2

Tombstone Records, 38

Warrant Registers, 72

York County Atlas (1876), 105

York Haven, 17
   Houses and Structures, 17

York Township, 19

Young, Henry James, 15, 41

-Z-

Zahn, Charles T., 42

Zarfoss, Franklin W., 42

Zemanek, Janet L., 60

www.ingramcontent.com/pod-product-compliance
Lightning Source LLC
Chambersburg PA
CBHW080335270326
41927CB00014B/3226